958.03

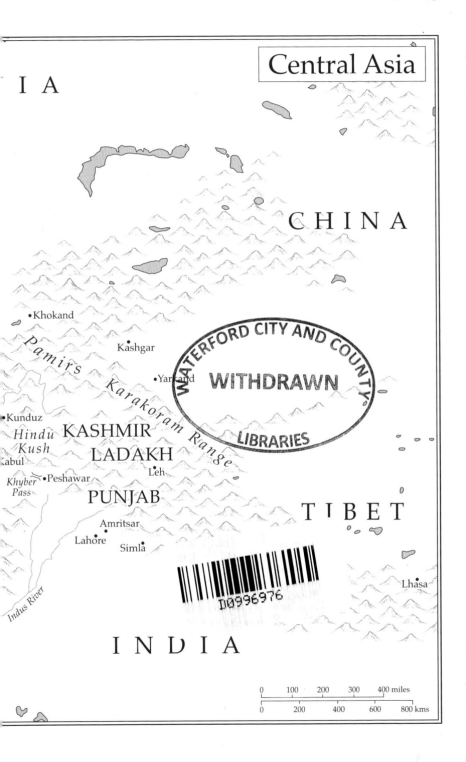

Central Asia

I A

CHINA

•Khokand

Kashgar

Pamirs

Karakoram Range

•Yarkand

•Kunduz

Hindu
Kush

KASHMIR

LADAKH

Leh

Kabul

Khyber
Pass

•Peshawar

PUNJAB

Amritsar

Lahore

Simla

TIBET

Lhasa

Indus River

INDIA

0	100	200	300	400 miles
0	200	400	600	800 kms

SABRES
on the
STEPPES

Danger, Diplomacy and Adventure
in the Great Game

John Ure

Illustrations by Toby Ward

CONSTABLE · LONDON

Constable & Robinson Ltd
55–56 Russell Square
London WC1B 4HP
www.constablerobinson.com

First published in the UK by Constable,
an imprint of Constable & Robinson Ltd, 2012

A copy of the British Library Cataloguing in
Publication data is available from the British Library

ISBN: 978-1-84901-667-4

Typeset by TW Typesetting, Plymouth, Devon

Printed and bound in the UK

1 3 5 7 9 10 8 6 4 2

'Something hidden. Go and find it.
Go and look behind the Ranges –
Something lost behind the Ranges.
Lost and waiting for you. Go.'

'Asia is not going to be civilized after the methods of the West.
There is too much Asia and she is too old.'

Rudyard Kipling (1865–1936)

For my grandson
ARCHIE BERTRAM RAMSAY
born into a tradition of adventure
as this book goes to press.

Contents

Maps

Acknowledgements

Anyone writing about nineteenth-century adventurers is deeply grateful for the fact that so many of them wrote at length (two thick volumes was the norm) about their own exploits. This first-hand material – long gathering dust on remote library shelves – has been the primary source for most of my chapters. But others who have written in more recent decades about some of these long-forgotten figures – notably Peter Hopkirk, whose encouragement has been much appreciated – have helped to bring them into sharper focus; Garry Alder for instance has pointed out the inadequacies of William Moorcroft's contemporary editor and has added much of his subsequent scholarly research to implement Moorcroft's own memoirs. Sir Fitzroy Maclean, whose inspiration and companionship during travels in Central Asia I have acknowledged elsewhere, has written about some of the characters who are protagonists in this book, using some of the same sources, but he did so more than fifty years ago, from a different angle and with a different perspective.

In obtaining access to my primary sources I am indebted to the staff of the British Library (where the India Office records are now housed), of the Royal Geographical Society library, and – more particularly – to Christopher Hurley and Gosia Lawik of the London Library.

My friend and former diplomatic colleague Sir Leslie Fielding was kind enough to read an early draft of this book and offer most valuable comments, based on his earlier experience of the region, with the well-developed critical faculties one would expect from a former university vice-chancellor.

Without the encouragement and constructive suggestions of Nick Robinson and Andreas Campomar (respectively chairman and editorial director of my publishers) this book would not have been embarked upon.

Last, but by no means least, I am grateful for the enthusiastic support of Toby Ward, the distinguished portrait artist who found time to do the line drawings which illuminate the text of this book (as they did of my last book) despite his other pressing commissions.

Introduction: Troublemakers
On Troubled Frontiers

'Personally I feel happier now that we have no allies to be polite to and to pamper.'

— King George VI in 1940

Relations between Britain and Russia have seldom been easy or relaxed. But there was a brief period after the Napoleonic wars when the two countries were not only allies but visibly friends. Tsar Alexander I – who had contributed so much to the downfall of Napoleon – was received in England with the acclaim due to a heroic partner. The hetman of the Cossacks was feted in Hyde Park. An era of detente appeared to be opening. But it was not to last.

Only ten years after the battle of Waterloo, Alexander was succeeded by Tsar Nicholas I, an aggressive imperialist, known for his frightening 'pewter gaze', with plans for expanding Russia's frontiers. In these plans the restless and independence-loving Islamic tribesmen of the Caucasus were to be subjugated and corralled within the tsar's domains; the Black Sea was to be converted into a Russian-controlled lake with access to the trade of the Mediterranean. In addition there was to be a steady encroachment southwards into Central Asia, toppling one khanate and emirate after another in an inexorable advance towards the frontiers of British India. The Great Game had begun.

Throughout the nineteenth century many young British adventurers were called to confront the spread of tsarist Russia into Central Asia and the Caucasus, considered as stepping stones on the road to British India. Many of these young travellers were there on the instructions, or at least with the encouragement, of the British government in England or the British governor-general in India. Some purported to be on leave when in fact they were fulfilling reconnaissance or espionage missions for their masters. The adventures of a number of these have been recounted in my book *Shooting Leave: Spying Out Central Asia in the Great Game* (2009).

As I was researching material for that book, I became increasingly aware that there were others who were undertaking ventures just as daring and dashing without the approval or encouragement of the government. They were a very different and distinct collection of people: they were all acting on their own initiative, frequently ignoring or defying the injunctions of their superiors. Their motivation was varied, but they all had a deep mistrust of the expansionist intentions of Russia and a determination to risk their lives by befriending local khans, emirs, chieftains and independence fighters who were inclined to resist this expansion.

Only a few of them were regular officers in the British or Indian armies; more of them were soldiers of fortune, enterprising journalists or merchant adventurers who were prepared to lay their lives and reputations on the line in a cause they felt was as worthwhile as any approved venture – and certainly as hazardous. These characters are a maverick collection with little in common with each other except a taste for danger and a sense of purpose.

Many of these were operating in Afghanistan or other parts of Central Asia, yet they were not restricted to that region. Some were in the Caucasus; others were in Persia, or on the frontiers of the Turkish Ottoman Empire. These were regions just as dramatic as the mountains and steppes of the Hindu Kush or the Pamirs. For these British pioneers, the legacy of Lord Byron's exotic adventures (both in life and literature) and Wordsworth's and Walter Scott's raptures over wild scenery, meant that regions of the world that would have appeared dauntingly grim to earlier generations seemed only enticingly romantic.

These imperial adventurers were not alone. Young Russian officers were also to be found in the same parts of the world. Just as to the British the north-west frontier of India was the natural stage for drama and adventure, so for the Russians it was more often the Caucasus that fulfilled this role. It was here that young tsarist guards and cavalry officers were sent when they were in disgrace – because of gambling debts, unsuitable love affairs or illegal duels – to retrieve their reputations and be restored to their former ranks by virtue of feats of bravery and leadership. It was here that Russian poets such as Pushkin and Lermonov, and novelists such as Tolstoy had had their earliest military experiences, and where they had fallen under the spell not only of the spectacular scenery – snow-capped mountains, raging torrents and narrow defiles giving way to sub-tropical valleys of vines, figs and lemons – but also under the spell of the Caucasian inhabitants who were and are a people of unusual beauty. Bold highlanders, bedecked in sabres, poniards and cartridge-belts under their fur hats and long silver-lace-trimmed cloaks, cut formidable figures, and their womenfolk – the

Circassian maidens so sought after in the harems of Constantinople – were no less admired. This was for the Russians a
backcloth as absorbing as the turbaned Pathan tribesmen and the
rock-strewn Khyber Pass were for the British.

The Russians had a long-standing tradition of expansion to
the south. Tsar Peter the Great was reported to have said on his
death bed in 1725 that his Cossacks would soon be watering
their horses on the banks of the Indus. And while many
regiments of Tsar Nicholas I's army were locked in conflict with
the Moslem independence fighter Imam Shamyl in the Caucasus
throughout the middle years of the nineteenth century, there
was also unremitting military activity in Central Asia, as
Samarkand, Bokhara, Khiva, Khokand, Geok Tepe and Merv
successively were either overrun or seduced into submission by
the tsarist expansionists. The Russians never doubted their own
superiority; as Anton Chekhov was to say, 'The Lord God has
given us vast forests, immense fields, wide horizons; surely we
ought to be giants, living in a country such as this'.

Britain was equally determined to protect the jewel in Queen
Victoria's imperial crown – India – while if possible avoiding a
military confrontation with Russia. Although the two nations
were at war with each other in the Crimea in the 1850s, no
formal conflict took place in Central Asia. Instead, both
imperial powers engaged in a 'tournament of shadows': their
explorers and spies, arms traders and mercenaries, diplomats and
dare-devils all pursued their national objectives and personal
interests among the mountain passes, wind-swept deserts and
corrupt courts of the rulers of the steppes. Because the action
was so often left to amateurs, it seemed not inappropriate that
this confrontation should be called the Great Game.

In reading the multi-volumed accounts of so many Victorian

travellers' adventures, I was also struck by the relevance to the present time of many of their exploits and of the regions where they were enacted. The border regions of Afghanistan, Iran, Chechnya and Ossetia, which were so central to the nineteenth-century dramas, are still as much in the news today: ideologies as well as nationalities confront each other in these places. My protagonists were men who felt that their own country had something to give to the rest of the world – a sense of liberty and liberal values – in the same way as Western participants in current conflicts feel they have today. Just as Lord Byron earlier had been incensed by the subjugation of the Greeks by the Ottoman Empire, so characters such as David Urquhart and Charles Christie, Arthur Conolly and Edmund O'Donovan, and many others had a sense of mission to protect the liberty and independence of isolated communities who were threatened by the rolling advance of an authoritarian, bullying tsarist regime. They were struggling not only to protect British India, but also to protect the more abstract idea of British values. The same idealism could be said to be a factor in the activities in the region today.

As I pursued these stories, I was struck by more parallels closer to home. When I was a diplomat many of the foreign correspondents and other journalists whom I had worked with and known were taking risks not just to get good stories for their newspapers, but also to expose incidents or policies that they felt were incompatible with their own standards and principles. They were exceeding their briefs as objective observers where they could rely upon the backing of their editorial bosses in London or New York, or upon the unquestioning support of local consular officers. One particular friend, having exposed what he saw as a hidden risk to peace and security, was murdered in circumstances that suggested assassination by a foreign intelligence service. Others were temporarily locked up in police stations or unceremoniously thrown out of the country. As a diplomat one could often learn much from such unconventional correspondents: they could reach out to those members of society – dissidents or troublemakers – who were usually not only off the diplomatic circuit but unreachable to those of us who had to play by the rules.

These characters were in the tradition of the protagonists in my book. Whereas 150 years ago the reason for their outrage might have been an Asian slave market or an invading army burning villages, now it might be the inadvertent bombing of an innocent wedding party on the Afghan frontier, an improper interrogation technique, or a concealed outburst of racial cleansing.

And it is not only among journalists that I have found echoes today of my nineteenth-century characters. As a sometimes-roving diplomat on the frontiers of the Soviet Union (as it then was), I encountered aspiring politicians of various nationalities who were ferreting out information that might force the hand of their own governments in directions they might otherwise have been reluctant to take. These would-be statesmen had a personal agenda. If they caused embarrassment at home, as David Urquhart did to Lord Palmerston in the 1840s, they did not greatly mind.

There were also businessmen – merchant adventurers as I saw them – who were committed to finding or establishing markets in hitherto no-go areas. Now as then, it is frequently the case that trade does not so much follow the flag, as the flag follows trade: it is the entrepreneur who, having established a business link in an officially closed market, often opens the way to more formal inter-governmental relations – whether in Cuba or Libya, China or Kyrgyzstan. James Bell, with his elicit trading of gunpowder and salt on the war-torn fringes of the Russian empire in the 1830s, has his soul-mates today.

So while *Shooting Leave* told the story of the good boys, the national heroes and role models of Victorian England, this book tells the murkier story of the bad boys – the ones who got out of line, who undertook missions risking embarrassment, who at best exceeded and at worst disregarded their instructions. Captain Christie – the son of the founder of the London auction house and a notable Great Game player – perhaps spoke for all of them when he tore up his orders and stayed to engage in combat with the Russians who were confronting the Persian troops he was training: 'If I am to be court-marshalled' [he is reputed to have said] 'it should be for fighting and not for running away.' He was not court-marshalled, but he was killed. I can think of officers I have known who would not only have said the same, but who would also have followed that path whatever the consequences.

Chapter 1

Charles Christie: The Officer Who Put Honour Before Duty

'I only regret that I have but one life to lose for my country.'
> – Nathan Hale, prior to his execution in 1776

On the morning of 1 November 1812, a small Russian foot patrol was carrying out a survey of the field of battle at Aslanduz on the banks of the Aras river, along the frontier between Russia and Persia in the Caucasus, and where – on the previous day and night – the tsar's army had inflicted a disastrous defeat on the Persians under command of their crown prince. The battlefield was littered with bodies: it was reported that 10,000 Persians had fallen – many as a result of having fired on themselves in the confusion following a night attack – while Russian losses had been limited to some 150. While searching for any remaining Russian wounded, the patrol was surprised to stumble on a seriously wounded officer who was neither Russian nor Persian but – it transpired – an Englishman. He had been shot in the neck and, although weak from loss of blood and unable to raise himself from the ground, he had lashed out with his sabre at the Russian who was approaching him. He clearly had no intention of being taken prisoner alive.

When the patrol reported back to their commander – General Kotliarevsky – that a live British soldier was still lying on the field and resisting capture, the general was astonished and infuriated. His country was not at war with Britain; quite the contrary: Napoleon's alliance with the tsar had faltered and his Grande Armée had invaded Russia earlier in the year. Britain and Russia were now allies confronting France together. What could such a British officer be doing leading Persian troops against friendly Russia? The general issued orders that, at whatever risk to his own men, the maverick Englishman was to be disarmed and brought in for questioning. The order was easier issued than carried out and a party of Cossacks set off to bring him in. But the wounded Englishman not only had his sabre, he had his pistol and he was said to have killed six Cossacks before one of them finally disregarded the general's orders and shot him dead where he lay. He was later buried on the spot where he had fallen. His name was Charles Christie.

In a book devoted to recounting the exploits of intrepid Englishman confronting tsarist Russia in defiance of their own government's policies and instructions, it may seem as strange to come across the name of Captain Charles Christie as it was to find his body on the battlefield. He was – by his background and previous record – the very model of an exemplary and disciplined servant of the British Raj.

He came from a family that was rapidly emerging in London as a byword for reliable and trustworthy business. For the first time, the wealthy citizens of London were entrusting their most precious possessions to a newly founded auction house which not only valued their family pictures, silver and furniture, but which attracted buyers from among the nouveau riche and even – a daring thought – from among rich foreigners. The house of

Christie, Manson and Woods had been founded in 1766, only a few years before Charles Christie was born. But as a young man he rejected the possibility of a career in the family business and enlisted at the usual early age – scarcely out of school – in the army of the East India Company in Bombay.

His first notable adventure was a signal of his later adventurousness. Together with a fellow officer, Lieutenant Henry Pottinger, he had been assigned the challenging task of reconnoitring the terrain between the western frontier of India (now Pakistan) and the eastern frontier of Persia (now Iran). This region, known as Beluchistan, was perceived as the likely line of advance for any invading army – from Napoleon's France or Russia – intent on seizing the rich prize of Britain's recently acquired Indian empire. He and Pottinger disguised themselves as Indian horse-dealers and, using their military training and experience, assessed the defensive potential of the forts and settlements in Baluchistan, and the rigours of the intervening steppes.

During their travels, for tactical reasons, the two men split up and each had his own adventures.[1] Christie's prime destination was the citadel and oasis-city of Herat, on the frontier between Afghanistan and Persia. There was only one Englishman still alive who had dared to visit this remote but strategically important junction. It was here that caravan routes from such exotic destinations as Samarkand and Bokhara, Kashgar and Khiva, Meshed and Isfahan converged and Herat was known as the gateway to India, its rich valley providing both pastures and provisions for an invading army, and also access to the vital Khyber and Bolan Passes.

Having parted from his companion, Christie faced not only the physical hazards of a desert and mountain journey, but also the human hazards of the bandit-infested region. Armed gangs of Afghans roamed the desert tracks in the hope of robbing travellers rash enough to venture into their terrain. The disguise of a Hindu horse-dealer, effective as it might be in allaying the suspicions of local elders and communities in Baluchistan, who would have dealt roughly and probably lethally with any detected spy, was no protection against predatory brigands. Indeed, it was a positive invitation to their attentions, as any merchant was assumed to be rich and vulnerable.

So Christie abandoned his horse-dealer pose and adopted that of a Moslem holy man returning from a pilgrimage; such a

---

1. For an account of Pottinger's adventures, see the author's book *Shooting Leave: Spying Out Central Asia in the Great Game*.

traveller would appear less of an inviting target. But the new disguise had a different set of problems: everywhere he went, people would accost him and engage him in religious conversation. This was a Moslem world where everyone was interested in the niceties of Islamic lore and behaviour, and a holy man was expected to pronounce on doctrine. Christie only evaded embarrassing and dangerous penetration of his fake role by purporting to be a Sunni Moslem to Shiites, and a Shiite to Sunnis; while the subterfuge did not endear him to his interlocutors, it provided an excuse for retreating into silence on theological matters. Thus he survived the twin risks of ambush and exposure.

When he approached the massive walls, moats and outer defences of Herat, however, Christie found it more convenient to revert to his Hindu horse-dealer guise. This gave him readier access to those who could inform him about the local resources necessary to sustain an army. He spent a month wandering around, covertly measuring walls and towers, and estimating how long such a desert stronghold could be expected to resist a modern, artillery-supported army. His conclusions were not reassuring, but were extremely valuable to his political and military masters in London and Calcutta. So far Christie's career had followed a commendably dashing and useful course: he might be seen as a model for future Great Game players.

But the very success of his mission was to lead him into uncharted waters as the European and Asian political scene was developing in unexpected ways. Soon after Christie's journey across Baluchistan, Napoleon and Tsar Alexander I changed from being fast allies to deadly enemies as an unsurprising consequence of Napoleon's invasion of Russia. Russia thus became a valued ally of Britain in the concluding years of the

Napoleonic wars. But it was still felt in London and Calcutta that the tsar and his imperial army remained the principal threat to the British Raj in India. The tsar's boasts of his Cossacks one day watering their horses on the banks of the Indus resounded in the salons of Belgravia on his visit to London in 1814. To combat this threat, Britain was intent on consolidating good relations with the Shah. Persia, a friendly buffer state, was seen as a prerequisite for the security of the jewel in the crown of the British Empire.

And consolidating good relations was not enough unless Persia was strengthened and given the wherewithal to resist Russian incursions. As early as 1807, General John Malcolm – the resident representative of the East India Company in Tehran – had written that 'the English have an obvious and great interest in maintaining and improving the strength of Persia as a barrier to India'. It was for this reason that Lord Wellesley (the elder brother of the Duke of Wellington, a former governor-general of India, and now in 1812 the British foreign secretary) decided that it was necessary to send a substantial number of British officers, NCOs and private soldiers to train and raise the morale of the Shah's army, and stiffen their resolve to contest any further Russian advance into the Shah's domains. The Persian army was at the same time to be modernized by the supply of arms and equipment, including muskets and horse artillery. Britain was to make it possible for Persia to defend herself against Russia, but it was no part of Lord Wellesley's policy for Britain herself to be directly involved in any confrontation between Tsar Alexander I and Fath Ali Shah.

It was not altogether surprising that the man chosen to lead the team of British military advisers and trainers was a proven and locally experienced captain in the Bombay regiment of the

East India Company – Charles Christie. While his former associate Henry Pottinger was allowed to go home and later pursue a high-flying career in the administration of the British Empire, Christie was sent to put some mettle into the Persian infantry. He was accompanied by Lieutenant Henry Lindsay of the Madras regiment, whose height (he was nearly seven foot tall) and commanding presence was said to remind the Persians of their own hero of antiquity – the giant Rustum.

Under Christie's gaze everything was done to bolster the Persians' self-confidence. Cannons were manufactured with the Shah's coat-of-arms emblazoned on their barrels; English-made uniforms in blue and scarlet replaced those earlier supplied by local or French sources, and almost gave the Shah's troops the appearance of British soldiers – only with lambskin hats rather than bearskins. A drum-and-fife band was created to raise the spirit of the troops with martial music. Shaving was introduced and the formerly bewhiskered Persians began to look like European soldiers. The Persian crown prince, Abbas Mirza, saw himself (like Peter the Great of Russia a century earlier) as dragging his country out of Asia and into Europe and a new century.

At first everything went well. The Persians managed to rout a small Russian force which was intruding across the Aras river in February 1812. The British guns proved as effective as hoped and the English officers had convinced the Persians that they could stand up to the Russians for the first time. The military advisers had won the respect of their Persian recruits and, for their part, had begun to feel affection towards and pride in the troops they had trained. But there was a built-in flaw in the arrangements, and this was the line of command that was laid down: the British officers were to be responsible on a day-today basis to the Persian crown prince (who was head of the Shah's army), but in the last resort they were to take their orders from the British Ambassador at Tehran.[2]

This was a new appointment. Sir Gore Ouseley had been sent out from England in 1810 as the first ever ambassador to Tehran; the journey had taken him and his family, staff and escort more than six months by sea, in two Royal Naval warships via Bombay, to Bushire on the Persian Gulf. (A cow from England had been part of the entourage to provide milk for the party.) A further eight-month overland journey by rough caravan routes and mountain passes to Tehran was to follow, in the course of which Ouseley's long-suffering young wife gave birth to a daughter at Shiraz – the first all-English child ever known to have been born in Persia. Now the ambassador was installed as a figure of prestige and authority. The authority over the British officers with the Persian army was to prove a crucial point when the Russians launched a serious offensive in the autumn of 1812. Aware of the sensitivity of Anglo-Russian relations, the British ambassador promptly forbade members of the British military training mission to take part in any further action against the Russians. The men were allowed to stay on in their training capacity but were ordered explicitly to leave the units to which they were attached in the event of hostilities breaking out again.

As it turned out, the Russian attack was sudden and unexpected. The Persian crown prince wanted the British – and Christie in particular – to stay and fight with the troops they had instructed; he maintained that the newly trained Persian troops

---

2. Such complex lines of command and training duties are not unfamiliar even today, where NATO officers training the Afghan army wish to give as much status and authority as possible to the Afghan military hierarchy but are themselves ultimately under NATO (US and UK) command.

were still dependent on their British mentors, whom they saw as leaders and not merely as instructors. Christie wanted to stay too. To abandon those he had spent so long trying to inspire would let them down in their hour of need, and would destroy at a stroke the respect he had won for himself and his British compatriots. It was a fellow officer, Lieutenant William Monteith, who reported Christie as saying: 'If he [Christie] was to face a court-martial for disobeying orders, it should be for fighting and not for running away.'

Running away was what almost everyone else seemed to be doing. Even the crown prince at one stage ordered his men to retreat and, seizing his own banner, rode with it off the field of battle. Christie rallied his trainees around him and refused to withdraw; he finally fell where he stood, wounded in the neck. His Persian recruits saw their mentor fall and, as Monteith later reported, 'more than half the battalion he had raised and disciplined himself' were killed or wounded while trying to drag him to safety. They doubtless knew he would have done the same for them.

The Englishman whom the Cossacks had tried to disarm and capture alive the following morning had died a hero's death surrounded by the very soldiers in whom he had instilled a fighting spirit. But he was not a hero to his own government. He had put his sense of personal honour before his duty to comply with his orders. His death had embarrassed the Foreign Office in London and the British ambassador in Tehran, so much so that the latter – Sir Gore Ouseley – felt obliged to accept an invitation to negotiate a peace treaty between Russia and Persia the following year. The treaty was a most unfortunate one in that it formally ceded to Russia almost all the former Persian territory in the Caucasus north of the Aras river. This was the price for restoring Britain's fragile diplomatic relations with the tsar after the disclosure of Christie's involvement – against instructions – in the battle of Aslanduz. Russia had, as compensation for the affront, achieved a significant step further towards the frontier of her coveted destination – India. The Persians for their part were to resent the treaty to which they had been persuaded to acquiesce.

Be that as it may, in the ultimate court-martial of public opinion in his own country, Christie was to stand acquitted. Insubordinate he may have been, but in death as in life he had behaved like an officer and a gentleman.

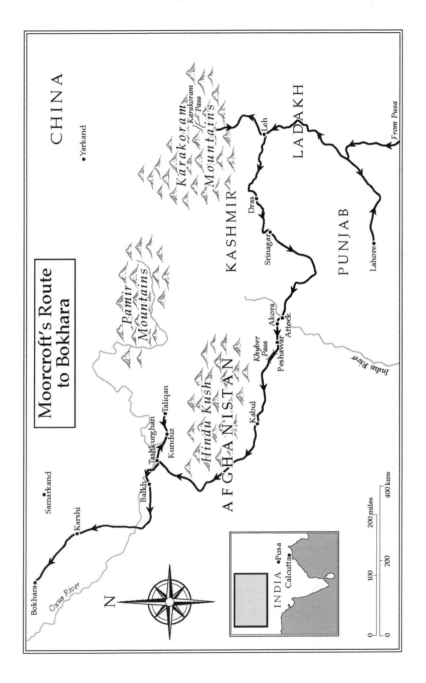

Moorcroft's Route to Bokhara

Chapter 2

William Moorcroft: The Uncontrollable
Stud Manager

'O! For a horse with wings!'
                    – William Shakespeare (1564–1616)

At the beginning of the nineteenth century, the Honourable East India Company ('John Company' as it was widely known) not only employed a wide variety of traders and merchants ('box wallahs' as they were later to be dubbed) but also a large number of soldiers in its own army. Horses of good quality, with stamina, speed and manoeuvrability were much in demand, particularly for the cavalry, and in consequence the management of the company's stud farm was an important and well-paid post. In 1808 the company took the unusual step of recruiting the most eminent horse vet in London and adviser to the royal mews to look after their stud farm at Pusa in northern India. They little knew what a problem they were landing themselves with.

Before he set off for India William Moorcroft had already made and lost a fortune in England. He had become disillusioned London life, having launched a financially disastrous horseshoe business. He was exasperated by legal complications arising from negotiations to buy horses that turned out to be unsound. In addition he had embarked on a less-than-joyous marriage. In these circumstances, the offer of the job of manager of the East India Company's stud farm at a salary of 30,000 rupees – an enormous sum on a par only with the salary of the governor-general and the commander-in-chief in India – was irresistible.

From the beginning, however, he had his own agenda for his new job. This involved not just supervising the company's stables, which was a difficult task in itself since horses, like men, suffered in health from the vagaries of the Indian climate on the plains, but also – Moorcroft decided – taking enterprising and unprecedented steps to improve the bloodstock line. He had heard, even before arriving, that somewhere in the hidden heart of the steppes of Central Asia was the homeland of a rare breed of spirited stallion which, if found and purchased, and brought safely to India, could transform the quality of the East India Company's cavalry. To obtain such fresh blood was a challenge that appealed to him much more than his routine veterinarian duties.

His first expedition in 1811, to Gurkha country in Nepal and returning through the Maratha region, took an unexpected eight months and was rather disappointing: he was more impressed with the emeralds he saw displayed by the local rajas than he was by the quality of their horses. To achieve his objective of robust cavalry stallions he would have to go further: beyond the limits of the company's sway and protection. For the first time he aspired to reach the fabled city of Bokhara, a city unvisited by any Englishman since the Elizabethan envoy and trader Anthony Jenkinson in 1557, and which lay – as far as Moorcroft was concerned – inaccessibly far beyond Afghanistan and the Oxus river. This was to dominate the rest of his life.

Moorcroft had hardly got back to Pusa from his first sojourn before he started lobbying for permission to make further trips. Of course the bloodstock question was the ostensible reason: he felt that for too long the stud had depended on unsuitable Arab horses. But there were other motives of which he was probably less consciously aware: at heart he was an adventurer and not an administrator. As a young man – he was already well over forty before he uprooted to India – he had put his life at risk by visiting France during the most turbulent times of the French Revolution. His itch to travel dangerously resulted in his setting off to Nepal again and to Tibet by the middle of 1812. He could not pretend that this was the most direct route to Bokhara and the home of the much-desired Turkoman horses, but the truth of it was that he had become almost equally obsessed by the prospect of opening a trade route between India and China, in particular the trade of goat's-wool shawls that came from Kashmir and the surrounding territories.

This time the Gurkhas were less friendly, and he and his companions were captured and held for several weeks on suspicion of being secret scouts for some invading force – why else should they be travelling without permission, apparently in disguise and so far from British India? Moorcroft was tempted to escape before his release, but calculated that the plentiful bears and tigers in the surrounding forests and mountains might prove more lethal than his Gurkha guards. Meanwhile, he made friends with his captors as best he could, mostly by treating them for venereal and other diseases; his veterinarian skills were versatile.

After this trip, the East India Company board of directors – his masters – expressed their displeasure at the risks he had taken and at his tendency to disregard the company's rules and follow his own interests and inclinations. He received a written reprimand from the governor-general himself along these lines, and afterwards the board took a lot of persuading that he should ever be allowed to take indefinite leave from the stud to travel in search of horses again. In fact it was eight years before Moorcroft managed to get the necessary consent to set off on his ultimate and most ambitious journey of all.

Meanwhile, Moorcroft's alarming experience of revolutionary France had left him with a deep suspicion of Napoleon's intentions. At first he, like those others who had sent Christie into Baluchistan, thought that Napoleon and Tsar Alexander might jointly invade British India; then (after Napoleon had broken with Alexander and invaded Russia) he thought that a French army in Russia would be 'so much nearer Hindoostan than at any former period' that it might tempt Napoleon to invade alone; later still (when Napoleon had been forced to retreat from Russia, and Moorcroft was back from his second expedition to Nepal) he still saw the tsar as an ongoing threat to India, despite the fact that the tsar was officially a friend and ally of England. In harbouring these fears he was ahead of his time; the Great Game had not been declared. As a result, no one in London or Calcutta was inclined to listen to his gloomy warnings.

While he was having these anxious premonitions about Russian intentions, his well-paid but routine administrative job at the Pusa stud farm was proving ever more frustrating. His disagreements with the board of directors might have led to the termination of his appointment had it not been for the outbreak of the Gurkha wars, which focused attention on the need for improved cavalry horses. The new governor-general, Lord Hastings, was himself a former soldier and more sympathetic than his predecessor towards Moorcroft's ambitions to improve the bloodstock line.

In 1819 it was Lord Hastings who finally was 'pleased to grant leave [to Moorcroft] to proceed towards the North Western parts of Asia, for the purpose of there procuring horses to improve the breed [. . .] for military use'. This was the message that Moorcroft had been waiting for ever since his return from Nepal in 1812, and which it had seemed might never be forthcoming. He also managed to get consent to taking goods for barter (rather than bills of exchange or gold bullion) to pay for the horses; he saw this as a means to set up the framework for future trade between India and her northern neighbours. This was part of his personal agenda, rather than his brief from the government or the company, and it was to cause serious trouble.

Moorcroft made the most of his licence to take goods for barter, taking strings of pearls for 'everyday currency'. For one stage of the journey alone he required six elephants and forty camels to carry all his merchandise and kit, the latter including his personal tent, rugs, writing desk and brass bedstead. Now aged over fifty, well beyond the age of most European travellers on the sub-continent in that era, he had no intention of being unnecessarily uncomfortable. At times his party numbered as many as three hundred, but there was a continual and insidious dwindling of personnel as the less robust defected and sought to return to the relative comfort of life on the plains. His staunch companion throughout however was George Trebeck, the nineteen-year-old son of one of his London friends from the Westminster Volunteer Cavalry. A doctor and a Persian secretary were among the other members of the team, as well as fourteen Gurkha soldiers who made up his official escort and who were paid from public funds.

His documentation consisted of letters of introduction in Persian, Russian, Chinese and English, all impressively embossed with the East India Company's seal and explaining his equestrian mission. What he did not have, and would never have been given, was any warrant to negotiate trade or other treaties on behalf of the government of India. Nor could his credentials from the company be expected to carry any weight beyond the confines of the company's extensive territories; and that was where Moorcroft was heading. He would be on his own, far beyond the protective reach of the Raj.

Bokhara was Moorcroft's ultimate aim, but he chose a circuitous route to get there. He decided to follow the traditional caravan trail, across what is now dubbed the Karakoram highway, north-eastwards into Chinese Turkistan. From there he planned to approach Bokhara from the east, across the Pamirs. Ostensibly the reason for selecting this very roundabout approach was that it avoided the dangers of hostile regions such as the Punjab, Peshawar and Afghanistan which contained extremist Moslem rulers who were notoriously unfriendly to the very rare European visitors who ventured into their domains. Privately, Moorcroft reckoned that since his preferred route lay through Ladakh there might be opportunities during his stay there to use the territory as a bridge for trade between China and India. This might open up a whole commercial dimension that would replace Russian goods with British or Indian ones throughout a great tranche of Central Asia. The factories of Birmingham and Calcutta, as well as the stables of the East India Company, would profit from his personal interpretation of the objectives of his mission.

On the first stages of his journey to Ladakh, Moorcroft describes in his journals some of the natural hazards of the route.

One district was so infested with tigers that the locals had developed their own special tiger trap: 'a small chamber of loose, heavy stones, with a sliding door at one end, and a loophole at the other [. . .] a rope passes over the roof of the hut and is tied to the neck of a goat [. . .] when the tiger attempts to carry off the goat [. . .] the door falling down secures the tiger [. . .] the animal is then shot through the loophole'. Wolves were also a local hazard, and the Persian secretary inadvertently disturbed a pack with 'long, lank bodies and bushy tails' that were in the process of pulling down a large deer. Even after the deer had been killed they continued to prowl around Moorcroft's party until 'finally dispersed with several shots'.[1]

There were other less natural hazards too. Moorcroft was so incensed by finding two young widows – the elder no more than fourteen years old – being burnt on their husbands' funeral pyres, that he intervened at some risk to himself to prevent it happening 'for a while at least'. Even before he set out on his travels he was aware of the dangers and wrote to a friend saying that he must 'push the adventure to its end'; little did he know how much these dangers were to escalate before he reached his destination.

By December 1820, he had already revised his route. He had left it too late to cross the mountain ranges that lay between him and Leh (the capital of Ladakh), so he needed to divert westwards and enter the Punjab – the kingdom of the fearsome

---

1. When the author first visited the British Embassy in Kabul in the late 1950s, wolves were so frequently encountered on Legation Hill, behind the embassy compound, that it was usual to take a supply of fireworks with one when out for a walk, and to disperse the wolves by throwing these at them. New recruits to the embassy were regularly asked to bring out a supply of such fireworks (rather than the customary marmalade or Marmite) from England on first appointment.

Raja Ranjit Singh who he worried would delay and detain him, or worse. They were now in territory where no Europeans had ventured before and where the small Gurkha escort was liable to be interpreted by the locals as the precursor of a vast invasion force. He had hoped to just cut across a corner of the Punjab and be on his way northwards, but it was not to be: Ranjit Singh's troops stopped him and refused to allow him to proceed without the explicit permission of the raja. The only way to obtain this was for Moorcroft to divert from his route and go alone to Lahore to face the raja in person and seek his approval.

Having set off on this diversion, he was further irritated by being held up for a month in great heat and discomfort – his tent was downwind of the local sewers – while permission to proceed to Lahore (permission to seek permission) was sought. Characteristically, Moorcroft passed the time by employing his medical skills to the advantage of the local population. On another occasion he managed to visit one of the raja's stud farms, and found that the stallions were only ever allowed out of their stables to cover mares, and consequently were so under-exercised and irritable that he was tempted to deploy his knowledge and advice in that direction too.

When he finally arrived at Lahore, Ranjit Singh extended a cordial welcome and invited him to an early audience. Seated on a golden throne, the raja motioned Moorcroft to a silver chair. The short, stout, one-eyed raja paraded his horses and his artillery for Moorcroft's entertainment and accepted presents of pistols (always a favourite gift); soon however it became clear his main interest in Moorcroft was to obtain medical advice for his own flagging sexual energy. Moorcroft prescribed a mixture of sensible suggestions and placebos. Having trusted Moorcroft with his most intimate medical problems, the raja also trusted

him to explore Lahore in his own way and his own time; Moorcroft took the opportunity to spy out the defences of the city, although he felt he was abusing his host's hospitality by so doing and recorded that he was indulging in 'more [...] espionage than is perfectly agreeable to my feelings'.

With all these consultations and activities, it was May before Moorcroft managed to leave Lahore and rejoin his own party, but he had succeeded in his objective. He returned with written consent to proceed towards Ladakh and, if necessary, to transit Kashmir on his way eastwards from Ladakh towards Bokhara. He accurately (and privately) forecast that when Ranjit Singh died the British would succeed in annexing the Punjab – a necessary step in his opinion to preclude a Russian advance in that direction. What he did not forecast was that, by the time he needed to take up Ranjit Singh's agreement to his passing through Kashmir, he would have taken other actions that were likely to upset the raja.

This was all some way ahead. For the moment it was he who was furious with Ranjit Singh, who had called him back to Lahore on the pretext that his son was ill when in fact it was the raja himself who was worried once more about his health; this ploy on top of the earlier obfuscation had altogether delayed Moorcroft for four months. His journey on to Leh – the capital of Ladakh – took from June to September 1820; he thought he was the first European ever to reach this highest inhabited country in the world (although it is now believed that two Jesuit priests may have done so more than a century earlier). Certainly the inhabitants were as intrigued with Moorcroft and his party as the visitors were with these smiling hill people. But even as he processed through the narrow streets and scrutinized the crowds of curious bystanders who had turned out to see him, Moorcroft was noting that among their number were traders with Chinese features from north of the Karakoram range, and others with more Semitic features from Kashmir to the west and from points further south.

This was undoubtedly a significant crossroad of caravan routes across Central Asia, and Moorcroft was already thinking about how this traffic route could be harnessed for the transport of British and Indian goods to new markets before the Russians. He was once again allowing goat's-wool shawls and Sheffield cutlery to interfere with his thoughts about Turkoman bloodstock and Arab stallions.

Moorcroft had hoped to press on northwards to Yarkand in Chinese Turkistan, but a number of reasons held him back: there was no invitation from the Chinese; it was too late in the year to face the ice and snow on the Karakoram passes;[2] and – possibly most decisive of all – he had run out of cash and credit. It said something about his diminishing credibility in India that Sir David Ochterlony, the government resident in Delhi to whom he appealed for an advance of funds against securities, prevaricated and failed to help.

But Moorcroft certainly did not waste time during his unwelcome delay at Leh. As usual, he dispensed medical help to those in need. He also was not impervious to the charms of the local girls, and a French visitor some ten years later remarked that 'Mr Moorcroft did not set an example of European continence here [. . .] his principle occupation was making love'. But more significant was his main self-imposed task. In this he set about doing something far beyond the reach of his brief or his powers: he set in train a commercial treaty between Ladakh and British India which was designed to implement his ambitions to establish a trade route through Leh to allow British goods to penetrate into China and Central Asia.

Despite fierce opposition at first from the Kashmiri and Tibetan merchants, Moorcroft managed to secure such an agreement on 4 May 1821, not only for British goods to enter Ladakh, but for them to be charged a much reduced customs duty and – if possible – enter the region without the necessity of passing through Ranjit Singh's Punjab. With considerable satisfaction, Moorcroft sealed the agreement with his personal signet ring 'on behalf of the British merchants of Calcutta', a vague body of which he was in no way the appointed

---

2. The author himself got stuck in snow and ice while trying to cross the Kunjarab Pass over the Karakoram range in early October 1996. Moorcroft had thought of making a dash for it alone, without his extended party, in October 1820 but was probably wise not to try.

representative. It was now up to the British government to give effect to his agreement; he stated the position in words that showed his feelings: 'Whether they [the people of Ladakh] shall be clothed with the broadcloth of Russia or of England [. . .] whether they shall be provided with implements of iron and steel, with hardware of every description, from Petersburg or Birmingham [. . .] is entirely in the decision of the government of British India'. He went on to characterize the attitude of his own government towards trade with Central Asia as one of 'misplaced squeamishness and unnecessary timidity'.

Moorcroft's commercial zeal was driven by his long-standing apprehensions about Russian military as well as commercial intentions in Central Asia. Never was this more the case than in Ladakh. Here he discovered a tsarist agent – now called Rafailov but originally of Jewish and Persian extraction – had been visiting regularly to exchange Russian manufactured goods for goat's-wool shawls, and possibly for the secrets of making the latter and for the chance of exporting goats for breeding in Russia. Rafailov had been much more than a merchant: he had been in the pay of the tsar's Foreign Ministry and received a medal and gold chain from the tsar for his services; he also carried rich gifts – emeralds and rubies – as well as letters from the tsar to the rulers of Ladakh and the Punjab. It transpired he had had a Cossack escort for much of his journey (no doubt necessary because of the gem stones in his baggage), just as Moorcroft had had a Gurkha escort.

Moorcroft much hoped to meet Rafailov and saw him as a fellow spirit as well as an opponent and admired 'his intelligence and enterprise'. He thought Rafailov might well have pioneered a route by a hitherto-unknown pass through the Karakorams which would bring the thrusting Cossacks much closer to India than had previously been realized and feared. Chinese Turkistan as well as Ladakh might become Russian dependencies.

It was therefore a considerable shock when he learnt that Rafailov had died or been killed – accidentally or otherwise (his death had been enigmatically described as 'sudden and violent') – when crossing the Karakorams in 1821. When Moorcroft managed to get a sight of some of the letters that Rafailov had been carrying on his last and fatal journey, he found Count Nesselrode (the tsar's foreign minister) had been trying to persuade the rajas of Ladakh and the Punjab to send envoys to St Petersburg at the expense of the Russian government. This was no innocent 'box wallah', any more than Moorcroft was an innocent vet. Rafailov and Moorcroft were both playing a lethal game, as the latter was also to discover all too soon.

Not only was Moorcroft running out of funds and embarking on commercial agreements beyond his competence, he also started meddling in political affairs. He approached the ruler of Ladakh and suggested that he should seek British protection against possible incursions either from the Punjab (Lahore) or from Russia, and he additionally wrote to Ranjit Singh in Lahore, in effect warning him off meddling in Ladakh's affairs. Such advice – unauthorized and provocative as it was – was bound to offend Ranjit Singh, and undo whatever goodwill Moorcroft had earlier gained by his medical attentions to that ruler and his subjects. This was not without risks to Moorcroft himself, since he might well have to travel on through Kashmir and other territories under Ranjit Singh's sway; no wonder he recorded that his rash action 'might introduce me to one of the oubliettes [prisons where the key had been thrown away] of Lahore, if not a more summary recompense'.

And it soon seemed that the latter – a summary recompense

in the form of an assassination attempt – might indeed be his fate. But in the event the first such attempt was made against his companion – George Trebeck – who was shot at in the early hours of the morning as he was working at his desk; fortunately for him, he had just moved from his chair or he would have been in the line of the bullet that was intended for him. Moorcroft also soon became the subject of attacks by three mysterious strangers. He shot at one of them at night with the pistol he now kept under his pillow, and 'the next morning I saw only two of the strangers'. When the attempts to shoot him were abandoned, they were quickly replaced by attempts to poison him. Someone was certainly trying to administer a 'summary recompense', and the aggrieved Ranjit Singh, with his reputation for murdering those who stood in his way, seemed the most likely suspect.

Whatever hand Ranjit Singh may or may not have had in these sinister happenings, there was one action he indisputably took against Moorcroft which did the latter much harm. He forwarded a copy of Moorcroft's ill-advised letter to Sir David Ochterlony, the Delhi official who had already proved less than co-operative with Moorcroft's requests for funds. Ochterlony predictably passed it on to the authorities in Calcutta where it was drawn to the attention of the governor-general himself. However well-disposed Lord Hastings may have earlier been to Moorcroft's travels, this gross interference in matters altogether outside his remit drew down an immediate expression of 'surprise and displeasure'. Lord Hastings did not pull his punches: 'It strikes his Lordship in Council as being the height of indiscretion in you to address any letter to the Maha Raja [Ranjit Singh] upon such a subject [. . .] to interfere and tender unsolicited advice in matters wholly foreign to your situation is the least reprehensible feature of the case.'

The governor-general went on to point out that Moorcroft's letter could only be construed as a threat that British India would claim rights over Ladakh; he denied this was the case, and more importantly he pointed out that any such suggestion was bound to upset Ranjit Singh, who was a valued but by no means reliable ally of the British. At a stroke, Moorcroft had undone all the good work he had put into devising the commercial agreement with Ladakh. He had not only made an enemy of Ranjit Singh, he had lost the support and goodwill of his own masters in Calcutta. As he recorded: 'The difficulties and dangers which subsequently beset my progress were mainly owing to the harsh, peremptory, and public manner in which discredit was affixed to my proceedings by the Resident of Delhi and the government of Bengal'. He was now on his own in every sense.

While all these diplomatic dramas were unfolding in Ladakh, Lahore and Calcutta, Moorcroft had still been pursuing the idea of crossing the Karakorams to Yarkand and Chinese Turkistan. Despite the lack of an invitation, the rigours of the passes, and his lack of credit and cash, he was still listening carefully to all reports of the state of the passes through the Karakorams. They were not encouraging: the leader of one caravan who was a mullah known to Moorcroft had – on his second attempt – fallen behind the rest of the party. Moorcroft takes up the tale in his memoirs:

> Just as they entered the gorge [. . .] a sudden gust of wind brought on such a cloud of snow, as to conceal the Mullah and a little girl riding on a couple of yaks, from the mountaineer who attended them as their guide. The latter threw himself on the ground, that he might not be blown off his feet, and upon getting up when the blast

had ceased, saw the yaks without their riders: they had been blown off their seats apparently, and were buried beneath the snow. After some delay the bodies were found: the girl recovered, but the old man was dead.

Because the mullah was also a man of property, his companions had felt it necessary to carry his body for forty days to Yarkand, in order to satisfy the Chinese authorities that he had not been murdered for his possessions.

On the rare occasions when Moorcroft and his companions ventured out of Leh into the hills, 'we were advised to be on our guard against hyaenas, who sometimes descend from the mountains at night, and to whom our baggage asses would be an acceptable prey'. Far from finding thoroughbred horses on these expeditions, he only encountered the 'kiang' horses, which he described as 'neither a horse nor an ass [. . .] his shape is as much like the one as the other'. The locals shot and trapped them and once he was presented with the head and feet and part of the skin of a kiang. His stud farm mission seemed a long way off and his absence from his post was once again becoming embarrassingly long.

By the end of 1822, it was clear that the Chinese were never going to allow him to travel through Yarkand. According to Gary Alder's scholarly and comprehensive life of Moorcroft, a wall painting had been erected there with a representation of a European (a virtually unknown species in those parts) and an invitation to seize the possessions and send the head of anyone looking like that to the Chinese authorities! Moorcroft finally had to consider his fall-back route to reach Bokhara. However much he had fallen out with Ranjit Singh, the latter's formal permission for him to travel through Kashmir and the Punjab was still nominally valid. So he now decided that this was the way he must go, passing on through Peshawar and the Khyber Pass to Kabul and the Hindu Kush, across the Oxus, and on through Balkh to Bokhara. It was not only a very roundabout way, but it also involved travelling through the territory of the dreaded Murad Beg (whose capital was Kunduz) and some of the most hostile country in Central Asia.

The first stage of the journey into Kashmir was not without its incidents. At one point, one of the horses carrying their equipment fell into a river and Moorcroft's much-prized collapsible bed was washed away downstream, and his note-books damaged by being soaked. More seriously, on the Dras river (between Leh and Srinagar) his horse fell from an icy track 'and we both pitched sideways upon a large slab of jasper, from the polished surface of which we rolled rapidly down a steep slope covered with snow [. . .] a slight check in our progress enabled me to disengage my feet from the stirrups but one leg remained tightly girthed [. . .] and the horse continued to slide along the slope dragging me down after him'. They ended up within a few feet of the edge of a precipice overlooking the river, Moorcroft badly battered but still able to carry on. As if that were not enough for one day, when they reached the small town of Dras they found that a party of armed bandits, led by the Raja of Hasora, had swept down the previous night and pillaged the settlement, leaving many injured behind them. Predictably, it fell to Moorcroft to use his veterinarian and medical skills to patch up the wounded and organize the construction of a stockade in the snow, while his Tibetan wolfhounds ranged outside the stockade to scare off any potential repetition of the raid. For one reason and another, he was delayed for ten days at Dras – the very first leg of his formidable itinerary.

He stayed much longer – over-wintering in fact – at Srinagar, the capital of Kashmir. Here he had to replenish his provisions and re-equip himself and his party for the arduous crossing of Afghanistan. Fortunately, Ranjit Singh did not unduly interfere with his visitor's plans. He undoubtedly would have done if he had known the extent of Moorcroft's espionage activities, how he was reporting in detail on the viability of routes through Kashmir into India from the north, and how he was speculating that Ranjit Singh might himself hand over Kashmir to the Russians as part of a wider deal. Indeed, Moorcroft was at his most neurotic during his stay at Srinagar, even imagining that a group of Frenchmen, who were actually residing there to train the Kashmiri army, were themselves tsarist agents preparing for just such a Russian invasion. Moorcroft's letters back to India about this would once again have put his life in danger had they been intercepted by Ranjit Singh's people; but they were not, and nor did they seem

to have any effect on their recipients in India, who were wearying of Moorcroft's endless and rambling warnings.

When it came to leaving Kashmir, all Moorcroft's earlier suspicions of Ranjit Singh surfaced again as one reason after another was put forward to prevent him and Trebeck from actually getting away. Even when the local chiefs stopped objecting to his departure, practical difficulties in the form of obstruction by the camel loaders and camel drivers cropped up in a sinisterly premeditated way. Just as before in Ladakh he had feared that he might be heading for an oubliette in Lahore, so now he feared that 'a mine would spring up under our feet before our party could reach Peshawar'. And this was exactly what appeared to happen.

Moorcroft and his party had crossed the Indus River near the fort at Attock and were nearing the outer extremity of Ranjit Singh's sphere of influence at the village of Akora, which was known to be the haunt of Khatak tribal gangs with a reputation for attacking passing caravans. Moorcroft's extensive party was likely to have attracted particular attention as unhelpful reports had been put around to the effect that the chests strapped on the camels (in reality holding medicines and ammunition) were stuffed with gold and rubies. Moorcroft's memoirs (edited by Horace Wilson and published by John Murray in 1841) give a vivid account of what occurred:

Upon loading our cattle the following morning, we saw a small body of horsemen assembled on the line of our route, and a message was sent to us from the Naib [the deputy leader of the Khataks] forbidding our advance, on pain of being immediately attacked. To this we determined to pay no regard; but before we moved the strength of the party had increased to about two hundred horse, and one hundred foot, whilst a mob of seven or eight hundred had issued behind us from the town. We nevertheless commenced our march, dividing our small

31

party into two bodies, one in advance, and the other in the rear, with the camels and baggage in the centre. The road was intersected by a ravine, which about seventy or eighty of the Khatak infantry were detached to occupy; but the head of our party gained the edge of it at the same time, and threatening, if they opposed, to open fire upon the Khataks, from a small piece of ordnance with the advance, they retired with great precipitation upon a body of horsemen in their rear.

At this stage the Naib, seeing Moorcroft was determined to proceed come what may, ordered his men off. But even then it was not the end of the affair, as some of the tribal horsemen turned up a couple of miles further down the track; but by the end of the day, Moorcroft was beyond their reach. And also – he concluded – beyond the reach of Ranjit Singh's retribution. Often slightly paranoid about plots against him – be they Russian or Punjabi – Moorcroft may have imagined the hand of the unfriendly raja behind this final attack as he was leaving his territory for good; it may have been merely a greedy attempt to grab the caravan's loot by the notoriously predatory Khataks. Be that as it may, the only fatal casualty his party had suffered in the Punjab was the death of one of his servants resulting from a snake bite, which Moorcroft – despite his promptly killing the snake and lancing the fatal incision – was unable to prevent.

By the night of 7 December 1823 Moorcroft and his entire party were firmly in Afghanistan. While at Peshawar (at that time within Afghanistan) a letter caught up with him from the authorities in Calcutta. It was a clear letter of recall, stating that as he had little prospect now of completing his mission and as he was urgently required back at the stud, he should 'make preparation for returning to the British provinces as soon as practicable'. The letter went on to say that only if he had already reached Kabul 'or the vicinity of that place' could he be permitted to carry on his journey to Bokhara. This was a chance for Moorcroft to return honourably to India and his well-paid job if he wanted to do so. But he did not; he was still intent on reaching Bokhara, finding the long-sought Turkoman horses, opening up further trade routes, and assessing the military and commercial threat to Afghanistan and beyond from Russia. Apart from the horses, none of these objectives were shared by his masters in Calcutta. Moorcroft resolved to ignore – or at least misinterpret to his own convenience – his instructions: he decided that Peshawar, although more than two hundred miles across difficult country from Kabul, could be described as within the kingdom of Kabul and so he qualified as being 'in the vicinity of that place'. He would ignore the letter of recall.

It was already June 1824 when Moorcroft and his party traversed the Khyber Pass and entered what is now Afghanistan proper. The locals – then as almost ever since – had a bad reputation for laying ambushes, but he felt the escort that he was offered was of almost as dubious a character as the Khyber tribesmen themselves. The latter he described as 'tall for mountaineers, and of a singularly Jewish cast of features', and – as always having an eye for the ladies – he found 'some of the young women had an arch, lively look, but we saw none that could be regarded as pretty'. He believed he was the first Englishman to travel through the pass, so he took more than usually careful notes of its potential as an invasion route or as a defensive feature. He refers, for instance, to the difficulty of getting cannon through the pass. There were mishaps – the demise of two of his dogs who succumbed to heatstroke: 'the wind was as scorching as if it had been blown from a blacksmith's forge', he recorded. Nor were the precincts of the pass a region where he felt he could sleep safely in camp; being continually alert by night, he became unnaturally sleepy by day and often dozed off in the saddle. Despite these precautions, they were surreptitiously robbed of a number of items; one of the party had his pistol taken from his holster by the man holding his horse as he dismounted, and 'due to the remissness of the sentries' Trebeck had a pistol stolen from under his pillow as he slept.

When Moorcroft reached Kabul itself, he found the city in its customary state of intrigue, plotting and counter-plotting. He and his party were to some extent a shuttlecock between the rival factions, being alternately the subject of excessive customs demands and special immunity from any customs payments. The confused political scene did not prevent Moorcroft appreciating the strategic importance of Afghanistan; he singled out Shah Shuja as a likely pro-British candidate for the Afghan throne – a view which was later to be shared by others with disastrous effects. Meanwhile matters moved from bad to worse, with open fighting breaking out in the streets of Kabul between rival factions. Taking advantage of a peaceful interval in this civil confusion, Moorcroft prepared his party to move on. But a number of locally engaged members of his team chose the moment to desert and make their own way back to India or elsewhere, including some of his hitherto-staunch Gurkha escorts. It was mid-August before he managed finally to get clear of Kabul and head off into the foothills of the Hindu Kush. He thought that leaving the kingdom of Kabul behind him meant he had weathered the most dangerous stage of his whole journey to Bokhara, but he had reckoned without Murad Beg at Kunduz.

Moorcroft feared being caught up in a civil war, and his baggage with its imagined riches being seized as a source of pay-roll money by one side or the other. However, 'man-stealing' as it was then called – kidnapping for ransom as it would now be known – was to become the main risk as they approached Kunduz. In fact one of Moorcroft's men, who had been straggling behind, was grabbed and carried off very early in their time in the Hindu Kush. While they were travelling through the mountains, they slept each night in caves and were not always able to check that the caves were free of robbers and wild animals before they dropped off to sleep.[3]

When they reached Tashkurghan, a little market town in the territory of Kunduz, they were disconcerted to be told by the local governor that Moorcroft was required to go eighty miles out of his way to Kunduz to present himself to the much-feared Murad Beg. Heavy hints were dropped that he would be expected to bring suitably lavish gifts with him. He set off across the bandit-infested country between Tashkurghan and Kunduz in a fairly nervous state, and on one occasion mistook – much to his embarrassment – a herd of cows for a party of raiders. A more serious setback was a message from Murad Beg that the whole of Moorcroft's party was to follow him to Kunduz, and they were all to be corralled under the authority of the notorious slave-dealer.

Murad Beg received Moorcroft in audience soon after his arrival at Kunduz, and from his close and unfriendly questioning

---

3. When the author was taken on a hunting trip into the Hindu Kush (by a friendly Afghan warlord) on his first visit to Afghanistan in 1958, the party slept in caves, presumably like those thought to have been giving shelter to Osama bin Laden after the events of September 2001. On one occasion the footprints of a leopard were found in the morning around the mouth of the cave. Such caves are not always the safest of shelters.

it was clear that he thought his visitor was engaged in espionage and also in possession of a vast treasure trove. Having dismissed Moorcroft, he subsequently questioned his Persian secretary in even greater detail: 'With regard to myself [Moorcroft recorded later] the chief remarked that he had been informed it was the practice of Europeans to send spies and secret emissaries into foreign countries, preparatory to their subjugation, and that he had been informed such was my real character'. However, Moorcroft was allowed to return to Tashkurghan, but not to leave the country until he paid extortionate customs levies on his whole caravan; days were spent at Tashkurghan trying to reach an agreed figure which would allow them to move on.

Just when everything seemed in place and Moorcroft was about to set off on the final leg of his mission to Bokhara, Murad Beg summoned him back to Kunduz ostensibly because he wanted medical help for some wounded soldiers. He also claimed that he would be ensuring the safety of the caravan and their goods while he made enquiries into the validity of Moorcroft's claims to be a horse-dealer and merchant rather than a spy. On arrival at Kunduz, no accommodation had been arranged for them, and Moorcroft and his party had to sleep on the floor of flea-infested quarters. As this point Moorcroft became convinced that Murad Beg's real intention was to seize all his trading goods, animals and alleged treasure and then to prevent any word of his fate getting back to India. It was a terrifying prospect. It seemed it was here rather than in Lahore that he would disappear without trace. He could not help recalling that Murad Beg's reputation included the murder of his uncle and his own brother, the handing over of his sister and daughter to the lustful purposes of a robber chief, and the selling into slavery of discarded concubines from his own harem. Consideration could hardly be expected from such a host, particularly once his greed had been awakened.

After so much enforced detention in Tashkurghan and Kunduz, Moorcroft and Trebeck thought seriously about trying to 'divide our party into two bodies, and fall upon the Uzbeks in the night, disperse them, seize their horses, and make a forced march out of the territory', fighting their way out. One drawback to this scheme was that a third European member of their party – Dr Guthrie – was not with them and would have been sacrificed to their escape. This was unacceptable to Moorcroft. He resolved instead 'to try a different scheme; to leave my tents privately during the night, and repair to Kasdim Jan [. . .] the spiritual guide and father-in-law of Murad Beg, and implore his intercession'. This spiritual guide, on whose goodwill and influence they decided to place all their trust, lived at Talikan – a considerable ride away. So Moorcroft surreptitiously stationed three horses in a hidden spot, managed to recruit two guides, and left his tent in the night, 'throwing an Uzbek silk dress over my own, with a sheep-skin cap upon my head, enfolded at bottom by a large turban, one end of which hung loose and the other was brought across my mouth and chin so as to conceal my face and want of beard'. Thus disguised, and 'concealing myself as much as possible by descending into ravines and hollows' he reached the rendezvous and set off with his guides to Talikan: 'we mounted and galloped until we reached the foot of the mountain' and went on skirting round the edge of Kunduz at night. They passed close to a fort without being observed, and at one point his guides nearly gave the game away by lighting up their pipes.

Eventually the terrain became too difficult for night riding, and they sheltered at the bottom of a ravine until they 'discovered a path by which we crossed the mountain as the day was beginning to dawn'. It turned out that it was just as well they had not tried to go over the mountains at night, because at the foot of the pass they found the remains of the fire made by a party of bandits who had obviously camped there overnight. They rode on all the following day, fording rivers at the right place by waiting to see where others forded them. When they had to enter a settlement to get food for the horses, Moorcroft 'lay down on a felt, and the guide who remained with me replied to those who inquired that I was his fellow traveller and very ill with fever'. This relieved him from the need to speak or show himself in any other way that might reveal him as a European. Once again they had to halt overnight because the guides had lost the way, and even when they re-found it they were obliged to travel through mud often up to the horses' knees. Moorcroft's horse was unable to manage any pace faster than a walk, because of 'being galled by my English saddle'. All in all, dodging both the authorities and random bandits, and coping with bad weather and rough terrain, it had not been an easy two days' ride to Talikan.

But it turned out to have been worth it. When they reached Talikan, the spiritual guide – or Khaja as he was known – quickly agreed to receive Moorcroft, who takes up the tale in his memoirs:

> I passed through a low porch formed of mats, and entered a circular chamber, on one side of which, close to the door, the saint was seated. I made the customary salutation, which was received with courtesy. I stated I was in some embarrassment as to what I had to state, as

38

it concerned a person with whom he was closely connected. The Khaja desired me to speak freely. I accordingly entered into a full detail of the vexatious detention and extortion to which I had been subjected by Murad Beg, after having been encouraged by him to enter his dominions, and threw myself on the equity and commiseration of the Khaja.

To all this, the holy man listened attentively and then, after a few questions, assured Moorcroft that he could count on his good offices. The fact that Moorcroft 'had thrown himself upon his protection and had become his guest' made such help a moral obligation. He further demonstrated his difference from his greedy son-in-law by returning the rich gifts presented to him by Moorcroft.

While he was awaiting developments, Moorcroft was approached by an emissary of Murad Beg, who tried to lure him out of the holy man's house to 'have some private conversation'. Moorcroft very sensibly declined to leave his sanctuary without the express protection of the holy man; by this precaution he was told 'he had taken the only steps that could have saved us' from being promptly abducted and taken back in custody to face the wrath and avarice of Murad Beg. Further attempts were made to lure Moorcroft out, ostensibly to show him some fine horses, but he remained adamant. Further envoys were also sent to prejudice the holy man against Moorcroft, including a man whose 'countenance was sharp and intelligent, but strongly expressive of malevolence' and who was accusing Moorcroft of various subterfuges. At this juncture, Moorcroft requested a second audience with the holy man in the presence of his accuser. The latter then maintained that Moorcroft was not a trader or a vet, but a general in the East India Company's army, and that he had been travelling on espionage missions for the past eight years. Even the holy man – the least military-minded of men – could understand that a general did not act as a spy, and that neither did a general desert his command for eight years at a stretch. A furious debate ensued, with the malevolent envoy accusing Moorcroft of 'taking the likenesses of mountains, rivers, towns and forts' and making illustrations of these features to help an invading army. This Englishman, he declared, had subverted the whole of Tibet and Kashmir, had imposed a levy on the Punjab and had stirred up trouble in Afghanistan – quite an achievement for a single individual! Winding up his peroration, he 'exclaimed at the top of his voice, and with a most satanic expression of countenance: "If you will not plunder and slay him, send him back to his own country!"'. Moorcroft for his part admitted to taking notes, and to the fact that other British 'government newsreaders' did the same as 'the necessity of counteracting the designs of the King of the French, who had declared his intention of marching to invade British India' (it was still only a few years after Waterloo); he also reminded his listeners that a whole host of merchants from Kabul and elsewhere could testify to his commercial credentials. It was Moorcroft whose protestations carried the day; the holy man concluded: 'The Englishman has spoken truth – thou falsehood – get thee hence!'

After this verdict, Moorcroft's accuser slunk away and rode back to Kunduz. Moorcroft himself retired to his apartment, where the holy man came to call on him shortly afterwards. The Khaja wasted no time in explaining to Moorcroft that – however pleased he might be to have won the argument – he should remember that he the Khaja 'was only a Fakir, and that my enemy was a powerful chief '. Moorcroft did what he could to reassure the holy man of his moral influence and power, but the Khaja pointed out that 'the exercise of that authority would dissolve the union which had hitherto subsisted between them [Murad Beg and his father-in-law], and would create him many enemies'. He therefore wanted to patch up an agreement which would leave Murad Beg with his dignity and cupidity at least to some extent gratified. A further payment was proposed as the answer. Advice was sought. After debate, an initial suggestion of a further six thousand rupees was reduced to two thousand, and a messenger was sent off to Kunduz with this offer as the price for Moorcroft and his party being allowed to leave peacefully for Bokhara. The messenger was forestalled by the unexpected arrival of Murad Beg himself in Talikan; the chief was at first disinclined to accept the proposed settlement and was demanding vast quantities of rubies, but his father-in-law (the holy man) eventually persuaded him to accept the earlier proposal with some modest modification. But even then the saga was not over; Murad Beg said that as he was about to set off on a military marauding excursion he could not allow Moorcroft to leave 'lest his [Murad Beg's] movements should be made known'.

Moorcroft sensibly declined a suggestion that he should return to Kunduz to await the chief's return from campaign, and opted instead to extend his sojourn with the Khaja at Talikan. Prolonging his visit had one unforeseen consequence: he became disillusioned about the nature of the holy man. It transpired that 'notwithstanding his saintly character, he was a dealer in merchandise and especially in slaves, of whom a portion taken in his forays were usually presented to [him] by Murad Beg [. . .] I saw a number of Badakhshani boys and girls detained until an opportunity offered of sending them for sale at Yarkand'. The slaves were sold in exchange for such commodities as tea, china, satin and porcelain. Another – though to most people less serious – fault which Moorcroft now found with the holy man was that he occasionally served up horse flesh at dinner – not an acceptable dish for an English stud manager.[4]

Moorcroft also spent part of his time staying at Talikan doing exactly the type of military surveying – 'espionage' would not have been a misleading description – which he had so hotly denied being involved with earlier (after all, he knew that Napoleon was no longer a threat to India even if his hosts did not): he noted that the local fort was 'a quadrangular building, with conical towers at the angles, and is of no importance [. . .] on the right bank of the Farkham river is a fort similar to that at Talikan' and so on.

When finally permission arrived for Moorcroft to move on, the holy man insisted on his staying an extra day till the omens were propitious for his journey; he then embraced Moorcroft – 'a mark of favour I had never seen him confer on anyone before' – and gave him his blessing. Moorcroft records he was sincerely grateful to him 'for an interposition which alone could have preserved us from destruction, and which had been exercised throughout the whole affair in a manner uniformly kind, benevolent and, though gentle, yet resolute'. It had been a brilliant idea of Moorcroft's to seek support in this quarter, and

---

4. The aversion of cavalry officers and their associates to eating horse flesh long persisted and probably still persists. The author recalls hearing of a relative who was 'singularly disadvantaged' during the siege of Ladysmith in the Boer War because the only meat available was horse flesh and – as a lancer – he felt obliged to abstain however hungry and starving he became.

his scheme had worked better than he had any reasonable expectation would be the case.

Now his last hurdle was to pass through Kunduz one final time and pay his departing respects to Murad Beg if need be. When the latter heard that Moorcroft had arrived, he promptly summoned him and – in marked contrast to his more unworldly father-in-law – immediately asked 'what had I got for him?'. Moorcroft replied by asking what he wanted, and on being told that his personal collapsible chair had taken the chief's fancy, told him that if he would send a man for it, it should be his. Murad Beg then went on to help himself to some medicines which Moorcroft had prescribed for someone else. But all in all, he was lucky to get away with his party intact: the chief had requested that Dr Guthrie be left behind – a suggestion which Moorcroft naturally refused.

Having finally shaken the dust of Kunduz off their camels' feet, Moorcroft and his party pressed on towards Bokhara, passing through Mizar-i-Sharif, Balkh and various smaller forts and settlements. When they came to cross the Oxus river some hundred miles south of Bokhara, they found it 'about as broad as the Thames opposite the Temple gardens'; they shot across it for target practice and found that a carbine bullet reached the other side without difficulty.

The only significant halt between the Oxus and their destination was the fortified town of Karshi; this was presided over by a sixteen-year-old prince-governor, who was the son of the Emir of Bokhara 'by a bondmaid'; the lad received them with all due pomp, ceremony and beard-stroking; throughout their journey from Kunduz they had found that the local rulers, almost without exception, deplored the bad manners and hostile behaviour of Murad Beg. This made them more confident about the prospects of being well received at Bokhara. Little did they know that the friendly and apparently innocent sixteen-year-old was a few years later – having murdered his brother and seized control of Bokhara in the interval – to become the evil emir who imprisoned and later executed Arthur Conolly (the subject of a later chapter in this book).

It was therefore with high spirits that Moorcroft reported 'with no slender satisfaction that on the morning of the 25th of February 1825 we found ourselves at the end of our protracted pilgrimage, at the gates of that city which had for five years been the object of our wanderings, privations and perils'. They had reached the holy city of Bokhara, where, according to legend, the light shone not down from heaven, but up to heaven from the domes and minarets of that sacred place.

The emir received Moorcroft in audience, who presented him with substantial gifts, including a cannon – the 'small piece of ordinance' which had proved so useful when they had been ambushed in leaving Ranjit Singh's domains at Akora. Not only was he friendly, but he also gave Moorcroft a licence to buy horses and sell his own trade goods. And Moorcroft soon observed some very fine horses indeed, mostly owned by courtiers around the citadel, but it turned out that such promising bloodstock was in short supply because so many of the best horses had been killed, wounded or worn out in the almost continual round of forays and military campaigns with which the emir indulged his ambitions. Indeed Moorcroft had hardly had time to identify and make offers for some of the best horses before they were whisked away by their owners on another such punitive expedition in the direction of Samarkand. Almost equally discouraging was the fact that the trade goods, which Moorcroft had so assiduously transported all this way, turned out to be unappealing to the local markets, which had grown accustomed to – arguably inferior – Russian goods. This was bad news for Moorcroft, because he was dependent on the cash generated by selling his own trade goods to have the funds to buy the horses that were the object of his journey. However, always alert to make the best of the situation and to pursue his personal agenda of opening up trading routes, he managed to buy some Russian goods to take back to India as an indication of what the markets of Bokhara were expecting.

And it was not only Russian commercial activities that occupied Moorcroft's attention. He was convinced they were intent on political and ultimately military domination of Bokhara, as of other regions of Central Asia. While the suspicious and paranoid emir was away on his campaign, Moorcroft was freer not only to make his own observations, but to set up a network of agents who could continue to report on the situation after he and his party had left.

Moorcroft now thought he had achieved all he could in Bokhara and asked for permission to leave. He was told he could not, until he had joined the emir at his campaign camp near Samarkand. He did not want to get involved in a military campaign, but had no option but to go as bidden. Once there, his medical skills were fully deployed tending to the wounded among the emir's followers, and he took advantage of the goodwill generated by this activity to seek leave to buy a few more stallions. But when he refused to take an active part – organizing the artillery – in the siege in which the emir was involved, the permission to buy horses was quickly withdrawn and he had to leave behind the best of those he had hoped to take with him. Even Moorcroft's disinclination to follow the rules did not allow him to engage East India Company personnel in a war that was nothing to do with him or his followers. He retraced his steps to Bokhara and then set out for home in July 1825.

But he had one further prospect in mind. When at Balkh he had heard rumours of wonderful Turkoman horses in the deserts or on the steppes some hundred miles to the west of that place, and he thought he could leave the main body of his party there and set off alone with just two or three companions – grooms and servants rather than armed escorts – to make a detour to locate and purchase these elusive steeds. The first stage was to return to Balkh, and the whole party set off with much less baggage; nonetheless, they still numbered some sixty men and horses with a few camels in support. He decided to leave the question of his ultimate return route until he had finished his private excursion from Balkh, but – whichever way he went – he was determined to avoid the clutches of Murad Beg. One way or another, he was anxious to cross the Hindu Kush before the winter snows made that impossible.

Having reached Balkh, Moorcroft left his party there and set off westwards, expecting to be away only some two or three weeks – longer than that, and he would put at risk his crossing of the Hindu Kush. It was at some stage before he left Trebeck and the others that Moorcroft received a letter from India (which was miraculously traced by Gary Alder when researching his life of Moorcroft) addressed simply to 'W. Moorcroft Esq, Samarkand or Elsewhere'; clearly the busy little vet, medic, horse-trader, entrepreneur and explorer had left his mark across a great swathe of Central Asia and was someone whose movements were known to many. But once he had set out from Balkh this last time, far from being widely known, his movements and everything else take on a strangely mysterious element.

The accepted version of the story is that he and his servants reached the village he was aiming for and there he fell ill with a fever and died three days later on 27 August 1825. His body – or at least a body – was brought back to Balkh where Trebeck (who did not identify the corpse, which would have been a grisly job after so many days in the extreme heat) arranged to have it buried in a Christian manner. These were for many years the undisputed facts regarding the end of a remarkable but largely unacknowledged career.

It was only some twenty years later that two priests (from the French mission to Peking) when visiting Lhasa were told that a man who had lived there from 1826 for twelve years, and who had then been murdered on his way to Ladakh, had left behind maps and papers revealing that he was not – as had been supposed – a Kashmiri but in fact an Englishman named Moorcroft, who had assiduously recorded all he had seen and learnt about the country where he had for so long been accepted as a resident. Someone then came forward who claimed to have been his servant during those years, and who had never realized he was not a Kashmiri as he spoke fluent Persian and behaved like a Moslem. Could this indeed have been Moorcroft?

The timing fitted with his departure from the scene; he was known to have an ongoing interest in Tibet and a desire eventually to retire in the Himalayas; he might have felt that his bloodstock mission had failed and his reputation with the stud in India had collapsed; nobody could be found who had actually witnessed his death or identified his body.

On the other hand, for Moorcroft to have deserted his companions (they had a terrible series of disasters – robberies, detention and fatal illness – after he left them) and abandoned any idea of pressing his case for opening up trade with Central

Asia, and of warning the authorities in India of the Russian threat as he so vividly perceived it, all seem completely out of character. So much so, that his biographer Garry Alder was firmly convinced that – even granted that Moorcroft's papers and maps may have turned up in Tibet – Moorcroft himself had behaved honourably to the end and lay buried where Trebeck had laid him.

The East India Company did little note, nor long remember, what Moorcroft – their recalcitrant stud farm manager – had done for them or for the wider concept of the British Raj in India. He had failed to produce the bloodstock for which they and he had hoped, and he had strayed far beyond the remit of his instructions, overstaying his leave of absence, embarking on trade agreements for which he had no authority, and involving himself and his masters in political controversy.

But future generations were to recognize aspects of his life and work to which his contemporaries seemed impervious, or by which they were less impressed. His geographical achievements alone were outstanding: he had been the first Englishman to reach Bokhara for over two centuries, and possibly the first ever to cross the Oxus and make himself familiar with the lands along its banks. And as a forecaster of the Russian threat to the khanates and emirates of Central Asia, time was to prove how solidly based his forecasts and fears were, as the Russian troops rolled over one after another of the territories he had explored.

He was not the first player of the Great Game, but he was the first who identified the threat correctly. Nor was it he who coined the phrase Great Game; that was to be done by Arthur Conolly (the subject of the next chapter). But however much Christie, Conolly and others might exceed or ignore their instructions, it was the little vet from Lancashire who tore up his employers' rule book more assiduously than anyone: this was an independent spirit who was to be a guiding light to many subsequent adventurers.

Chapter 3

Arthur Conolly: The Soldier Who Exceeded His Orders

'Show me a hero and I will write you a tragedy.'
    – F. Scott Fitzgerald (1896–1940)

Lieutenant Arthur Conolly of the Bengal Native Light Cavalry started his military career as a model player in the Great Game; indeed it was he who first coined that phrase to describe the struggle between tsarist Russia and the British Raj in India for mastery of Central Asia. But he was to end not only his career but his life after exceeding his instructions. An officer who once had enjoyed the full support and confidence of his superiors, he was to be murdered in circumstances in which his own government could not help him and was set on disowning his enterprise.

In late 1829, returning after home leave, the twenty-four-year-old Conolly had set out overland from England through Russia, the Caucasus, Persia and Afghanistan bound for British India. He had already served in India since the age of sixteen when he had been sent out by sea, after finishing his schooling at Rugby, to join his regiment. Now his role was to observe Russian troop deployments, to assess the terrain that any army would have to cross if planning to invade India, and to make contact with the Khan of Khiva and Afghan leaders whose domains lay across the line of any such advance towards India.

All went smoothly for the first stages of the journey. The carriage drive from St Petersburg to Moscow took five days and nights on a very bad road, 'sandy, muddy or over the trunks of trees which had been laid across it'. After four days in Moscow, where he lamented the 'gross and idolatrous superstition which can scarcely be imagined by a Protestant', he pressed on and crossed the River Don into Cossack country and then continued over the steppes towards the Caucasus, sleeping at night in the carriage 'buried in furs'. As he approached the Caucasus however, security considerations arose. He waited to join up with a larger party that could justify an escort of Terek Cossacks, some infantry and even a twelve-pounder gun. He was now entering a region where 'the Russians do not yet command free passage [...] for they are obliged to be very vigilant against surprise by the Circassian sons of the mist, who still cherish the bitterest hatred against them'.

Even the Cossacks were nervous, as sixteen of their number had been ambushed and killed very shortly before. For once Conolly's military judgement was mistaken: he predicted that 'the Russians will find it an easy task to reduce them [the Circassians] to obedience' since they had set up forts on the coast and were imposing a blockade which would mean that supplies could no longer reach the insurgents from Turkey.

Conolly was still the guest of the Russian commanders, who entertained him at Tiflis – the Georgian capital – and who impressed him with their hardiness and bravery. But he was already beginning to feel that, although they might be Orthodox Christians and thus in principle to be preferred to the followers of the Prophet, they did not share his particular brand of religious conviction. His own beliefs – which were to play a crucial part in his later disastrous decisions – were largely the result of exposure at an impressionable age to Bishop Reginald Heber, the charismatic preacher and author of such popular hymns as 'Holy, Holy, Holy! Lord God Almighty' and 'From Greenland's Icy Mountains to India's Coral Strand'. For Conolly, Anglicanism was a mixture of evangelicalism and patriotism: to rescue a fellow countryman and to die for one's faith were to prove commitments that transcended any military instructions.

The first real dangers and tests of his endurance were to come when he left the protection of the Russian authorities and of the Persians to set off across the Karakum desert from Astrabad on the Caspian Sea to Khiva on the Oxus river. This was Turkoman country, where caravans were regularly waylaid by armed parties of slavers, and where to travel as an Englishman was to invite both the cupidity of hostage takers and the hatred of a population who feared (often correctly) that foreigners were pathfinders for invading armies. Up to now, he had travelled as himself; now disguise was required. He decided that if he went as a local merchant this would not only conceal his nationality but would also give him a plausible reason for making the trip; accordingly he set about buying goods which he thought appropriate for the Khivan market: red silk scarves, shawls, furs, pepper, ginger and other spices. It was difficult to persuade his guide and servant to go with him: the latter seemed to think the Turkomans would eat him.

The fear engendered by the Turkomans, though they were not cannibals, proved to have plenty of justification. Conolly and his companion had not gone far into the desert on their camels in their search to find and join a larger caravan, when they were overtaken by a small armed gang who – under pretence of protecting them – effectively took them prisoner. They then led them off their path towards Khiva on an alarmingly circuitous route which seemed to be taking them ever further from help. When questioned about why they were doing this, their captors confessed that they had heard from one of the desert tribal chiefs that Conolly was really a Russian agent, loaded with gold bullion to bribe support for his cause. Conolly records in his account of his travels that at this stage 'we told them to examine our baggage, and convince themselves that we had no wealth, and then escort us to the caravan [. . .] or two of their number might come with us to Khiva, where Russians would certify that I was not of their country'. Although the armed gang were at pains to avoid taking them to settled encampments, they stumbled on some other camps in the desert. At one of these their captors took up their offer of allowing them to search their baggage for the supposed stock of gold ducats; the only gold they found was the few coins they carried in belts round their waists, but – more disturbingly – when they unwrapped a brass astrolabe they assumed this was solid gold and were with difficulty persuaded that it was not an object of intrinsic value – however much value it held for Conolly, for navigational purposes.

Eventually Conolly concluded that all the prevarication and delay was a prelude to deciding either to murder them or to sell them into slavery. Their so-called protectors continued to avoid contact with other desert travellers wherever possible, explaining that such travellers were likely to be enemies, but Conolly remarked that he was not sure what such enemies could do to him that was worse than the attentions of his 'protectors'. However, contact with outsiders at a desert well revealed the

fact that their captors had 'given out a report of our murder' to see what the reaction would be: 'if our friends appeared resigned to our loss', then Conolly and his friend could be safely sold on; if on the other hand 'it should appear that we had patrons influential enough to cause annoyance', then they would 'produce us as [having been] saved from attack'. While all this negotiation, aimless travel and constant menace was going on, Conolly gained some local credit by offering medical cures to those with ailments; in some cases he was able to give genuine help, and in others he made wishful promises in the conviction that – by the time they were proved to be unfounded – he would either be dead or gone.

While on these gyrations round the desert, Conolly learnt some useful tips for travellers in Central Asia. For instance, he nearly gave away his European origins at one point by carelessly throwing two lumps of sugar into a cooking cauldron; such extravagance with a rare commodity could only – his hosts speculated – be evidence of extreme (European) wealth. He also learnt that when selling a horse, it was incumbent on the vendor to explain to the buyer where the horse had been stolen; if such information were not passed on, and the purchaser was later challenged about the true ownership of the horse, the vendor would have to pay compensation. Conolly wryly remarked that it sounded just like Yorkshire to him!

It was random contact with some Persian merchant travellers that eventually led to their being escorted back to Astrabad. Conolly had failed to reach Khiva, but he had survived his desert ordeal and had learnt a considerable amount about the problems of crossing the Karakum desert. He had learnt also that Khiva still retained its independence and that the Russians had not yet properly established themselves on the eastern side of the Caspian Sea. Now he contemplated an alternative route to India, one that might equally be used by an invader. He turned southwards and headed for the Persian town of Meshed, and after that across another bleak region to Herat in Afghanistan; for part of this journey he managed to travel under the protection of an Afghan military unit, and so was able to observe at first hand the practicality of moving an army across the harsh terrain. The experience of travelling with the Afghan army also gave him a disturbing introduction to their methods of discipline: noses were cut off those who had broken ranks to go marauding or who had proved to be sleepy sentries.

Once in Herat, he again abandoned his merchant guise and reverted to his increasingly familiar and well-practised role of a man of medicine; this proved sufficiently convincing to save him from further scrutiny by the despotic ruler. The next stage before he reached India was across Afghanistan from Herat to Kandahar, and here again it was slave-raider country. The distinctive feature of the bandit gangs in this area was that they made a practice of cutting off the ears of their prisoners, in the belief that this would so embarrass the latter that they would be less likely to try to escape and make for home where their disfigurement would prove a humiliation to them. Mindful of his lack of protection in the Karakum, and no doubt alarmed at all the mutilation he had witnessed or heard about, he took the precaution of ensuring that he was accepted into a party of Islamic holy men before venturing beyond the walls of Herat. From Kandahar it was another long march to the Indus and the frontier of British India.

Conolly had not completed his journey along the intended route. But he had switched to another route which was equally relevant to the possible invasion of India. He had followed his instructions and returned with valuable intelligence. So far he had been a model officer, so much so, that he sat down on his return to write a postscript to his account of his travels, analyzing the threat to India from Russia, as well as outlining the routes that any invading force might take. Furthermore he suggested broad foreign policy objectives which might serve to frustrate such an invasion. He argued not only that Britain should set up and support a friendly regime in Afghanistan, but also that she should endeavour to bring the khanates and emirates of Central Asia into an alliance with each other and with Britain which would serve to provide a buffer zone and which – also an important objective for Conolly – would involve their giving up their trade in slaves. Conolly felt that the abolition of slave capturing and the slave markets would not only ensure that the khanates were less provocative to their powerful northern neighbour (many of the slaves were captured Russians), but would also be a stepping stone to their adopting those Christian values that played such an important part in his faith.

Now that he was established as an intrepid and resourceful traveller (his two-volume account of his journey was published in 1838), Conolly was determined to seek authority for further ventures into Central Asia. But not everyone thought his ambitious plans to unite and convert the khans and emirs was realistic. Among his critics was Sir Alexander Burnes – 'Bokhara Burnes', whose own travels in the region were already legendary – who saw Conolly as an over-emotional trespasser on his own established ground: 'he is flighty, though a very nice fellow [. . .] he is to regenerate Toorkistan, dismiss all the slaves, and looks upon our advent as a design of providence to spread Christianity', he wrote. Burnes suggested that the only way such ambitious and vague objectives could be achieved was by waving the wand of Prospero. And Burnes was not alone in his scepticism: more powerful figures were also set against any such wild projects and plans.

Chief among these powerful figures was the governor-general of India himself, Lord Auckland. The governor-general did not want to act in a manner that the Russians would find provocative, and nor did he want to get too involved with an unsavoury bunch of khans and emirs whom he viewed as basically untrustworthy. Perhaps an even stronger motive behind his letter vetoing Conolly's plan was that he did not want to have another British officer being held as a hostage by a psychopathic Central Asian ruler. Because there was already one such hostage being held in Bokhara by Emir Nasrullah.

This hostage was a certain Colonel Charles Stoddart, who had arrived in Bokhara in December 1838 with a brief from the British government (or at least from the British ambassador to Persia) to secure the release of any Russian slaves (always a provocation to the tsar) held by the emir, to offer British assistance if the emirate was attacked by a foreign power, and to reassure the emir that British intentions towards him were benign. Stoddart was a brave soldier but no diplomat: from the moment of his arrival at the emir's court he put people's backs up – riding in a cocked hat through the Registan (main square) where no one but the emir himself was permitted to remain mounted, and failing to dismount and bow when greeting the emir. It also transpired that Stoddart had no appropriate presents for the emir and no letter from Queen Victoria – a monarch whom the emir apparently considered as no more than his equal in status. After such an inauspicious start, it was only a matter of days before Stoddart was arrested and thrown into the infamous reptile-infested pit where the emir kept his enemies while they awaited execution.

Under imminent threat of death – probably being buried alive in the grave that was dug in front of him – Stoddart's morale finally collapsed and he abjured his Christian faith and declared himself a believer in Islam. Even after this 'conversion', the emir's conduct towards him was erratic in the extreme: sometimes he was received and given employment at court; at other times he was daily reminded that he was a prisoner and hostage. Some of his letters were smuggled out and even reached his family in England, but still there were no letters reaching Bokhara from Queen Victoria or any other recognition of the emir's status. It was a stalemate, in which Stoddart's safety depended from day to day on the emir's assessment of Britain's military strength. Bad news from Afghanistan could at any moment prove fatal.

This was the story that reached Conolly as he formulated his plans and negotiated with the governor-general and other British officials about whether he was to be permitted to venture again into Central Asia. And it was to add a further strand to his ambitions. Not only now did he wish to go to Khiva and Khokand, but he also saw as part of his mission penetrating as far as Bokhara to release the unfortunate Stoddart and secure his reconversion to Christianity. It was a noble aim. But Burnes and others were even more determined to prevent Conolly attempting to reach Bokhara; this was after all the destination that Burnes himself had managed to reach after so many difficulties in 1832 (eight years earlier), as a result of which he had earned the sobriquet of 'Bokhara Burnes'. It was not a distinction that he wished to share with a younger officer, and he spoke sarcastically about Conolly wishing to become 'Baron Bokhara' and predicted that if he were allowed to go ahead with the project he would end up keeping Stoddart company as a prisoner there.

But Conolly was set on his objectives. Although Burnes and the governor-general were against his proposals, he found support in England and an ally in his cousin Sir William Macnaghten who was British minister at the Afghan court and – as such – Burnes' immediate superior. Macnaghten managed to persuade a somewhat reluctant governor-general that Conolly should be allowed to proceed, but only as far as Khiva and Khokand. A dispatch was sent to Macnaghten setting out the conditions:

> As in the present aspect of affairs it does not seem necessary to continue the restriction which had at first

been imposed, the Lordship in Council authorizes you to permit Captain Conolly to proceed from Khiva to Khokand, if he should think it expedient, and if he finds that he can do so without exciting serious distrust and jealousy at the former place. In his personal intercourse with the Khan of Kokand, he will be guided by the instructions which have been issued [...] Captain Conolly may, in such a journey, find increased means of using a useful influence at Bokhara for the release of Colonel Stoddart; and, his Lordship in Council need not add, that he would wish every such means to be employed with the utmost earnestness and diligence for that purpose.

Conolly was delighted, not least because he desperately needed an adventure to take his mind off a personal unhappiness. His proposal for marriage had recently been rejected by a young lady in England, and when he thought his travel plans were to be thwarted he had written to a friend explaining that 'I felt the blank that a man must feel who has a heavy grief as the first thing to fall back on'. Now he knew he was going, he wrote again asking his friend to explain to the lady in question that he was 'about to undertake a journey which is not without risk to life, and if mine should end in Tartary, I would not have her fancy it shortened or carelessly ventured in consequences of my disap-pointed love for her'. Despite these protestations, it seems all too likely that he was indeed in a frame of mind where he was inclined to take risks that a man more at peace with himself might have rejected.

Be that as it may, Conolly set about collecting the team for his journey. This included a Khivan envoy whom he described as his 'croney', and a rather treacherous-looking envoy from the Afghan court. To ease the rigours of the journey they had an immense baggage train with some eighty bearers. So it was that, in September 1840, they set out, with reluctant consent rather than official blessing.

They headed first for the city of Merv – the crossing point for so many caravan routes and the site of a large slave market. Conolly, whose Christian values were shocked by the way in which female slaves were herded into pens and handled by lascivious purchasers, was even more shocked when he found that the Khivan envoy – his 'croney' – was quietly buying up children in the market as a speculative investment. As soon as possible he moved on from Merv and headed towards Khiva.

At Khiva he was received by a smiling and friendly khan, but he made no progress in trying to persuade him to enter into any confederation or even loose alliance with his neighbours in Khokand and Bokhara. The khan was feeling self-confident, having recently witnessed a Russian invasion force obliged to turn back without reaching his capital. As for the slave trade, the khan pointed out that he had freed those Russians who might have been a pretext for further incursions from the north, and the remaining traffic was a vital part of his state's economy. Disappointed by this response, Conolly and his sizable party moved on across the steppes to Khokand.

Here he fared no better. Far from wanting closer links with his neighbours, the Khan of Khokand was actually in the process of launching a military campaign against Bokhara. Conolly was concerned that he was to have very little to show for all his efforts. But while he was enjoying the hospitality of Khokand for two months, there was a development which was to set him off on unauthorized tracks.

Colonel Stoddart in his detention in Bokhara was experiencing a period of enjoying the favours of his despotic host. And, being aware of Conolly's relative proximity at Khokand, he managed to get letters smuggled out to him there. One of these actually contained an invitation from the emir to Conolly to visit him on his way back to India. Stoddart appeared to endorse the invitation, saying that he thought Conolly could expect to be well treated if he came. He mentioned this proposal to his host, the Khan of Khokand, but the latter warned him on no account to trust the Emir of Bokhara. The Khan of Khiva had earlier spoken in very similar terms, but Conolly was inclined to disregard these warnings: had not both khans shown a long-standing hostility towards their Bokharan counterpart, and was not Khokand even fighting with him at this very moment? Surely such negative advice was self-interested.

Conolly was well aware that he had no official authority to go to Bokhara. Indeed, it had been made clear to him that this emirate was out of bounds: there were enough difficulties already with Stoddart's detention there. But several considerations conspired to encourage Conolly to disregard his own authorities. First was his personal desire to have a solid achievement to report when he returned home, and so far he had singularly failed in this. Second was the encouragement he had had from Stoddart, and by extension from the emir himself, to extend his travels in that direction. And third was the nagging weight on Conolly's conscience: Stoddart had been coerced into renouncing his Christian convictions, and surely it was Conolly's divinely appointed role to rescue him from this lapse and see him accepted once more into the Christian fold. All these factors contributed to the decision of this hitherto well-disciplined soldier to fly in the face of his orders and undertake a venture that both he and his government were to regret.

It was not easy to go from Khokand to Bokhara when the two states were at war with each other. But adopting a devious route he managed to arrive at the Bokharan frontier at the moment when the emir was returning from his campaign, and he succeeded in entering the city in November 1841 in the wake of the triumphal ruler. This was a much better start than Stoddart's arrogant-seeming ride across the Registan square. He was installed in accommodation provided by the emir, where he and Stoddart were lodged together.

During the weeks that followed, the emir received both Englishmen in audience on a number of occasions. Gradually his questions to his visitors became less friendly. Why had Conolly come here? Had he been plotting with the neighbouring khans against Bokhara? Was he reconnoitring a route for an invading army as the English had done in Afghanistan? Where were Conolly's credentials? Why had no reply been received from Queen Victoria to the emir's friendly letters? But what really tipped the emir's sentiment against his English visitors was not so much the somewhat unsatisfactory replies to these questions but the fact that he was getting news from Afghanistan of a British defeat there. Indeed, the news was the worst possible as far as the visitors were concerned. The First Afghan War had been a disaster: the British protégé on the Afghan throne had been deposed; the British envoy to Kabul – Sir William Macnaghten – and Sir Alexander Burnes had both been murdered by the Afghans; General Elphinstone's army was in full retreat and being decimated by the tribesmen in the passes; Britain – it seemed to the emir – was no longer a power to be feared in the region. By December he was becoming openly hostile to his two hostages.

An incident then occurred which made matters worse. A Jewish visitor from Persia arrived with a packet of letters for Stoddart which he delivered to the emir's vizier. The latter passed the letters to Stoddart with a request for a translation of them. They turned out to be a dispatch which had been sent some months before by Lord Palmerston – the British foreign secretary – acknowledging the receipt of the emir's letter to Queen Victoria, but going on to say that this had been passed to the governor-general in India to deal with as he saw fit. Stoddart felt he could do nothing but forward an accurate translation to the emir, while putting the best gloss on it he could. This was not the response that the emir had expected: he felt that as a head of state – a state which he believed to be of equal standing with England – he should have been granted the dignity of a direct reply from Her Majesty.

Having received this imagined insult, and having absorbed the bad news about the British defeat in Afghanistan, the emir now felt at liberty to treat his English visitors as prisoners of little consequence. At the next audience, he made a heavy-handed remark about Conolly's gold watch, which resulted in his visitor feeling obliged to present it to the emir as a gift. But even that gesture failed to placate the vicious ruler. The next day they were arrested and imprisoned in a private jail, and Conolly's numerous servants were also rounded up, and while some were released others were executed. The British hostages were left in no doubt about the psychopathic tendencies of their host.

Deprived of news from Bokhara, and preoccupied with the appalling reports coming back from Afghanistan, the British authorities in India and London lost track of the fate of Stoddart and Conolly. The two Englishmen were being held in truly terrible conditions: hungry, clad in filthy rags, in vermin-infested cells, and suffering from tropical fevers. Those letters they endeavoured to get out by private messengers to Persia told a sorry tale of suffering. One such letter written by Conolly in March 1842 eventually surfaced and described their plight:

> This is the eighty-third day we have been denied the means of getting a change of linen from the rags and vermin that cover us [. . .] At first we viewed the emir's conduct as perhaps dictated by mad caprice; but now, looking back upon the whole, we saw instead that it had been just the deliberate malice of a demon [. . .] But God is stronger than the devil himself, and can certainly release us from the hands of this fiend [. . .] We wear our English honesty and dignity to the last, within all the filth and misery that this monster may try to degrade us with [. . .] We hope that the British and Afghan Governments will treat him as an enemy; and this out of no feeling of revenge. [. . .] We hope and pray that God may forgive him his sins in the next world. [. . .] Stoddart and I will comfort each other in every way until we die.

And die is what they did. Their last hope had been the intervention of the Russian diplomatic mission on their behalf. Although the Russians realized that the English emissaries were working to frustrate their territorial ambitions, and although Conolly had long ago outgrown his initial regard for the Russians as he became aware of their hostile ambitions in Central Asia, nonetheless the Russian mission used its best endeavours to keep in touch with the two English prisoners and to indicate their concern about them. They recognized that Christians and Europeans had to stick together in the face of oriental brutality. But now the Russian mission were themselves withdrawing from Bokhara after the emir had insulted them by insisting they did business with his butler rather than with his vizier; so this last lifeline was lost.

Ironically, it was confirmation of the Emir Nasrullah's psychopathic tendencies that held out the last shred of hope for Stoddart and Conolly. The emir had embarked on yet another of his campaigns against his neighbour at Khokand, and reports reaching the prison at Bokhara indicated that this raid had been unusually successful; in fact, the emir had killed in cold blood not only the Khan of Khokand but also his son, his brother and his uncle. He was now returning in triumph once again to Bokhara, and Conolly hoped that his success might induce a more benevolent turn of mind towards his captives. But it was not to be.

The only thing that might have saved them at this moment was a personal letter from Queen Victoria. Somewhat belatedly, consideration was finally being given in Westminster and Whitehall to drafting such a document, but meanwhile the only communication sent to the emir was an unhelpful dispatch from Lord Ellenborough (who had taken over from Lord Auckland as governor-general of India) describing the two Englishmen as innocent travellers and asking for their release. This probably arrived too late to be relevant, and in any case the emir did not even deign to answer a missive from someone who was not a fellow head of state.

At some stage (probably in June 1842) the emir appeared to have decided that he had nothing to lose by disposing of his two hostages. Stoddart and Conolly were led out of their confine-ment and ordered to dig their own graves in a public place in the main square in front of the citadel while a large crowd looked on. Stoddart took the opportunity publicly to denounce the emir as a cruel despot; he was promptly beheaded by the public executioner. Conolly was now told that if he renounced his Christian faith his life would be spared. Even if it had not been for the disheartening example of Stoddart, who had converted under extreme pressure to Islam and had then been cruelly imprisoned and executed, there would have been no prospect of Conolly renouncing his Christianity. His faith was central to his whole life – to his motivation in coming to Bokhara in the first place and to his concept of his patriotism. He declared himself ready to die, and his head was struck off, joining Stoddart's in the dust.

It was a while before news of these deaths reached England. But a few months after these events a young Persian, who had at one time been employed by Conolly, arrived at Meshed and reported that he had been given a first-hand account of the Englishmen's fate by one of the executioners himself. The truth of the story seemed far from certain, and eventually another Englishman – a clergyman called Dr Joseph Wolff – raised the

necessary funds and set off alone to reach Bokhara and verify the details of what had happened. His is another story, and is the subject of a later chapter in this book.

But even before the deaths were fully authenticated, the British and Indian governments were busy distancing themselves from the tragedy. Conolly had never been authorized to go to Bokhara, and now the authorities said that he had been expressly forbidden from doing so: 'in all probability [Conolly] owes all his misfortunes to his direct transgression of that instruction', it was declared. The Indian government stated that while it was prepared to meet some of the costs of the expedition – such as the wages of Conolly's servants – for the journey as far as Khokand, it was not prepared to meet any costs for the subsequent unauthorized extension of the trip; indeed any such expenses would be chargeable to Captain Conolly if he were alive and to his estate if he were not. Public sentiment in England was more generous to Conolly than official comment: one fellow officer and friend declared that in previous reigns any such insult and harm inflicted on an Englishman would have been promptly avenged. But the country was still reeling under the disasters of the First Afghan War – an army of 16,000 men destroyed – and the fate of the two visitors to Bokhara was somewhat overshadowed.

Captain Arthur Conolly was an officer who started his professional life considerably in awe of tsarist Russia: he had been their guest; he was attracted by the courteous and gentlemanly behaviour of their officer caste; he was impressed by the military stamina of the Cossacks and their other military units; he was prejudiced in favour of any Christian – as opposed to Moslem or Hindu – society. But his attitude towards India's northern and menacing neighbour underwent a radical change.

After his long overland journey through Russia, the Caucasus, Persia and Afghanistan he became aware of just how real a threat Russia was to the British Raj in India, and he became disillusioned about the religious credentials of a country whose church was so far removed from the Anglican and Protestant values of Bishop Hever and Victorian England.

Conolly felt he had a personal mission to identify this Russian threat, and he fulfilled this mission by spelling out the threat in the appendix to his travelogue, by trying to implement schemes to consolidate the khanates and emirates of Central Asia into a confederation to resist the southward advance of the tsar's domains, and by attempting to rescue an Englishman who had been engaged in a similar mission to his own and who appeared to have been disowned or ignored by his compatriots. In these circumstances he decided to follow his conscience rather than his orders, his patriotic and religious principles rather than the cautious remit of his superiors. He did not complain when his maverick attitude led to his untimely and cruel death.

Chapter 4

David Urquhart and Edmund Spencer: The Aspiring Politician and His Disciple

'What is morally wrong cannot be politically right.'
— Donald Soper (1903–98)

A biography of David Urquhart, written in 1920 by Gertrude Robinson, describes him as 'a Victorian knight errant of justice and liberty'. It is ironic that, of all the British adventurers in the Caucasus in the early nineteenth century, we know more about Urquhart as a man than about any of the others, but less about what he did in Circassia than we do of his successors and disciples. His diplomatic and political careers are well documented, but he did not write at length about his Caucasian adventures as so many of his followers were to do.

He was always destined to be an unusual character. He was born in 1805 on the family estate in the Scottish highlands, the son of a chieftain with a fierce loyalty to his clan, a characteristic which he was to recognize and admire among the highlanders of the Caucasian tribes. He was educated privately by tutors, as his mother took him around Europe to France, Switzerland and Italy, and then sent to a Benedictine college where he studied classical and modern languages from five a.m. until seven p.m. every day 'and sometimes his anxiety is such that he gets up at

3 a.m. and studies'. At sixteen he matriculated at St John's College, Oxford, but rather than complete his university course he joined the navy and later sailed in 1827 with Lord Cochrane on a mission to the newly liberated Greece.

From Greece, Urquhart went on to Constantinople, where his knowledge of mineralogy (acquired by this ever-industrious student during his vacations from Oxford) brought him to the attention of the sultan, a contact that he was to develop to his advantage later. Meanwhile, he set off for home via Albania, a country notorious for being a nest of brigands and which was additionally – in 1830 – in the throes of revolution. On his return, he published his findings in a series of articles in the press, which in turn came to the attention of the sailor-king William IV. The king was greatly impressed by a young man of such obvious intelligence and enterprise, particularly as he knew Urquhart had, like himself, a naval background.

But Urquhart's real interest had been aroused not so much by Albania as by the Ottoman Empire centred on Constantinople. At the first opportunity he returned there and settled into a wholly Turkish environment, living in the Turkish quarter surrounded by Turkish friends and speaking Turkish all the time. His aim – an ambitious one for so young a man – was to extend the good relations he enjoyed with the sultan into good relations between the Ottoman and British empires; he even drafted a commercial treaty between the two powers. But while doing all this, he became increasingly convinced that the Russians were working assiduously behind the scenes to disrupt Turkish-British relations; in particular, he saw the Russian blockade of the Black Sea coast of Circassia (the northwest Caucasus) as an impediment to trade as well as an interference with the liberty of the Circassian peoples. Thus he applied for an official post in the British embassy at Constantinople, aspiring to become a diplomat. Apart from his local contacts, he had two considerable other assets for the job: he was a personal friend of Lord Ponsonby, the ambassador, and he had the support of King William IV in London. Lord Palmerston, who was the king's foreign secretary, somewhat reluctantly agreed to this unorthodox appointment.

Urquhart's diplomatic career was not a success. He singularly failed to adapt his lifestyle to that of a member of a diplomatic mission, continuing to circulate exclusively with his Turkish friends, wearing Turkish dress and invariably eating Turkish food. Even the friendly Lord Ponsonby became exasperated by the behaviour of his young protégé. But already before he had arrived to take up his post, he was in trouble. It was discovered he had followed up a contact with the Turkish ambassador in Paris to pursue the idea of British warships passing through the Dardanelles; this he did entirely on his own initiative and with no authorization. Not surprisingly, Lord Palmerston told him off in no uncertain terms: 'a private person may act on his own impulse, but a commissioned officer must wait till he is told to act'. This was a message that Urquhart was never to fully accept.

But things came to a head over the question of support for the Circassians in their resistance to the Russian invasion of their Caucasian homelands. Urquhart took the unprecedented step of actually visiting the region in 1834 to get a first-hand impression of what was going on. He was in fact the first recorded English visitor to contact the highland tribesmen of Circassia, and he went entirely alone and without any official backing or authorization. Ostensibly his visit was a secret commercial mission 'to collect what may be called statistical information'. In reality, it was a perilous undertaking, open to every sort of misunderstanding, and likely to provoke just the sort of row with Russia that Lord Palmerston was so anxious to avoid.

Predictably, two things happened. Firstly, the Circassian chiefs were so encouraged by Urquhart's presence that they begged him to become their leader both in council and in the field of military operations against the Russians. They called him 'Daoud Bey' (Prince David) and saw him as a David figure who could confront the Russian Goliath. More worryingly for the British government, they also saw him as an emissary of England and a living proof of British support for their cause.

Secondly, Urquhart himself fell totally under the spell of the Circassian independent fighters. Here were a gallant, handsome people, defending their families, their homes and their flocks and herds against a bullying super-power. They were – it seemed to him – living a pure and simple life, founded on a long tradition of native craftsmanship and civil liberties; and furthermore they were doing this against the most romantic of backgrounds; wild mountainous scenery which a few decades earlier would have seemed daunting and austere, now – in the romantic era of Turner's landscapes and Wordsworth's poetry – seemed the very essence of all that was most worth struggling to preserve. He wrote passionately about what he had seen and heard: 'Russia has never been able to conquer the Circassians of the Black Sea. Still in sight of the Russian fishers of Anapa [a Russian fort on the coast] peasant girls tend their flocks, and warriors meet in the open air in solemn deliberation'. He goes on to argue that because no other state had ever possessed Circassia, there was no legal validity in the argument that Russia had in the past ceded Circassia to Turkey and that – by subsequent treaty – Turkey had passed it back to Russia. This was a wholly spurious Russian justification for their territorial aggression.

Despite Urquhart being an awkward misfit at the embassy in Constantinople, Lord Ponsonby fully supported his Circassian venture. He shared Urquhart's indignation at the injustice being done to this small independent community and saw it as Britain's role to champion the oppressed, and he offered to send Urquhart's report of his trip as a dispatch to the Foreign Office in London. He warned that 'if we do not take care, Russia will possess the Caucasus and all the power that that will give her'. Predictably, Lord Palmerston in London was less enthusiastic about Urquhart's exploits and wrote to Ponsonby 'expressing some alarm' at Urquhart exciting the tribes to revolt. Ponsonby responded vigorously and replied to the foreign secretary:

It is evident you have not attended to the facts [. . .] the Circassians could not be excited to revolt, because they were at the time, and had long been, in arms against Russia [. . .] there are 3 or 4 millions of people determined not to be transferred like herds of swine to the Russians, but resolved to assert their rights and liberty. I do not know the Englishman alive who would not, when asked, have given advice to such people how to act and render legitimate their virtuous, noble and just resistance to a yoke which Russia had no right to impose upon them. His [Urquhart's] words nor his acts could not implicate His Majesty's Government, and lastly, it is wholly a secret to everybody that he is employed at all by the British Government.

Lord Ponsonby ended his letter by saying that he had heard from a Captain Lyon who joined Urquhart that, far from inciting the tribes, the latter had argued that they should act with caution and warned them against expecting any aid from any foreign power. It could not have been a more robust defence of Urquhart's controversial mission.

Stout-hearted as this defence was, it did not stifle some elements in Britain from continuing to complain that Urquhart's exploit had 'endangered the peace of Europe'. But Urquhart had an even more powerful ally than the ambassador in Constantinople: as long as King William IV was on the throne, he had a champion in the highest place of all.

So he continued to push his luck. In 1836, ostensibly to assert the right of free trade between Britain and the Caucasus, he arranged for a ship called the *Vixen* (which was owned by a firm of English merchants based in Constantinople and controlled by friends of his) to run the gauntlet of the Russian blockade, carrying a cargo of salt and other vital provisions. The *Vixen* safely made the voyage to the Circassian coast and had begun a lively trading activity with the local resistance forces when a Russian warship sailed into the bay where the *Vixen* was anchored and seized control of the ship. The Russians claimed that not only had the *Vixen* violated the blockade, but she had made her landfall on a part of the coast 'occupied' and ruled over by them. The owners of the ship requested the British government to intervene on their behalf to restore their confiscated property to them. Lord Palmerston, who as foreign secretary was responsible for handling any such representations, was less than helpful: he postponed any action until the British parliament had risen for its recession and then – when there was no pressure on him – did not in his turn press the Russian government about the matter. Furthermore, he was furious when he heard about Urquhart's hand in the affair. This was for Palmerston the last straw; he had already taken against Urquhart's independent and unauthorized activities; now he saw his way to dismiss him once and for all from the British diplomatic service. And alas for Urquhart, his protector was no longer to hand: King William IV had died a few months before the matter came to a political head and he had no reason to expect favours from the young Queen Victoria.

Urquhart would later turn from diplomacy and adventure to politics and literature. On his return he toured the north of England making speeches attacking the government's lack of support for those who resisted Russian expansion, and he eventually got himself elected to parliament and became an enduring thorn in the side of Lord Palmerston.

All that was in the future. For the present – the remainder of the 1830s – there was no shortage of fellow adventurers to take up cudgels on behalf of the oppressed peoples of the Caucasus. Urquhart's friends such as James Longworth (a correspondent of *The Times*) and James Bell (a merchant and part-owner of the *Vixen*) were to venture where he had blazed the trail. They too were to run the Russian blockade, to fraternize with the Circassian tribal leaders, to aid them in practical ways with weapons and advice, and even to risk their own lives by fighting alongside them in their struggle against the Russian occupying forces. Their stories are better documented than Urquhart's, their adventures more dramatic, their accounts more sensational. But without Urquhart, without 'Daoud Bey', none of this would have happened.

Even before Longworth and Bell had ventured onto Urquhart's domain, a more mysterious figure was to appear on the scene in the person of Edmund Spencer. For someone who was to undertake daring adventures directed against Russian activities in the Caucasus, Edmund Spencer started his familiarity with the region in very odd circumstances. He was the guest not just of the Russians but of a pillar of the Russian establishment – Count Worrenzow, the governor-general of Southern Russia, which was deemed to include the disputed Caucasian region. He had met the count at Constantinople and been invited to join him in the summer of 1836 on his steam yacht, the *Peter the Great*, on a voyage around the Black Sea. Other guests included not only the British consul-general to Constantinople but a selection of very senior Russians including Count de Witt (commander-in-chief of the Russian cavalry), Prince Galitzin 'and other princes whose names I never could pronounce or write'. This was to be a presentation of the Black Sea from the viewpoint of Russian imperial ambitions.

After some ports of call in the Crimea, the voyage began to be seriously interesting for Spencer when they approached the coast of Circassia – the north-western shore of the Caucasus. Here they made landfall at the Russian fortress of Anapa. The count's yacht and its escorting corvette were welcomed with a 'deafening gun salute from the fort', but Spencer could observe even from the deck that the hills behind the fort were alive with armed warriors who, at the approach of the vessels, galloped off in all directions to warn their compatriots that an armed body of men appeared about to land. A few sentinels were left behind on the hilltops to observe the movements of the Russian visitors.

Spencer, who had hoped to go ashore himself at Anapa, was surprised that only the count and his immediate entourage were allowed to land there. It transpired that the garrison were 'excessively unhealthy'. They were cooped up in a fort where the water supply was 'brackish and unwholesome', and when they needed to go out in search of fresh water from a nearby mountain rivulet, they needed to be escorted by 'a park of artillery with lighted matches, as a defense against the determined hostility of the natives'. They had also recently suffered some disastrous military setbacks. These were attributed to reports that an English officer who had served in India was directing operations against the Russians, and that copies of a 'proclamation from the King of England calling on the Circassians to defend their country' were circulating freely. When some of the distinguished Russian guests on the count's yacht heard these reports, they became decidedly cool towards Spencer, but Count Worrenzow himself took the view that these rumours were unfounded. He attributed them to Poles who had defected from the Russian army. After all, the count said, what would be the point of distributing seditious literature among a people who are 'not only ignorant of every foreign language, but unable to read their own'?

The count also told Spencer that while he had been ashore at Anapa he had received one of the Circassian princes – originally a Tartar from the Crimea and a fierce opponent of the Russians. The prince had come to the meeting ostensibly to seek 'the assistance of the garrison in a love affair, as he was anxious to carry off the daughter of a neighbouring prince'. But the count had reckoned this was merely a pretext to visit the fort and spy out the nature of its defences. The Circassian prince had clearly been nervous that he himself might be kidnapped during the encounter, and his 'squire' (or attendant) had held a cocked pistol in his hand during the interview 'ready to be discharged at the head of his excellency, in the event of any violence being offered to his master'. Mutual trust was clearly non-existent between the two parties.

Spencer got a clearer idea of the extent of the Russian occupation when they went on to another fort some thirty miles further south down the coast. This had only just been captured by the Russians a few days before the arrival of the count's yacht. He found that as well as regular Russian troops there were Kuban and Don Cossacks, brilliant in their Astrakhan hats and scarlet uniforms, and also a smattering of Life Guards officers 'glittering with jewelled orders' who had volunteered to come to the Caucasus for the summer campaigning. This was where the action was to be found and the glory won. But not all the aristocratic Russians were in such privileged circumstances: Spencer was introduced to one soldier of former social and literary distinction who had been involved in the Decembrist insurrection against Tsar Nicholas I and who had in conse-quence been dispatched to serve for twelve years in the ranks as a private soldier in the Crimea and the Caucasus (an alternative to exile in Siberia) to exculpate his sins. Spencer also met a very handsome and well-dressed Circassian prince who had defected to the Russians but who was under constant surveillance, because there had been a number of defectors who had received gifts and weapons from the Russians but who had 'on the first opportunity [. . .] scampered off' with a lot of valuable information about the Russian deployments.

While the troops paraded for the benefit of the visiting commander-in-chief, while aides-de-camp were galloping round, bands were blaring out martial music, and the officers playing cards, there were also less happy signs of this military occupation: the surrounding hills were lit up by the light of blazing villages, recently torched by the invaders. Various officers confided to Spencer that it was the Russian intention to build or capture a whole series of such forts along the western

(Black Sea) coast of Circassia, and thus to reinforce their blockade and cut off supplies sea-borne from Turkey to the mountain tribesmen. They also told him that the local tribesmen were 'all robbers by profession' and so treacherous that 'they will not hesitate to slay with one hand, while the other is extended in friendship'. Spencer – who had already resolved to visit the region later under his own steam – could not help but be deeply apprehensive on hearing all these reports.

In the meanwhile, Spencer sailed on with his Russian hosts to yet more strategically placed fortresses along the coast. Like many Englishmen encountering the region for the first time, he waxed lyrical about the beauties of the scenery: 'surely any man possessed of the slightest spark of courage, who calls this beautiful land his home, would die to defend it'. Spencer admits to being under the influence of Sir Walter Scott's romantic vision of highland life.

Everywhere they landed, he was struck with the contrast between the restricted life of the Russian garrisons in their 'miserable little cabins' and the free-ranging life of the gallant mountain chieftains galloping around in glittering armour in the encircling countryside. But the countryside too had its own sad sights: some villages had been completely laid waste or set on fire as reprisals against locals who had kidnapped Russian soldiers and sold them on into slavery in the markets of Turkey or Persia. Even the placing of sentries outside the forts was considered too dangerous, and dogs were let loose instead to raise the alarm if tribesmen approached the walls. And some of the forts were so overlooked by the surrounding hills that the Russians were not only shot at when they went out to gather water or supplies, but were picked off by sharpshooters even while they were within the forts themselves.

Once Spencer's party put to sea again, their ship also came under intermittent rifle fire and they had to 'steer a course at greater distance from the shore'. Everywhere there was evidence that the Russian blockade was causing formerly prosperous trading stations – some of them starting points for long caravan routes – to close down, and in some cases to relocate to the Turkish coast.

Eventually, Count Worrenzow's steam yacht turned back to the Crimea, and Spencer meditated on the difference between what he had expected to find on the Black Sea coast of the Caucasus and what he had observed. The native chiefs had conspicuously failed to come forward to greet the count, and instead they had found 'a whole people in arms fighting for their independence'. Back in the Crimea, the Russian hospitality was warm and lavish; the palatial residences of the aristocracy were thrown open to Spencer, trips were arranged to Tartar sites such as Bakche Serai, the wine flowed and the gossip at card tables was as sophisticated as ever. But Spencer was no longer in sympathy with any of this. His emotions had been involved by his exposure to the romantic resistance movement of the Circassians. Now his mind was turning to how he could help these 'champions of liberty', how he could perhaps bring to them some evidence that they were not alone in their struggle, how he could bring them comfort if not supplies. His tourism was over; his real adventures were about to begin.

After an arduous journey across the Crimean steppe, Spencer took a ship across the Black Sea to Trebizond and from there planned his escapade to the northern Caucasus – Circassia. His friends at Trebizond tried to dissuade him from going, pointing out what a dangerous enterprise it would be, not only because of the risk of being intercepted by Russian warships on the way

there, but also because once he arrived there 'the freebooting mountaineers would probably detain him, or sell him as a slave'.

But Spencer was determined to go ahead with his plan, and the one concession he did make to the anxieties of his friends was to assume a false nationality: 'I waived, for the first time in my life, the proud privilege of my birthright as an Englishman'. The disguise he decided to adopt was that of a Genoese doctor; he had been told that the Circassians held the Genoese in high regard as former trading partners, and he rightly assumed that the guise of a doctor would open the prospect of a friendly reception.

Without too much difficulty he found a Turkish brigantine bound for Circassia. This was no ordinary Turkish coaster. It was equipped with four 'long swivel brass guns, at first stowed from observation', and the cargo largely consisted of weapons and ammunition for the insurgents and – a universally marketable commodity – salt. The expected return merchandise in exchange for these goods was 'a cargo of beautiful girls to replenish the harems of Constantinople'. The captain was a battle-scarred veteran, the crew was considerably larger than was necessary for the management of the ship and all of them were armed like pirates with pistols and poniards; this was clearly a serious gun-running operation.

Predictably, having set sail, they soon found that they were pursued by a Russian brig. Spencer feared that if they were hit by a shot from the Russian vessel, his whole ship might explode, in view of all the powder and ammunition they were carrying. He also feared that if they were boarded and he was captured 'although my visit was one entirely of curiosity, yet it might be misconstrued'; this was a considerable understatement – he would have indeed been in the direst trouble as an Englishman

in disguise on an illegal ship loaded with arms for Russia's enemies. But neither disaster happened. They outran the Russian brig and when, as a result of the chase, they found themselves on a coastline far from their destination and heavily occupied by Russian forces, they managed to set to sea again in weather that deterred any further pursuit.

When they approached the shore, the captain of the Turkish ship 'hoisted a signal well known to the Circassians' and thousands of local tribesmen appeared from the forests as if from nowhere and rushed to greet them on the beach. After all the cautionary tales he had been told, Spencer was not a little nervous. 'These were the people to whom I was now about to confide my safety: they had been represented to me as perfidious and cruel [. . .] I banished every distrustful thought, and, with a firm reliance on their good faith, landed'. The desirable cargo was rapidly unloaded, and the ship itself was 'snugly concealed' from view in a small river overhung with majestic trees.

Spencer quickly became aware of the problem of communicating with his hosts; their own language was 'without the slightest affinity to any other on the face of the earth', and Spencer's own knowledge of Turkish was both limited and of limited value. But one thing he could do was to adopt the local costume: a lamb's-wool turban and a massive cloak protected him from sun and rain and made him more acceptable. He was escorted through dramatically wild scenery and noted that the highlanders' huts were concealed from view by dense foliage as effectively as his ship had been: these hills could at any moment become a war zone, and camouflage was everywhere necessary. To add to the dangers of precipices and ravines, there was visible evidence of wolves, bears and jackals (which were later to keep him awake at night) and reports of occasional visits from tigers.

When he reached the tented residence of the principal local khan, his sword, rifle and ammunition were all taken from him and hung on the walls – only his poniard was left tucked into his belt as this was considered part of his natural clothing and never to be discarded. Because the Turkish sea captain who had transported him to the Caucasus was well known in the region as a reliable source of salt, gunpowder and other necessities, Spencer was accepted as a friendly – if somewhat mysterious – visitor. He also had a letter of recommendation to some of the more powerful chiefs. But none of this saved him from intermittent suspicion – especially if he were spotted writing in his notebook or sketching. Such behaviour immediately raised doubts as to whether he might not, after all, be a Russian spy. A meeting of the elders was convened to consider whether he was someone who could be trusted 'to journey any further through the land'.

At this point, Spencer began to regret that he had followed the advice given to him and claimed to be a citizen of Genoa rather than truthfully admitting to being an Englishman. He found the Circassians did not now seem to know anything of Genoa and 'entertained no respect for any other nation or people under heaven except the Turks and the English'. Nor did they understand his motives for coming to the Caucasus: why should a stranger have any interest in their customs and manners unless he had some sinister purpose in mind? The elders examined all his papers and these – amid growing alarm – were declared to be written in Russian; however, when some Russian prisoners were produced to translate them, they confirmed this was not the case. He was allowed to proceed – under escort – further into the interior to meet an even more influential chief who was a local prince.

Genoese nationality might have proved to be a broken reed, but his claim to be a medic was a more useful subterfuge. Everywhere people brought their ailments to him, and as the natives were mostly of healthy constitutions and had had no previous exposure to medication, even the smallest doses of the most basic remedies effected 'instantaneous and decided improvement'.

When he reached the mountain prince's lair he was impressed with its strategic situation and defences. It was at the summit of a formidable hill and surrounded by rocks; three sides were quite inaccessible and the fourth could only be entered by a gorge so narrow that only two horsemen could ride abreast. From this lookout, the prince could plan ambushes of the Russian garrisons when they emerged from the fortresses whose access passes he overlooked. He could also send signals to other insurgent outposts by lighting bonfires on his hilltop. The prince had about a thousand warriors under his command, and – although the strength of the Russian garrisons in the region amounted to over fifteen times their number – hardly a day went by without some skirmish in which the tribesmen usually came off best. Not only did he deter the Russians from making sorties, but he also hindered their efforts to consolidate their fortifications. Just as Spencer waxed lyrical about the beauties of the Caucasian mountain scenery, so now that he had encountered a fighting prince at his mountain redoubt, he waxed equally lyrical about the martial qualities of the hill tribesmen. Their equestrian skills are said to outshine those of Western circus performers; their chivalry results in single combats with Cossacks; their indefatigable spirit means that none are ever captured unless already so badly wounded that they can resist no longer; their patience is such that they can lie in ambush for days or creep like snakes in the grass to overpower a sentry; in short, during his stay in the prince's camp he witnessed exploits that were straight from 'the pages of romance'. This was a visitor who had fallen totally under the spell of his hosts.

Hardly surprisingly in these circumstances, Spencer could not resist invitations to take part in some of the prince's 'reconnoitring' expeditions. Such exploits were 'too daring not to be attended with considerable danger', and he describes in his letters one such when they became surrounded by an overwhelming force of Cossacks who had hidden themselves in the long reeds and sedges along the banks of the river. Fortunately for Spencer, the prince's clansmen had been keeping a vigilant eye on the operation from a distance, and as soon as they saw the trouble that the reconnaissance party were in, they flew to their assistance. Even as it was, Spencer's party suffered several casualties and lost three horses. He himself was hit by a bullet and only avoided a fatal injury by being protected by one of the cartridge belts he had slung across his body: 'the pistol-shot completely shattered one of the metal tubes filled with bullets, leaving no other bad effects than a slight contusion'. He had proved himself in action.

But the most worrying aspect of this whole incident was that he thought the Cossack trap had been laid specifically to capture him. If they were going to such pains to seize a Genoese visitor, how much more so – he reckoned – would they have been anxious to apprehend a rogue Englishman! He reported his suspicions to the prince on his return, and these might well have been discounted by his hosts as evidence of his own self-importance had it not been for the fact that – when a strict watch for traitors was set up – the clansmen caught a self-styled Pole who had previously deserted to the insurgents returning from the Russian camp. The deserter had clearly been passing information about the stranger who had come among the tribesmen. Spencer comments in his letters that such traitors were almost never native Caucasians, unless they were Armenian merchants – 'a sordid race [he comments with traditional prejudice] who would at any time sacrifice honour and probity for gold'. This was not the first so-called Pole to turn out to be a Russian double agent.

Spencer thought himself fortunate in being invited to accompany his prince to a gathering of tribal chiefs. When he arrived, he found each chief surrounded by a body of armed clansmen, all of them intent on military training of the most classical type: some were hurling javelins at a target; some were practising archery; some were learning to be dextrous with their poniards; some were wrestling or running; some were training their horses to swim across rivers; gunsmiths were repairing weapons and tiny children being taught to ride; the whole complex was one heaving mass of military activity. When it came to the assembly itself, the chiefs seated themselves under a grove of sacred trees and took it in turns to make emotive speeches, reviling the Russian invaders and pledging themselves to permanent resistance. Spencer was deeply moved by the whole procedure, and makes comparisons between the Caucasians' stand against the Russians and the Swiss cantons' stand against the powerful house of Hapsburg.

After listening to the deliberations of the elders, Spencer allowed himself some speculation about the conduct of the war between the invaders and the clansmen. He thought that the main Russian fort in the interior – at Aboun – was more of a liability than an asset to them, since it was out of range of effective communication with either the Cossack bases along the northern banks of the Kuban river, or the Russian forts along the Black Sea coastline. The garrison of Aboun either languished starving behind their defences, or risked their lives by venturing out.

Spencer was now taken on an overland trip north to the banks of the Kuban. Bivouacking among the thirteen-foot-high reeds along the river bank, he was kept awake all night by 'the howling of dogs, wolves, and jackals [. . .] the chirping of myriads of reptiles and insects [. . .] and the momentary expectation of a visit from the Cossacks'. He found that, although the river itself rushed like a torrent, both Circassians and Cossacks frequently swam across it on horseback 'to carry away everything within their reach – men, women, children and cattle'. To fail to do this was a sign of cowardice, and maidens would taunt their lovers with accusations of unmanliness if they failed to bring them a cow from across the river from time to time: 'to spoil an enemy is the very perfection of virtue!' he was told. This was less a formal war-zone front line than a border – like that between Scotland and England a century earlier, where reavers regularly raided across the frontier to rustle cattle and loot the home-steads.

Spencer was also aware – from his time on Count Worren-zow's yacht – that the official Russian hierarchy was not in sympathy with the Cossacks: they were viewed as rough soldiers of fortune who might be hired to do the Russians' dirty work but who could not be trusted in the long term to remain loyal to the Romanovs. (Past events, such as Pugachev's revolt in the eighteenth century, and future events such as their partial defection during the Revolution and the Second World War, were to prove such fears justified.) Spencer speculated that if the Cossacks were ever to break with the tsar and join the Circassian insurgency, then Russia would be in deep trouble and her Caucasian ambitions permanently thwarted.

When he left the Kuban river and regained the coast, Spencer was made aware of just how narrow an escape he had had during the storm that obliged Count Worrenzow's yacht to keep away from the rocky coastline. One of the other ships in the squadron – a naval corvette – had been obliged to seek shelter from the high winds in the little bay of Soutcha, which was occupied by the insurgents. When one of the latter saw the Russian vessel anchored offshore, he swam out through the heaving seas and managed to cut the cable between ship and anchor. As the corvette imperceptibly drifted towards the shore, she was boarded by a heavily armed band of Circassians who made the crew their prisoners and appropriated all the weapons on board – a valuable cache of Russian muskets – and then set fire to the corvette. So profitable had been this venture, that they posted lookouts along the shore to see if any of the Count's other vessels were equally vulnerable. Spencer would have had a very different reception had he been captured on a Russian ship, rather than arriving independently on a Turkish ship a few months later with letters of introduction and gifts: the slave markets of the East would have beckoned.

As he travelled around the country, Spencer was struck by many of the distinctive features of the countryside and its inhabitants. Everyone rode everywhere, and they were as deeply attached to their horses as the Arabs are reputed to be to theirs. Their steeds were not only handsome and fast, but also expert at scrambling up 'craggy rocks and down steep glens'. Once broken in, the horses were never beaten or punished, but always encouraged to share the hardships and adventures of their masters: a horse would swim rapid rivers alongside its master, lie silently hidden in ambush positions, and even 'submit without resistance to having his head adopted for a rest for a rifle'. Spencer was also impressed with the amount of wild game to be encountered: swans and geese haunted the rivers and marshes to such an extent that if any man had a rifle and ammunition 'it was his own fault if he goes to bed without supper'. For those with more ambitious sporting or culinary requirements, wild boar and deer were everywhere to be found. But the country was not without its wildlife hazards: not only did jackals keep Spencer awake at night, but bears, wolves, vultures and eagles made the lives of the shepherds difficult; and tarantulas, scorpions and twenty-foot-long snakes had to be avoided in the rockier desert parts of the interior.

The Russian blockade of the Circassian Black Sea coastline had one bizarre effect which came to the attention of Spencer. Although the mountain tribesmen valued their liberty above all, this did not discourage them from selling their daughters and sisters to the highest bidder. Sometimes such a bidder would be a local chieftain, but more often it would be the owner of a harem in Constantinople or elsewhere in the Ottoman or Persian empires. The comfort and luxury of such harems was such that often the girls themselves would be only too anxious to embark on a voyage that would result in their ending up in such an institution: 'the fair lady who has spent her youth in the harems of a rich Persian or Turk, on returning to her native country, decked in all her finery, never fails to create in the minds of her young friends a desire to follow her example'. But with the Russian blockade impeding all sea passage from the Caucasus to the Porte, the market forces were not able to function properly; while Spencer was there the price of an attractive Circassian maiden fell from a hundred cows to twenty-five, 'which is lamented over by those parents who may have a household of girls, with the same despair that a merchant mourns over a warehouse full of unsold goods'.

Unlike later travellers such as Longworth and others, Spencer does not relate just how he managed to get safely away from the Caucasus. His lack of specifics about this and one or two other aspects of his Caucasian adventures led some of his more sceptical contemporaries to question whether he had ever really returned to Circassia after his comfortable coastal cruise with Count Worrenzow. Such scepticism seems hardly justified: he would have to have had a very remarkable imagination indeed to invent all his detailed adventures and his vivid impressions.

Spencer devotes his final letters to rhapsodizing about the Circassians and their way of life. Not only, he concludes, are they physically the most beautiful people on earth, but they are generous to the poor, considerate to the elderly, gallant towards the ladies (this seems to him entirely compatible with selling daughters and sisters into opulent harems), given to healthy vegetarian diets, and brave to the point of exemplary heroism in defence of their liberties and independence. He argues forcefully against the Russian claim to have negotiated from the Turks a right to occupy the Caucasus, since it never was within the gift of the Ottoman Empire in the first place. He calculates that the dozen or so tribes of Circassia are, between them, capable of putting some 200,000 warriors into the field against the Russian invaders, largely because no one is too old or too young to take up arms. This is a cause – he declares – which all true Englishmen should support!

Chapter 5

Alexander Gardner: The Loose Cannon

'Life is a gamble at terrible odds – if it were a bet, you
wouldn't take it.'

– Tom Stoppard (1937–)

There have been many explorers, travellers and scholars who
have doubted the truth of every word written by Colonel
Alexander Gardner, of the Maharaja of the Punjab's artillery.
Indeed there have been some who even doubted his very
existence: to them he was a phantom figure like Sir John
Mandeville, whose spurious account of his fourteenth-century
travels was only discredited after his own time. There are those
who believe that he was a deserter from the British army and
therefore set about creating a false personality for himself to
cover his tracks. The weight of evidence however suggests that,
although he may have been more than usually given to
exaggeration and embroidery of the facts, he was in fact a
remarkable – if disreputable – adventurer, who explored more
by force of circumstances than by design (he was frequently in
flight from some violent and questionable exploit) many of the
remotest corners of Central Asia and the north-west frontier
region of the British Raj. In addition, he was a war lord who
would have been more at home as a *condottiere* in Renaissance
Italy than as a British officer in the early nineteenth century.

Gardner's own account of his origins places his birth in 1785 'on the shore of Lake Superior which is nearest to the source of the Mississippi'. His father was a doctor who came from Scotland as a first-generation immigrant to British colonial America, and took an active part in the struggle for independence. The young Alexander Gardner started his travels early in life; the family moved to Mexico, and while his father practised medicine the young boy was taught Greek and Latin at a Jesuit school. As an Anglo-Saxon Protestant American, he felt lonely among the Spanish Catholic community in which he was brought up, and he spent much time reading stories of adventures among the American Indians in the Wild West. He later was to write that 'from this early period in my life the notion of being a traveller and adventurer, and of somehow and somewhere carving out a career for myself, was the maggot in my brain'. After Mexico, Gardner spent several years in Ireland where, for some unexplained reason, he acquired a knowledge of gunnery, which was to be significant in his later career. In 1812, at the age of twenty-five, he returned to America, but found that there was little to hold him there as his father had died. He then resolved on embarking on the career of adventure to which he had always aspired.

His first thought was to seek employment in Russia, where his elder brother had been engaged as an engineer in Astrakhan, and after some circuitous travels he arrived and lived with his sibling while he studied mineralogy in the hope of being employed in a supervisory role in the government-controlled Russian mines. Promises were made of a good job once his studies were completed, but again ill fortune dogged his steps: his brother was killed in a fall from a horse, and the Russian authorities promptly reneged on their undertakings. His brother's house was seized by creditors and his Russian contacts were not only unhelpful but discourteous and unsympathetic. He was left homeless and jobless. For a year he tried to sort out his brother's affairs, at the end of which time he was so disillusioned with all things Russian that he had no desire to live and work there. Instead he resolved to devote his itinerant energies to undermining Russian ambitions in Central Asia.

It was at this point, in 1818, that Gardner met up with two travelling companions who were equally disenchanted with Russia and set out with them intending to go through Persia and Afghanistan to the Punjab. But he was deflected from his route and eventually set off on what turned out to be twelve years of apparently aimless wandering through the wilder parts of Central Asia. He tells his own troubled story in his memoirs, written much later and – possibly for that reason – full of the sort of inaccuracies, vagueness of specifics and surprising omissions that have led later critics to doubt their authenticity.

Gardner pretended to be a native of Arabia, as he felt this assumed nationality made him less conspicuous and less likely to be sold for ransom (he had survived one attempt to do this already) than if he had claimed to be a European. Also, he met very few Arabic speakers and when he did he always pretended to come from the opposite corner of Arabia and, for this reason, to speak the language in his own peculiar way.

When they were about ten days' journey from Khiva, Gardner and his caravan had their first really serious encounter. They had brushed off a marauding party of some twenty horsemen, telling them to get lost 'like dogs', only to find that the horsemen were the advance guard of a much larger troop of Turkoman warriors who duly plundered their possessions – Gardner losing his pony. They were however relieved that 'our lives were to be spared, and we and our women were not to be sold into slavery, the ordinary doom on such occasions'. One of the Jewish merchants in the caravan sought to protect his own interests by suggesting that Gardner was a Russian spy – something that was much feared in an area where Russian incursions were already beginning to be a feature. The Khan of Khiva sent 'three learned men who had travelled over half the world' to cross-examine Gardner and get to the bottom of the accusations.

Gardner thought it best in these circumstances to forget his Arab disguise and declare himself an American. He was then asked 'could I go by land from America to England?' When he said firmly 'No!', this was considered sufficient proof of his American identity. His original travelling companion, Mr Stursky, who had gone separately to Khiva, had been less fortunate: this 'hapless man had only bought his escape from Khiva at the price of circumcision in a public ceremonial'. Nothing daunted by all these escapades, Gardner and Stursky pressed on to the Aral Sea, crossed the steppe to Alexandrovsk, and took ship across the Caspian Sea to Astrakhan.

Gardner stayed in Astrakhan for more than a year, but here 'imbibed a prejudice against the Russian method of conducting business, and preferred to remain his own master'. His dislike of Russians was also probably enhanced by the fact that he spent or lost all the small fortune left to him by his brother. In 1823 he set off on his travels again – once more across the Caspian and the steppes – declaring that 'he could not rest in civilized countries'. He exchanged his Russian furs for the garb of an Uzbek – a black sheepskin coat and black boots and puttees – and was joined by another footloose traveller whom he suspected of being an escaped convict from Siberia.

As they approached Samarkand, where one of Gardner's party claimed to have good connections, they were confronted by a band of freebooters who 'on the pretext we had intruded without leave in their territory' first made a demand for the handover of their horses and a share of all their goods, and then – when this was not forthcoming – stole these things from their camp. Gardner organized a reprisal raid and prowled around the camp of the robbers for two nights 'being fired on once or twice in mistake for wild animals'. Eventually they managed to recapture their own horses. When some pursuers ordered them to yield up their booty 'in the name of the government', Gardner recorded that 'we slew them and fled on'. By now the whole surrounding steppe was up in arms. It was little wonder that at this point they decided that, despite any promising introductions, Samarkand had become too hot a destination for their safety.

They decided instead to strike south, crossing the Oxus, making their way to Kabul, in the hope of offering their services to Dost Mohammad, who was in the violent process of establishing himself as ruler of most of Afghanistan. En route they were living off the country in the most literal way: 'Food we obtained by levying contributions from everyone we could master, but we did not slaughter unless in self-defence'. One such self-styled defence involved the killing of three armed men.

When approaching Kabul and before they had any opportunity of offering their services to Dost Mohammad, Gardner and his party were intercepted by a mounted guard representing the ruler's rival – a certain Habib-ulla Khan who was a nephew of the ruler. Realizing that 'nothing but audacity and tact could save us', Gardner appealed for this rival's protection, which was generously granted. It transpired that Habib-ulla Khan was himself an outlaw, but a very charismatic one with a large and strong following. He was in fact the perfect patron for Gardner, who declared that 'being favourably impressed by his appearance and manner, I proffered the services of myself and my followers, which were readily accepted, and I was engaged as commandant of 180 picked horse to be employed in forays into the enemy's country'. Gardner had in fact signed up with the opponent of the man he had intended to serve, but with the sort of remit to range, rove and plunder which suited him well.

In his memoirs, Gardner records that: 'From this date for a period of two and a half years I led a life in the saddle, one of active warfare and continual forays'. Habib-ulla Khan (or 'the chief' as he was henceforth labelled by Gardner) and his warriors managed to dominate all the mountainous region to within twenty miles north of Kabul; his followers were not paid a salary, but expected to live off their takings and share the proceeds of such loot as they could acquire. The chief was their leader in every struggle and every fight; his war cries struck terror into his opponents; he had personally saved the lives of most of his followers by his courageous interventions; he was clearly Gardner's hero.

One of the chief's objectives was to settle old scores with his uncle Dost Mohammad. He saw an opportunity for this when his spies informed him that one of the ladies of Dost Mohammad's harem with an escort of some fifty horsemen was about to return from pilgrimage to Kabul, passing through territory dominated by the chief. (The purpose of her pilgrimage had been to seek holy intercession for her fertility.) Dost Mohammad had sent additional troops to secure most of the passes to protect his wife, the princess. Gardner takes up the tale: 'By a clever ruse [. . .] we induced the lady's escort to divert their route to the Ghorband Pass where Habib-ulla lay in wait [. . .] we attacked them front and rear [. . .] eventually we made off with the camels laden with treasure and those on which the lady and her attendants were carried'.

The chief entrusted this entire prize caravan to Gardner while he himself covered their retreat. They were soon engaged in fierce conflict with 'the Kabul cavalry', but the chief's courage and dash extricated them from their pursuers.

In the course of all this marauding and fighting, Gardner caught sight of a beautiful girl who was one of the kidnapped princess's attendants. When it came to dividing out the spoils, he refused his share of the gold and 'begged this girl to be given to me in marriage as the only reward I desired'. She turned out to be of royal birth on her mother's side, but notwithstanding that Gardner had his request granted, and was additionally given a fort in which to install his new bride. The kidnapped princess was also installed with dignity in a fort of her own and eventually ransomed for 3,000 gold pieces, five horses and three large falcons. She was returned for this price 'with her personal honour untarnished'. But the rivalry and warfare between uncle and nephew persisted.

The next major initiative in the conflict was taken by Dost Mohammad. He sent two mullahs to the chief's camp, ostensibly to bring about a reconciliation and to convert the chief to 'the right faith'. The mullahs stood on the road waving and accosting passers by and establishing a reputation for being crazy eccentrics with 'fanatical airs'. But later they were seen to be standing on the top of one of the turrets on Gardner's fort and signalling to 'armed strangers who had been skulking about the ravines'. Whistled responses were heard from the valleys. It was immediately clear that the mullahs were spies and traitors within the fort. One of Gardner's fort wardens promptly shot them dead; thereafter the label of 'saint-killers' was added to the other insults heaped on the chief and Gardner by the Kabul government.

Dost Mohammad now sent his whole army, some 12,000-strong, to destroy the chief's raiding parties and his forts. In the course of a bloody campaign in March 1826 while the snow was still lying deeply around the Panjshir Valley north of Kabul, Gardner's own fort was attacked and his wife and baby son killed – the former by her own hand to preserve her honour, and the latter (despite the efforts of a loyal mullah to protect the child at the cost of his own hand being severed) by a blow from an attacker's sabre. On hearing the news, and shortly afterwards seeing for himself the bodies of his slaughtered family, Gardner sank to his knees and vowed vengeance. To the end of his life, he was never able to retell the story without shedding tears for his dearly loved wife and child. And to the end of his life he held a bitter grudge against Dost Mohammad which, as the latter became increasingly inclined to flirt with Russian patronage at the expense of British India, stoked his hatred of Russia and all things Russian.

Habib-ulla Khan – Gardner's chief – now withdrew in despair further into the mountains and slew his wives and female slaves with his own hands 'to preserve them from dishonour'. He died shortly thereafter, and Gardner – severely wounded in the recent fights – was left once more without a protector. He set off, virtually destitute, with just eight companions. They slept in caves in the hills, frequently too frightened even to light a fire in case they gave their position away: it was all 'a wild and sickening dream'. They were so desperate for food that they robbed anyone they encountered – often the only such people being other bands of equally unscrupulous robbers, but happily for him, Gardner and his mates proved faster on the draw than those they encountered. On one occasion the mouth of the cave where they were hiding was blocked by an avalanche, but the avalanche had also killed a 'hyena-like animal', which they considered as a godsend as they set about eating it half raw.

Eventually things were getting so desperate that they decided their best hope of survival was heading for a place of sanctuary, a shrine on the south bank of the Oxus inhabited by hermits. They abandoned their Afghan disguises (which had replaced the earlier Arab ones) and dressed themselves as a bunch of itinerant Turkomans. When they reached the shrine, they were well received, had their feet washed in warm water and were fed and clothed, Gardner himself being given a leopardskin cloak by the leading hermit. They promptly joined the pious group of his disciples. But even here they did not feel safe from the long arm of Dost Mohammad's pursuing squadrons of cavalry. Gardner, who had once again been confirmed as leader of the party, decided that they should move on, not least to protect their shelterers from reprisals by troops from Kabul.

At no point in all his rambling tales of his adventures and travels is Gardner more elusive about precise locations. 'I will not weary you with details of our marches', he writes, drawing down on himself the suspicion of some subsequent travellers that his unwillingness to be specific about place names suggests that he had never undertaken some of the journeys and adventures he recounts. At this point, however, he tells us that he was on the way to a place called Takht-i-Sulaiman. His main problem was that while he wanted to put as much space as possible between himself and the forces of Dost Mohammad in Kabul, there was a considerable stretch of open land between the

relative shelter of the Hindu Kush and the Oxus which was patrolled by roving bands of gunmen answering to Murad Beg, the ruler of Kunduz (also in Afghanistan), who was almost as menacing a figure for Gardner as the ruler of Kabul.

So it was not surprising that when a considerable body of apparently hostile horsemen approached them, they galloped for the nearest pass at full speed, only to find it cut off by another body of horsemen who ordered them to halt in the name of Murad Beg. Gardner's party laid into them with their spears and Afghan knives. But by then the earlier party of horsemen had caught up with them. Gardner recalls: 'The fray now became general, as the main body charged us, trying to save their comrades. This fortunately prevented their using their matchlocks [. . .] their overwhelming numbers, however, soon broke our ranks [. . .] there was no room for orderly fighting, and it was a mere cut and thrust affair.' Gardner himself was badly wounded again and reported that with his two new wounds, one of which was bleeding freely, and with two older wounds still raw, he was so weak that he nearly fell from the saddle; but he did manage to ride to safety through the pass with the five survivors of his party of thirteen. He concluded that the only reason their attackers had not pursued them further was that they were too preoccupied stripping the bodies of those who had fallen of any arms or other objects of value.

As they proceeded on their haphazard flight, punctuated by skirmishes and robberies, they became aware of the extent to which the inhabitants of the territory around Kunduz were living in terror of Murad Beg's raiding parties: whole villages had been carried off for sale in the slave markets of Kunduz, Khiva or Bokhara. Everyone was – understandably – suspicious and frightened of them: hospitality was rare. River crossings were a problem too: at one point where a bridge had been destroyed, he managed to 'bind blocks of ice together with straw ropes, which when covered with grass formed a means of crossing for us and our horses'. At another point, they ran into a pack of wolves that were intent on stealing the carcass of a sheep shot by Gardner's companion; even when they hid the carcass under a pile of rocks, the wolves managed to drag it out and devour it. It was all they could do to stop the wolves devouring them too. Doubtless this episode, like others, did not lose anything in the telling.

The baffling feature of Gardner's rambling and at times improbable stories is that some of them bear verification from other sources. His description of a tribal wedding among the Kirghiz people is a case in point. On the other hand his untraceably confusing journeys through the Pamirs and Kafiristan leave curious gaps and test the credulity of the reader. Despite his earlier dread of Dost Mohammad, he apparently reached Kabul at one stage on his travels, where he not surprisingly found that there were too many Afghans whose close relatives – fathers, brothers or sons – he had killed or wounded in his earlier escapades; in a country 'where blood-feuds were a sacred duty' this made it far too dangerous to linger longer than necessary: somebody would have found it necessary to settle an old score and he would have been the victim. But his capacity to survive and depend on no one but himself seems to have extricated him from a remarkable number of tight spots. As Sir Henry Durand (a one-time governor of the Punjab and hero of the First Afghan War) remarked: 'Gardner seems to have been indebted for life, and that many a time over, to his cool audacity, which never failed him for a moment, be the straight what it might'.

Indeed, Sir Henry Durand and Sir Henry Rawlinson (a president of both the Royal Asian Society and the Royal Geographical Society) were both clearly impressed with his story, despite the vagueness of some of the details of his travels; and Sir Alexander 'Bokhara' Burnes also might well have spoken up for him had he – Burnes – not been killed in Kabul in 1841, and had not many of Gardner's papers (which were lent to Burnes at the time) been destroyed in the ensuing hostilities. Some of his papers which did survive, at least for a while, were the notes he scribbled on his travels and concealed by interleafing them with the pages of the Koran he carried on a cord round his neck while travelling in Islamic dress. Anyone who was brazen enough to look closely at these scribblings was accused of being disrespectful to his 'additional prayers'.

What we do know for certain is that after all his nefarious escapades Gardner settled in the Punjab, where he was entrusted with charge of the Maharaja's artillery, though even in his capacity as an artillery officer he was skating on thin ice and – as confessed in his own memoirs – relying 'on a small printed slip of paper giving instructions' (which he conveniently found enclosed in a bundle of fuses and other material) to establish his reputation as a master gunner. Nothing with Gardner was quite as it appeared. Later still he was to return to Kashmir and settle there until his death in extreme old age.

In this last stage of his life, his real or embroidered experience of Central Asia won him wide acclaim and ready audiences. He sat in Kashmir decked in tartan (bought from a visiting highland regiment) from head to foot – or more accurately from turban to spurs – in a curious uniform of his own design. He used his influence to warn against the dangers of Russian advances towards the vulnerable frontiers of British India, and to alert British and Indian authorities to the realities of Russian territorial ambitions. He speculated: 'May it not be suggested [. . .] that Afghanistan may fall to Russia if attacked [. . .] an army might steal its way down the Chitral valley, and suddenly dash on the astounded and probably weak garrison of Jalalabad.' He also wrote extensively on the theme of the Russian threat and was an advocate of a 'forward' policy to pre-empt incursions from the north. He pressed his views on Lord Lawrence when the latter was Viceroy of India in the 1860s. He had never forgotten or forgiven his harsh treatment by the Russians as a young man before he began his peripatetic and dubious career.

While most of the protagonists in this book, although they may have acted occasionally outside their instructions, were essentially honourable officers or respectable professionals of one sort or another, Gardner was essentially a rogue and a chancer. British he was by descent; an adventurer he was by inclination; a confronter of tsarist Russian policies he was by conviction and reasons of personal animosity. But as Major Hugh Pearse, the retrospective editor of Gardner's memoirs in 1898, concluded, 'as a student of "the great game in Central Asia" he was in the front rank'.

Chapter 6

James Longworth: The Intrepid Journalist

'Dangers by being despised grow great.'
                                    – Edmund Burke (1729–97)

The enduring mystery about James Longworth's perilous year-long visit to Circassia – the western Caucasus – in the late 1830s is why he went there at all. His friends in England were baffled; his companions in the enterprise were confused; the Circassians remained mystified and surprised; the Russians were highly suspicious and hostile; and even the readers of his two-volume, seven-hundred-page account of his exploits (published in 1840) find it difficult to work out quite what he thought he was doing.

Longworth was at pains to try to rationalize his adventure. He wrote that 'lest the reader should appreciate no better than the Hadji [his pilgrim guide] my motives for breaking through the Russian blockade, and penetrating into countries hitherto deemed scarcely accessible to Europeans, I shall here take the liberty of adding a few words of explanation'. He goes on to explain that while living in Constantinople (the Porte) he had become enthralled with the strange and romantic image of Circassia. He had also been affronted by the brutality of the Russian incursions – amounting to full-scale invasion – of this independent land which had 'lived in jealous seclusion for centuries'. The Russians were pursuing a policy of 'war to the knife'. He was incensed by the unequal nature of the conflict, where simple tribesmen from the hills were confronted with the full force of a superior military power. He felt that the Russian naval blockade of the Circassian coast amounted not only to a crippling trade embargo for the inhabitants, but also denied Turkey – and by extension her trading partner England – an important market. But none of this really amounted to explaining a one-man mission with only the vaguest of objectives into a war zone in which Britain had no direct involvement.

One other possible explanation was professional ambition. The concept of a war correspondent was totally undeveloped at the beginning of the nineteenth century; indeed, it was only with the appearance of R. H. Russell as the correspondent of *The Times* during the Crimean War (some twenty years later) that reporting from the front line became a feature of British journalism. But Longworth had long been a writer for *The Times* and contributed occasional dispatches from Constantinople and elsewhere. He doubtless thought that he would have a great story to tell if he could play a role in the insurgency and resistance of the mountain tribesmen of the Caucasus against the onslaught of the Russian military machine. He would be the first to tell the story to the outside world. This would provide not only material for dispatches but for a substantial book.

So it was that, for all or any of these reasons, he set about trying to secure a passage on a ship through the Black Sea from Constantinople to the beleaguered coast of Circassia. It was not an easy task, because the Porte was filled with Russian emissaries keeping a vigilant eye on shipping that might be intent on evading their blockade. Russian consuls bullied the

Turkish authorities into helping them frustrate such endeavours or, if that failed, into punishing with fines, imprisonment and destruction of vessels any seafarers who attempted to run the gauntlet of their Black Sea fleet. Longworth, who spoke fluent Turkish, eventually managed to contact some rough Turkish sea captains who were prepared to negotiate a passage for himself and some trade goods – mostly salt and gunpowder – if he would meet them on board their vessel. The vessel was already under suspicion, as it was distinguishable from the ordinary run of shipping around the Golden Horn, being 'built to run low in the water, or, as the Turks say, like a thief'. In fact, one of the reasons for this design of blockade-running vessel was so that it could be more easily dragged up on the beach and hidden on the Circassian coastline than a more conventional ship. After making these arrangements, the Turks 'went away as stealthily as they had come' and Longworth had to sneak off and get a caique to take him to the rendezvous. Even when he got to the ship, he had to meet with the captain and his five crew below decks, 'where we might confer without being seen from the shore'. Having agreed the extent and nature of the cargo, and the price for chartering ship and crew, they agreed to sail in four days' time.

Longworth spent these few days in recruiting a dragoman – in addition to his Hadji guide – who allegedly had some knowledge of local Caucasian languages and who could 'mend and wash, dress a dinner and serve it, and, if necessary, fight'. He also gave some thought and time to collecting provisions that could act as currency or gifts. In addition to salt, gunpowder, lead (for bullets), steel (a euphemism for swords and sabres), they also loaded bales of a coarse white calico (used for clothing and other purposes); these goods, he reckoned, would be readily exchangeable for 'all other property – slaves, horses and guns'. Thus equipped he set out for 'the land of heroism and adventure'.

The voyage was not without incident. They gave Trebizond (on the north Turkish coast) a wide berth, because it was known to have a vigilant Russian consul who would try to get the vessel impounded or otherwise frustrate onward progress. Soon they were within sight of Mount Elbruz (though some of the crew mistook it for a cloud formation) and Longworth allowed himself to be lost in classical reveries about the landscape – Prometheus 'bound and bleeding on his rock' and Jason navigating his Argonauts through these waters. However, he was soon recalled to reality. A boy at the masthead reported sighting a warship bearing down on them, which turned out to be a Russian corvette. Every scrap of sail was unfurled and every man took his turn at the oars to distance themselves from the approaching predator, apart from one pilgrim who decided that vocal prayer was likely to be more effective than sail or oar. The corvette got within firing range of them, but – after a four-hour chase – the Turkish ship managed to pull away from its pursuers before nightfall. By the next morning they were within sight of the beach where they planned to land, and friendly figures could be seen on shore.

The reception accorded to Longworth came fully up to his expectations. A lone horseman on a white stallion rode into the water and with a flourish made clear that they were welcome ashore. Soon the beach was crowded with tribesmen from the surrounding mountains and forests, who conducted Longworth and his companions to a hut where more formal salutations were exchanged. From the outset, he was left in no doubt that he was among warriors: they were all dressed in sheepskin bonnets,

bedecked with cartridge belts, and in addition to the muskets slung over their shoulders they had silver-mounted pistols and daggers stuck into their belts and ebony-hilted sabres slung beside them; to complete the attire they wore 'gaily-gartered galoshes'. While his guide went off to arrange where to stay, Longworth was provided with a horse with a curious saddle having 'an upright piece of polished wood four inches high' before and aft, on which he nearly impaled himself on mounting. The stirrups were also absurdly short and uncomfortable. But Longworth soon realized that whatever the discomforts, this was a saddle on which he could easily turn completely around and shoot behind him at any pursuing foe.

News of the impending visit of an Englishman had clearly preceded his arrival, and he was taken to meet a local nobleman, or bey, who was somewhat upset that an English bey was not staying under his roof, but with a merchant (chosen by the guide for reasons of personal profit). From the start his visit was welcomed as evidence of England's concern for the plight of the independent Caucasians in the face of Russian invasion and attempted colonization. And from the start there was confusion about his precise role. Everywhere he saw little groups of people in discussion, and soon found that they were speculating among themselves as to 'in what degree of relationship I stood to the King of England' (William IV). When Longworth started to distribute some of the merchandise he had brought as presents, the recipients were uncertain as to whether they were indebted for these gifts to the sultan of Turkey or to the king of England, and when Longworth explained that he had come as a private visitor to find out what was happening in this inaccessible land, and that his gifts were – in part – to test the market for a development of trade between England and Circassia, he was met with polite deference, because 'everyone here has the undisputed right to tell as many falsehoods as he pleases', but with total incredulity. They just could not believe that anyone could be induced simply by sympathy and curiosity to face the Russian blockade and expose himself to the dangers and fatigues of a journey in the Caucasus.

The reluctance of both the beys and the tribesmen to accept Longworth's reasons was enhanced by the conduct of his guide and dragoman. These followers of his were continually hinting that Longworth was really a person of great importance and in some way an emissary of the sovereign and government of his country; they did this largely to inflate their own importance and attract attention, gifts and hospitality. The Circassians themselves preferred to think of their visitor as representing government rather than trade, because they suspected that a merchant once established might prove to be a wooden horse within their Trojan defences – an illusion encouraged by the fact that many of them believed themselves to be descended from the inhabitants of Troy.

It did not take long for Longworth to realize the intensity of the Circassians' hatred of their Russian oppressors. Russian prisoners of war were to be found doing the most basic manual labour, and they were pointed out to him as having 'piggish eyes and a shuffling gait [. . .] a compromise between the peasant's slouch and a military strut'. The Russians had brought this hatred on themselves by their brutal and vicious behaviour: knowing that all Circassians felt particular reverence for the dead, and that they went to enormous pains to retrieve the bodies of their fallen comrades, the Russians had deliberately mutilated the bodies of local fighters they had killed. They were also reported to have burned Circassian prisoners over slow fires.

In the months before Longworth arrived, Russian tactics had changed: whereas previously they had mostly engaged in cavalry skirmishes using Cossack units along the Kuban river, now they had started making prolonged sorties with infantry and artillery from their forts along the Kuban and penetrating far into the tribal interior. One of the chiefs was pointed out to him as the marksman who had picked off a Russian general riding in the middle of his regiment in one such sortie, and brought him crashing from his saddle. The Russians' use of grape shot from their cannons had caused great damage and resentment within the ranks of the tribesmen, who no longer felt they could confront the enemy on a battlefield but were reduced to guerrilla warfare in the hills. Also the Russians had started making military highways through Georgia and Abkhazia; since such roads were not in continual use by the invaders, they were a two-edged asset: the insurgents used them to move quickly around their own country and they also placed ambushes on them to surprise Russian columns on the move. Indeed, the gorges and defiles of the Caucasian mountains provided the ideal terrain for guerrilla warfare – a permanent hinterland into which the tribesmen could withdraw to reform and consolidate.

But the most visible and immediately provocative evidence of the Russian presence was their string of forts along the Black Sea coastline. These were extending steadily southwards, from Anapa (not far from the Crimea) to the mountain ranges in the mid-Caucasus. They were instrumental in enforcing the blockade, and they were also the jumping off point for punitive raids – slashing and burning villages and stealing cattle – into the mountains and the heartlands of the tribes. But a posting to these forts was highly unpopular with the Russian garrisons, who felt holed up with meagre rations in confined quarters from which they seldom dared to sally forth. As a consequence, there was a steady trickle of deserters from the garrisons, soldiers who felt that anything – even labouring as prisoners of war or, worse, being sold on as slaves to the Ottoman empire – was better than the claustrophobic and brutal regime of Tsar Nicholas I's army. The largest element among these deserters were Poles who had been conscripted into the tsar's army and who felt little patriotic allegiance to it. But many who described themselves as Polaks to the Circassians were in fact Russians who thought – hardly surprisingly in view of the atrocities they had committed – that they would be less harshly treated if they concealed the fact. Indeed, so many alleged Poles were reaching the independence fighters that they thought of trying to form a regiment of them to fight against the Russians.

Against this background of fear and hatred, it was especially alarming to Longworth to find that from time to time he was under suspicion of being a Russian spy. These suspicions surfaced as a consequence of his hosts' bafflement at the purpose and sponsorship of his visit: if he was really not an agent of the British government, what was he doing there? Were such suspicions to crystallize, he feared that the first intimation he might have that something was wrong might be 'an apology for the necessity they were under of selling me to the Abasseks or of throwing me into the sea'.

The best way that Longworth could think of disproving such suspicions was to offer himself as a front-line combatant against the Russians: he wanted to join in some daring raid and put his life as much at risk as his hosts were doing; it was easier said than done. Time and again he was frustrated by promising forays being aborted at the last moment. But he did manage to join in reconnoitring the defences of one or two of the Russians' coastal forts, being shot at in the process, and consequently became a friend of the most rash and dashing of all the guerrilla leaders, a chief invariably known as 'the Wolf'.

Throughout these adventures, Longworth was not entirely a lone Englishman in this part of the world. Mr J. S. Bell (the owner of the ship *Vixen* whose passage to the Caucasus had provoked David Urquhart's row with Lord Palmerston) was also in Circassia at the same time, but was less inclined than Longworth to risk his person in conflict with the Russians, since he had ongoing commercial interests which he did not want to jeopardize. Longworth wanted to meet up with Bell, and was delighted when this was arranged by his hosts, but – part way through Longworth's stay – another unknown Englishman appeared on the scene who was also assumed to have a close link with King William IV and to be a precursor of official British aid to the beleaguered independence fighters. This figure is referred to throughout Longworth's book as Nadir Bey (the title and name allotted to him by his Circassian hosts). He was in fact a Mr Knight, of whom little is known, but who was such a charismatic character that he instantly established a reputation for being a quintessential English gentleman: he out-rode the locals, shot better than them, bestowed lavish gifts, and – when cornered – was capable of setting his horse at any ditch, hedge or barricade and clearing it in the best Leicestershire-hunting-field style.

In addition to the presence of these three loose-cannon Englishmen on the Black Sea coast, there was another factor which persuaded the Circassians that the king of England and his government stood firmly on their side in their conflict with Russia. A message had been received by one of the chiefs from no lesser person than Lord Ponsonby, the British ambassador to the Porte. Ponsonby urged them to send a placatory message to the Russians, offering to stop all hostilities if the Russians for their part withdrew beyond the Kuban river and dismantled their forts along the Black Sea coast. They were authorized to offer in support of their terms 'the guarantee of England'. The terms were to be offered three times, and if consistently rejected by the Russians, the Circassians were to report the fact back to Lord Ponsonby. They took this as a clear indication that Britain was standing behind them in their troubles, and two 'heralds' set out immediately under a safe-conduct to deliver the message to the Russian commanding general. In fact, the chiefs probably read much more into the message than was intended by the British government or even by Ponsonby himself.

Predictably, the Russian general who received these advances did not react favourably. He treated the suggestions with derision and spoke of the British government in disparaging

terms. As to Longworth and his fellow Englishmen on the
ground (of whom it seems they were well aware through their
own spies) the general said 'they were unprincipled adventurers
who were endeavouring to mislead [the Circassians] for their
own ends, and the best they could do was to cut them into
pieces'. Submission to Tsar Nicholas I was, he said, the only
serious option open to the rebellious chiefs; the alternative was
an immediate slash-and-burn operation by the Cossacks.

When this was related to Longworth, he commented that the
Russians seemed to think they were addressing the 'crouching
and defenceless population of the steppes' rather than 'a hardy
race of mountaineers' who could plunge into their native forests
and fastnesses and defy the Russians to follow them. With his
encouragement, a bold and provocative response was sent back
to the Russian general: 'You seem proudly to imagine you can
do as you please; but, though we be but a small nation, with
God's blessing and the succour of England, we will resist you
still'. The chiefs went on to declare the war against Russia a
jihad: everyone who died would be a martyr to whom the gates
of paradise would promptly swing open.

Islamic practices also involved Longworth in one or two
embarrassing incidents. When he started trading the goods he
had brought with him to test the local market, he received – as
well as wax, butter and fox-furs – 'a buxom damsel of
seventeen'. The girl was terrified when she learnt that she had
been sold to a Westerner, because a malicious Islamic friend had
told her that Christians had cannibalistic tendencies and that her
new owner was likely 'to roast and pickle her'. When during the
subsequent night an alarm was raised, everyone thought a
Russian attack was imminent; only the night before, a slumber-
ing elderly sentry had been aroused by two Cossack scouts who

had threatened to kidnap him. But on this occasion the disturbance turned out to be caused by the seventeen-year-old girl effecting an escape. She was eventually found and returned to the camp. The young man who, it turned out, had eloped with her, gave a solemn assurance under oath on the Koran that she was 'undamaged'. Nonetheless the deal regarding the girl was called off and Longworth had his trading goods returned to him – somewhat to his relief.

But all these exchanges with the Russians and the bartering for goods were proving distractions for Longworth, who really wanted to be involved in some active operations against the enemy. It seemed his time had come when one of the chiefs invited him to join a 'reconnoitring' party intent on attacking, or at least disrupting, the garrison of a small Russian fort and military colony. Ten of them set off together on horseback, and soon found that – even as so small a body of men as that – they were attracting cannon fire from the fort, so they split up and Longworth found himself riding alone along the edge of a ravine when he spotted four horsemen riding along the skyline of the ridge opposite. Convinced that these were part of the Circassians' own raiding party, he descended into the ravine to join them on the other side. But the bottom of the ravine was marshy and he was slowed down, which was just as well for him as it enabled one of his own party to overtake him and point out that the four figures he had seen on the ridge were not their own men but Cossacks. He had been on the point of blundering into the hands of an enemy who would undoubtedly have captured and hanged him, no doubt causing immense embarrassment to the British government.

While Longworth was surviving this narrow squeak, one of the tribesmen of his party was deliberately putting himself at equal risk. He had spotted the Cossacks and rode straight at them, being the next moment 'sword in hand among them', doubtless reckoning that odds of four to one were odds that he could manage. He was right. The Cossacks – possibly because they saw he had other supporters following on – took to flight, but not before the tribesman had overtaken one of them and stripped him of his carbine and sabre. Longworth thought this fellow could have captured the Cossack if he had not been so intent on acquiring his weapons. The operation was only called off when they observed that 'a body of infantry, which, judging from the lengthening line of bayonets flashing in the sun, amounted to not less than five hundred men' was advancing to cut off their retreat – a gratifying reaction to a reconnaissance by ten men! Even then, the chief made a feint of charging the enemy 'apparently to see if I [Longworth] would accompany him'. Longworth kept abreast of him until the last moment, proving his courage and horsemanship. It was the sort of experience he had been wanting, to prove his commitment to his hosts and to himself.

But in the weeks that followed he was more than ever conscious of the Circassians' disappointment in the performance of the British government. They were continually looking out to sea to search the horizon for ships of the Royal Navy on their way to break the Russian blockade or to escort trading vessels that were doing so. There were rumours that the British had a fleet in the Black Sea. On one occasion a red flag was spotted on an incoming vessel and the tribesmen were exultant at the prospect of welcoming a merchant ship sailing under the red ensign; unhappily, the flag turned out to be a red signal flag on a Russian ship. Worse still, there appeared to be a real threat of a raiding party being landed from a Russian corvette to ambush and capture Longworth or his Circassian hosts – conjuring up horrific fears of 'captivity, death, or more than death, the gloom of Siberian banishment'. An unlit bonfire was discovered on a headland which looked as if it were intended as a guiding beacon for the incoming corvette; when the tribesmen dismantled the bonfire, it was sinisterly reassembled a day or two later. Even when lookouts were posted along the coastline, there was a continual anxiety about surprise attack from the sea.

Sometimes the tribesmen took the initiative. When a landing party from a Russian corvette put in to the shore close to where Longworth was staying, the Russian sailors claimed to be wanting to buy mutton, having seen sheep on the shore line. In a bargaining exchange – carried on at a safe distance without contact – the Russians made it clear they knew an Englishman was in the region. The Circassians were convinced the whole episode was a trap to lure them within range of the Russians' rifles and capture prisoners – hopefully including Longworth. So they reversed the trap and when the next party of Russians came ashore, the tribesmen came out of hiding and opened fire on them. The shooting continued even after the Russians had regained their landing craft and 'many of the men in the boat were killed before they could regain the vessel'.

On another occasion, a small Turkish ship that had evaded the blockade was spotted on the shore by the Russians and subjected to intensive bombardment. It was for this reason that the tribesmen tried to conceal – with leafs and branches in the rigging – any such vessels that were sheltering by the shore. Longworth himself was caught in one such bombardment 'shut in between the cliffs and the sea' where he could find no shelter until he managed to escape inland up a path leading to a ruined fort; but he did not venture far, because of the number of poisonous snakes encountered. All these maritime events increased distrust on both sides, and alarmed Longworth.

They also proved beyond doubt that there were Russian agents or spies acting on their behalf in the tribal areas. The principle suspects were always the Armenian traders. They were despised and mistrusted in the same sort of way the Jewish community was blamed for mischief within Russia.

Longworth himself, who – despite his generally liberal views – could be very prejudiced, comments in his book that 'Armenians are the bane of all those who admit them to their bosom'. He also subscribed to the view that it was through the Armenians that Russia was informed of everything that took place in Circassia. To their credit however, both Longworth and Bell tried to dissuade their tribal hosts from routinely robbing Armenian caravans of their trade goods.

When Longworth moved from this rugged coastal region to a more fertile plain, in the hope of seeing more action against the Russians, he finally encountered Nadir Bey, the nom de guerre already bestowed on the new arrival Mr Knight, who was suffering from fever, brought on by the extreme exertions and alarms of the voyage: Nadir Bey's ship had been intercepted by no less than three Russian 'cruisers', one of which had succeeded in getting between them and the shore. It had been a question of all hands to the oars, and Nadir Bey had 'set a steady example to the crew'. A Circassian merchant who had cadged a lift on the ship with his cargo had not rewarded Nadir Bey's efforts with any great generosity of spirit: he had suggested that – to lighten the ship's load and add to their speed – the Englishman's baggage should be jettisoned overboard rather than his own. And to add to Nadir Bey's exasperation – and no doubt aggravating his fever – the same fellow passenger on discovering that the Englishman had a valuable pocket watch had made a practice of asking him the time every hour of the day and night until, in desperation to be left alone, Nadir Bey had succumbed and given him the watch in question. Altogether it had not been a good introduction to the more greedy practices of the country.

Longworth for his part immediately assumed that the visitor was an agent of the British government, just as the locals had made the same assumption about himself, but he was not. It transpired that he was – in Longworth's words – 'a volunteer to the cause, a gentleman of fortune [. . .] impelled thereto solely by the genuine spirit of chivalry'. He had come prepared for action, bringing with him no less than sixteen large chests of powder and lead, which he declared he was happy to give to any local chief who would allow him to join in some worthwhile enterprise, such as the storming of a fort or an incursion into Russian territory.

Nor did Nadir Bey have long to wait before seeing some action. The Russians, who had clearly been informed by their spies of the arrival of an Englishman with a cargo of military material, sent a frigate to the point on the coast where he had landed with instructions to capture or burn the gunpowder and bullets even if they could not capture the visitor. When he heard what was afoot, Nadir Bey rose from his sick bed to go down to the beach and rally his supporters among the tribesmen, who turned out in such large numbers that the Russian frigate commander thought better of the attempt and instead sailed a few miles further up the coast and set fire to another Turkish ship which had taken refuge there. A desperate cavalry gallop up the coast by the tribesmen to forestall this arrived too late to stop the burning, but not too late to kill twenty of the Russian landing party.

As soon as he was well enough to be more active, Nadir Bey decked himself out in a garb that he must have realized was likely to increase the local view that he was an official representative or ambassador of his government: he wore a scarlet yeomanry uniform with gold and green facings, which – even in comparison with the colourful attire of the local warriors – must have looked spectacular. As with Longworth, the tribal chiefs could not be persuaded he was a private adventurer: either he must be an envoy of England, or a spy for Russia. His hyperactivity against the invaders made the latter seem implausible. Both Longworth and Nadir Bey saw one of their main roles as being credible witnesses to what was happening in the Caucasus, at a time when there were no other first-hand reports reaching England. But they soon got news from home which made them very despondent about how much attention would be paid to their reports in high places. King William IV had died. The king had always been seen as sympathetic to the independence of the Caucasus – 'one who sincerely resolved to stem the tide of Russian aggrandisement'; his ministers – notably Lord Palmerston – were less so. The two Englishmen assured their hosts that, despite this bad news, they still had plenty of friends in Britain.

With his newly arrived compatriot so full of aggressive energy, Longworth was more than ever determined to engage in military action. Nadir Bey was set on storming a major Russian fort, and had earmarked Fort Shapsine as his intended target: it was set on a river bank in a forest, had walls fifteen feet high, was crenellated, flanked by bastions and boasted heavy guns. He and Longworth decided to do a private recce together at dawn. They crept from bush to bush along the river bank as the sun was beginning to rise. By the time it was fully light they were within musket range of the battlements and could 'distinguish the features of the sentinels on duty'. Having spied out all they could, and worked out the best line for a serious assault, they retraced their steps to where they had tethered their horses and galloped back to the tribal camp from which they had set out – no doubt expecting to be congratulated on their escapade. But they were to be disappointed. The tribal chiefs were furious that they had embarked on this exploit on their own and without a proper escort. In fact, they went so far as to suggest that 'such early visits to a Russian fortress might be misinterpreted'. They could never quite shake off the idea that they might, after all, be Russian spies.

Perhaps the Circassians had special reason to be nervous at that moment. They had just learnt that the Russian tsar himself – the formidable Nicholas I, renowned for his terrifying 'pewter gaze' – had arrived in the Caucasus to assess the situation and was lodged with a garrison only some three miles away at Ghelendjik. A formidable force of Cossacks and infantry, leaving behind them dead and wounded as well as cattle and provisions, had arrived by forced marches to give protection to their sovereign; the hills above them were bristling with Russian bayonets. But all was not well at the Russian camp, and while the tsar was there a fire broke out, destroying much ammunition and vital food supplies, and obliging the tsar to return to his ship and go further along the coast.

There were sinister rumours about the cause of the fire, some people thinking that it had been started on the orders of General Williamanoff, the commander of the base, to avoid the tsar discovering the 'wholesale fraud and spoliation' that had been going on there. (Nicholas I was on another occasion publicly to humiliate and drive to suicide one of his senior officers of whose conduct he disapproved.) Whatever the truth, in the confusion of the fire a large number of Russian soldiers deserted. However brief and troubled the tsar's visit, it still gave time for him to issue an order that if any of the three English soldiers-of-fortune in the region were captured, they were to be unceremoniously hanged. Longworth comments in his book that were that to have happened he was confident that 'the people of England would have called him [the tsar] to a strict account'; and it was possibly bearing in mind the need to alert British opinion to what was happening that Nadir Bey offered to finance from his own funds the sending of a Circassian embassy to London.

The tribal chiefs had for some months now pursued a policy of non-provocation towards the Russians, partly as a result of the advice given them in Lord Ponsonby's letter. But the Russians had conspicuously failed to respond: their aggressive behaviour on land and sea and their tenacious holding on to all their forts showed that a policy of reconciliation was not for them. The Circassians therefore resolved, with much encouragement from Longworth and Nadir Bey, to be more active themselves. As a preliminary step, they insisted that their supporters took a solemn oath on the Koran promising full support; many did this only reluctantly because they realized they were putting their lives on the line by signing up in this way.

Spring was coming and the solid ice across the Kuban river would soon begin to melt, making any forays northwards into Russian territory more difficult. The Wolf and other tribal chiefs therefore decided that this was the moment for a major raid which would concentrate on capturing Russian cannons and ammunition, rather than on the more usual and popular objective of carrying off plunder in the form of sheep and cattle. Five thousand horsemen, reminded of their oath of loyalty to the cause, were assembled; the hills, which earlier had been crawling with Russian infantry, were now illuminated by the campfires of the insurgents. Longworth and Nadir Bey toured some of the campsites and found the tribal warriors gathered around their minstrels listening to war songs and in high spirits.

Longworth tells how they rode back to their own watch-fire and attempted to get some sleep on the night before the crossing. He explains that this was not easy 'less owing to apprehension for my personal safety, than conscientious scruples as to how far I was justified as an Englishman to take part in the wild sort of warfare I was now enlisted in'. But he comforted himself with

the thought that there could be no nobler cause than the independence of these mountain people, and that if he did find himself witnessing some horrors then at least his presence would be likely to have the effect of mitigating them. He also felt that however wild and ruthless his fellows in arms might be, the Circassians were not given to slaughtering their enemies in cold blood, nor to violating women.

It was two hours after midnight when the Circassians began their march towards the Kuban river. Longworth struggled to keep up and not to lose sight of his companions in the thick brushwood through which they had to 'flounder and scramble' on their horses; he was scratched by branches and brambles and his horse sank into half-frozen bogs. Strange and unknown warriors loomed up out of the darkness, with just the muzzles of their rifles and the tails of their horses appearing from the folds of their poncho-like capes. When they halted in a hamlet, Longworth dozed in his saddle while his horse quietly munched the roof of a thatched cottage.

As dawn broke, they found themselves on a hill overlooking the Kuban river. It was then that an advance scouting party brought back the disturbing news that the river ice had already begun to melt and a passage across was problematical – and the return even more so. Disheartened by these reports, most of the infantry and about a third of the cavalry immediately gave up, and set off for home. The remainder was not so easily deterred from 'an enterprise from which they had promised themselves such glorious results'. They went forward, through about a mile of reeds along the bank, to judge for themselves whether bridges of interwoven branches could not be constructed over the broken ice. Longworth went with them and when he reached this point he was not surprised to find that it was the

Wolf (whose real name was Tougouse) who was leading the work of bridging the ice, and he was relieved to find his compatriot Nadir Bey also there – as he had lost contact with him and feared that he had been somehow lost in the approach march.

While some of the other chiefs conferred on the bank, the Wolf led a party of some three hundred horsemen over the rickety bridge and the broken ice into the Russian territory on the other side. Among the first to push forward were Long-worth and Nadir Bey 'not doubting we should be followed by the whole army'. But the others did not follow. They listened to the council of chiefs, who concluded that 'it would be madness to persist in the expedition' because they reckoned that the return – hopefully laden with booty – would involve fighting their way through Russian troops and then trying to re-cross the river, which would be quite impossible. Also, they thought the silence of the Russian guns on the far bank was an ominous sign that an ambush was being prepared. They feared – as always – that spies had given away their plans and that large reinforce-ments of Russians were lurking in the reeds on the other side of the river, ready to attack the tribesmen the moment they became 'entangled in the marshes'. The expedition was formally abandoned.

But what had been decreed too risky for the majority was now to be attempted by the 'chivalrous handful' who had already crossed the ice. The Wolf was determined to press on, and he crossed and re-crossed the river to persuade a few of the bolder spirits on the southern side to join him on Russian territory. The party on the north of the river dismounted and offered a prayer to Allah before springing again into their saddles. Two chiefs from the south bank went so far as to cross the river to try to persuade the two Englishmen to withdraw, but when they failed in this – Nadir Bey declaring he and Longworth would stand or fall with their companions – decided to stay on themselves with the 'chivalrous handful'.

The party then moved forward by a path that led from the river bank through the forest of reeds. There was an eerie silence which made them fear they were indeed walking into an ambush. But Longworth was impressed by the orderly way in which they steadily advanced for two miles into Russian territory. Then, quite suddenly, the path they were following changed direction and it became clear they were riding into a trap: a narrow causeway led to a battery of Russian guns guarded by infantry and Cossacks. To charge down this only open way would be to charge to almost certain death: it was a Light-Brigade-at-Balaclava situation twenty years before that event.

The raiding party came to a standstill and the chiefs conferred. Most felt there was no alternative but to retreat. The Wolf, on the other hand, asked what they were stopping for: had they not come to attack the enemy, and there was the enemy in front of them! The question was resolved by the appearance of a chief called Pakako; he was renowned for his courage and also for his ferocious looks (he wore his full-length sheepskin coat inside-out which made him look like a wild animal). 'Waving his standard high over his head, he broke with a scornful yell from the council, and, followed helter-skelter by the Deli-Kans [mounted tribesmen], dashed up the avenue'. Close behind him were both Longworth and Nadir Bey 'being curious to see how this mad career would terminate'. But halfway towards the Russian guns, their horses became bogged down in heavy mud and while they were floundering another chief – also a man

whose courage was beyond question – caught up with them and said if they could not get through the mud and reeds they must turn back. 'We will try, however', he added, and plunged ahead among the reeds, sinking up to his stirrups in the bog. There was nothing for it but to give up, retrace their steps to the river and retire to join their more cautious brethren on the southern bank.

No comparable adventure was to occur again. Nadir Bey decided to leave just as soon as he could arrange a passage to Constantinople. Longworth records that his companion's 'gallantry and proficiency in the exercises martial and equestrian' had greatly endeared him to young people of both sexes in Circassia. He managed to get a ship to take him from the blockaded coast to Trebizond in Turkey, where the Russian consul persuaded the local Pasha to impound the ship; but Nadir Bey (always willing and able to do the generous thing) paid an indemnity which secured its release. Mr Bell too disappeared from the scene; he went south in connection with some trading deal and was not able to rejoin Longworth before the latter fell sick with ague. Disappointingly for Longworth, it was while he was on his sick bed that the Circassians mounted a successful assault on one of the Russian forts close to Anapa in the north. They had seized the opportunity by repulsing a Russian sortie in quest of plunder, and then attacking the fort from which they had emerged, scaling the walls and either killing or capturing the entire garrison. The tribesmen themselves lost twelve men. This was exactly the sort of escapade in which both Longworth and Nadir Bey had so long sought to be involved.

After the disappointment of missing this action, Longworth felt at last that it was time too for him to return home. He was exasperated that even now, whenever something happened to arouse apprehensions that intelligence had been passed to the Russians – as it did when a Russian fleet of twenty-seven sails appeared off the coast – the finger of suspicion always pointed towards him. On this last occasion, suspicions were once more allayed, this time by one of the chiefs, revealing that the Russians had in fact offered him a large bribe – two haversacks full of gold – if he would 'either betray me into their hands, or make away with me privately'.

Leaving was never going to be easy, but Longworth was fortunate in that a Turkish ship had been forced to run ashore near the Russian fort of Anapa and had managed, with the help of oarsmen, to sneak a little further up the coast to be 'hastily dragged on shore, and so completely disguised by the number of boughs attached to her mast and rigging, as to present only the appearance of a tree'. The ship was now only waiting for a north-westerly wind to slip away and evade the blockade by night. They agreed to take Longworth with them, and he started saying his farewells. His friends declared that he had been so long among them – in fact it had been over a year – that they had begun to consider him as one of them.

Lookouts were posted on the hilltops and, when the coast seemed clear of Russian warships, the vessel was stripped of its leafy covering and dragged, with the help of rollers and pulleys, across the beach. Just as Longworth had ruminated on the voyage out about the classical legacy of these waters, so now he meditated about the inextinguishable liberties of the natives of the Caucasus. Once again, more practical matters intervened: a Russian ship had been spotted, and Longworth himself climbed up the rigging to find it was not one warship but two. An eight-hour chase followed and when eventually they shook off their pursuers, Longworth – who was by now playing an active part in running the ship – discovered that the captain's compass was not working: they had no idea in what direction they were sailing. This would not have mattered so much if the Black Sea had been encircled by friendly ports, but the opposite was now the case. To make matters worse, they became becalmed and fresh water supplies were running out. While the crew were gloomily speculating on their likely fate, an unidentified vessel passed in the darkness within a cable's length of them. Then, at dawn, a familiar coastline hove in sight and Longworth was put ashore very close to the point from which he had set off a year before. A small boat took him along the north coast of Turkey to Trebizond where he was welcomed at the British consulate. His adventures were over.

Back in Constantinople, Longworth was encouraged by his friends to write his two-volume report of his year among the Circassians, on which the above account is largely based. With the withdrawal from the region of himself, Mr Bell and Mr Knight (Nadir Bey), the Circassians decided that there was no immediate prospect of the Russian invasion being discontinued or reversed as a result of diplomatic pressure from England, and it was therefore necessary for them to take matters into their own hands, disregarding the more cautious advice that had been given them by Lord Ponsonby.

So – somewhat ironically – it came about that, no sooner had Longworth withdrawn from the scene than they started to undertake a whole series of attacks on the Russians, just the sort of operations in which Longworth had been longing to participate while he had been there. The fort at Shapsine, which he and Mr Knight had reconnoitred earlier at some peril to themselves, was now made the subject of a full-scale attack; the Wolf had collected together some 7,000 men and – after placing a cordon round the fort to intercept any escapees – had made an advance through the forests under cover of darkness and then made a dawn attack, storming the walls and killing over 2,000 of the Russian garrison and hangers-on, and capturing the remaining 500. The Circassians lost 350 killed themselves. Perhaps Longworth and Knight, had they been there leading the attackers from the front as was their wont, might have been numbered among the casualties. As it was, they lived to tell a tale which was to cause no small ripples of disquiet in London and St Petersburg, but was to be an inspiration to other adventurers.

Chapter 7

Joseph Wolff: The Crazy Cleric

'Madness need not be all breakdown.
It may also be break-through.'
                                        – R. D. Laing (1927–89)

Wolff said: 'What humbug is that? You cannot dare to put me to death. You will be putting to death a guest.'

The mullahs of Doab [in Afghanistan] replied: 'The Koran decides so.'

Wolff said, 'It is a lie. The Koran says on the contrary that a guest should be respected even if he is an infidel.'

The mullahs replied: 'Then you must purchase your blood with all you have.'

And thus Wolff had to surrender everything . . . naked like Adam and Eve and without even an apron of leaves to dress himself in he continued his journey.

This is the Reverend Joseph Wolff's own account of one of his many curious and alarming adventures as he crossed and re-crossed Central Asia between 1830 and 1844. He was someone who courted trouble from an early age. Born in 1795 in Bavaria, the son of a rabbi, he had early in life rebelled against the teaching of his Jewish faith in the face of violent opposition from his family (an aunt threw the fire irons at him when she heard of his blasphemous intentions). Between the age of seven and seventeen he developed a reputation as a disputatious convert to Christianity. Having explored the doctrines of the Catholic and the Protestant churches, he initially threw in his lot with the Church of Rome, and after being expelled from a succession of academic institutions in Germany, he arrived in Rome and became a theological student in the Vatican. But he remained as contentious as ever, denying the supreme authority of the Pope and finally obliging the Inquisition to expel him from the Holy City as he had been expelled elsewhere so many times before.

Eventually, in 1819, he came to England where his perversity was regarded as endearingly eccentric, and where he found both a wealthy patron who could help him – in the form of Henry Drummond – and a church that was broad enough to accommodate his peculiarly personal theological views. After further oriental studies at Cambridge, he toured the Middle East trying to convert Jewish communities to Christianity, and then returned to England where – somewhat surprisingly – he successfully courted and married the aristocratic and well-connected Lady Georgiana Walpole. They visited Jerusalem and other places together, and then, in 1830, Wolff resolved to go off on his own to Central Asia in search of the lost tribes of Israel. So started the first of Wolff's two memorable trips to Bokhara.

At first sight, he may not have seemed to be a very convincing British adventurer confronting tsarist Russia. But by now this cosmopolitan character of Jewish origin had become a naturalized British subject and no one could deny that he was an adventurer. He was also confronting tsarist Russia by the mere act of travelling – at immense personal risk – along the fringes of the Russian empire; this was already a region in which Russian influence in all matters commercial and political was largely unchallenged. This was made explicitly clear to him on his first visit to Bokhara: the emir told him at an early encounter 'we wish you to know we are great friends now with Russia, and they give us, in all respects, every assistance in their power'. Wolff comments in his memoirs that 'it is worthy of note that they have in Bokhara introduced the hours of day, as in Russia, from 1 to 12'. While there, Wolff met many of the principal citizens and he recorded that 'they were all acquainted with Russia [. . .] their merchants go chiefly to Makariev, Astrakhan and Saratoff in Russia'.

There was another way too in which Wolff, who was always primarily on a religious rather than a political mission, distanced himself from the influence of tsarist Russia, and this was in doctrinal matters: although by now he was an Anglican missionary, he had experience with the Catholic and Jewish faiths and spent much of his time trying to persuade the followers of Islam that he understood their misguided beliefs, but – although he sometimes preached in front of Orthodox Christians – he had no such links or sympathies with the Russian Orthodox church.

It is also significant that those whom he encountered in his travels assumed that he was anxious to champion British interests at the expense of Russia. The ruler of the Punjab went so far as to say to him 'Now, we come nigh unto God, by making an alliance with England in order to keep out the Russians from India'; even to Wolff this must have seemed a slight over-simplification of the way to heaven, but he did not contradict it. Wolff's heart was with God rather than with the viceroy of India, but he was always conscious of travelling as an

Englishman in a regrettably Russian-dominated sphere, and of the need to try to redress this balance.

Wolff's first journey to Bokhara, to find and convert the lost tribes of Israel, really started at Constantinople. He had dined there with Sir Robert Gordon, the British representative, who procured letters of introduction for him from the Turkish sultan, and who (according to Wolff, one not given to modesty) 'never had a more pleasant evening than in his conversation with him [Wolff]'. He hired a Tartar guide and set off on horseback, requesting 'an old decrepit horse – the only sort he dared to mount'. When he reached Tehran he dined with the British Ambassador and collected more letters of introduction, this time from the shah of Persia to the chiefs of Khorasan through whose turbulent country he would need to travel.

The introductions would have reassured him more, had not one of the ambassador's guests said to him over dinner 'Now you have got all the letters; but, in spite of them, we shall hear, two months hence, the sad tidings that Joseph Wolff has been made a slave in Khorassan by the Turcomauns [sic], and sold for sixty shay'.[1] And these gloomy prognoses were to continue: some visiting Afghans forecast that if he survived Khorasan, he would fall victim to the Turkomans at Sarakh or Merv and, if he did by some miracle reach Bokhara, he would either be held there indefinitely or killed 'as they killed Moorcroft' (who appeared to have become part of the unsavoury legend of Bokhara). Besides which, the Afghans added, 'You have physical impediments, because you are short-sighted, and do not see when robbers are coming'. This last point was to prove all too accurate.

---

1. The value of one 'shay' was the twentieth part of a farthing.

As Wolff progressed further eastwards, and entered the dreaded Khorasan, he travelled in a caravan which included his own four hired camels, all loaded with bibles sent to him from Bombay for distribution on his route. As predicted, it was not long before shrieks from his fellow travellers alerted Wolff to the fact that something was wrong. When he enquired what the matter was, his companions said 'Are you blind? Look there! There are Turkomans coming on horseback.' When the marauders caught up with the caravan 'to the surprise of all, they did not fire, nor make any attack'. Instead they asked where the caravan came from. Wolff promptly replied that they came from a certain part of Persia, knowing that there was an outbreak of plague there. When Wolff saw that this greatly alarmed them, he boldly approached them as if to embrace them, upon which they turned their horses round and rode off as fast as they could. His imaginative handling of the situation had more than made up for his short-sighted unawareness of the impending danger. On other occasions when danger threatened, he presented his opponents with a bible and started speaking volubly about religion, which (as he confesses in his book) 'he always did on the slightest opportunity'.

But his luck was not to last. When they set out from a village called Sangerd, Wolff – who was riding on ahead of his companions – suddenly heard firing from all sides and dreadful yelling and screaming. He resisted the temptation to ride on and save himself, returning instead to join his companions and found 'his servant and all the rest were already tied to the horses' tails of the banditti who surrounded them'. All the prisoners had already been stripped naked, and soon one of the robbers rode up to Wolff with a gun in his hand and demanded his money. They forced him to dismount and stripped him naked too, and

tied him with a long rope to a horse's tail, and a man with a whip came behind and flogged him. He notes in his memoirs: 'Wolff prayed! – in such hours one learns to pray'. His prayers appeared to be answered, because when he boldly declared – in answer to questions about who he was – that 'I am a follower of Jesus', instead of further tormenting such an infidel, the robber chief gave orders for him to be untied and allowed to ride one of the horses. They even put a few rags around his body to restore his modesty.

But his troubles were not over and soon they were speculating among themselves as to what price he might fetch in the local slave markets. When they searched his baggage and found the letters of introduction from the sultan and shah, they said, 'Now this is a dangerous man; we see from his looks and from these letters that he is not a common man'. They concluded that if they held him there would be others coming to seek his release and that of the other captives; they would therefore do much better to kill him quickly and say that he had been taken away by Turkoman robbers. All this was said within Wolff's hearing, so he immediately went up to them and said 'Your reasoning is very good [. . .] but you are too late'; he then went on to explain that he had written in the bibles he had sent to His Royal Highness Abbas Mirza, the commander of the Persian army, telling him: 'In case these Bibles reach you without me, you may be convinced that I have been made a slave, with my servant, and fifteen muleteers, not by Turcomauns, but by your Highness's subjects, the Kerahe [. . .] who wander about to make foray, against the orders of their chief.'

The inscription then went on to ask Abbas Mirza to rescue Wolff and his companions from the Kerahe. As soon as his captors heard this, and had it confirmed by the other prisoners, 'they became as pale as death' as they feared retribution. Wolff took advantage of their disarray to start negotiating a price for their release, based on notes promising a ransom would be paid. But still his captors were nervous, and decided that, although it might be too dangerous to hold on to him or kill him outright, 'a fatal accident' could be arranged. Having noted that he was no horseman, they therefore put him on the wildest horse they had, with no saddle or bridle, and whipped the horse into a gallop over rough country. Somehow Wolff managed 'to sit his horse like the colonel of a regiment' and reached the gates of the next village intact.

By good fortune, or divine intervention as Wolff would have interpreted it, the village in question had a large Jewish community whom he recognized as such and greeted in Hebrew with the words 'Hear, Israel, the Lord Our God is One Lord'. They gave him shelter and comfort, but soon the Kerahe robbers caught up with him once again, this time shackling him to other slaves 'in the most painful manner'. They still seemed determined to finish him off one way or another, and this time he was denied any food and thought he might be left to starve to death because 'dead dogs tell no tales'.

But rescue was at hand. A Persian officer of the Great Khan arrived unexpectedly in the village and on hearing that an Englishman was among the captives immediately demanded his release and that of all the other slaves, declaring, 'Away with the chains from the Englishman and all the rest, for slavery is at an end throughout [the province]!'. More than two hundred others were set at liberty and, attributing their release to Wolff, roamed the streets calling out to him, 'Oh, thou hast been an angel sent from the Lord!' Wolff would not have dissented.

The Persian officer who had liberated them was himself however no angel. He declared to Wolff that he had no religion but was a man of justice. To prove this, he asked Wolff to tell him the exact amount of money that had been taken from him. Wolff obliged, and then the Persian officer had the Kerahe mercilessly flogged until they surrendered every last coin; 'and then, putting the money into his own pocket, without giving Wolff a single penny, he added, 'Now you may go in peace.' So, much the poorer but undaunted, he continued his journey.

When he reached Meshed in eastern Persia, Wolff was able to meet Abbas Mirza and the latter paid so much attention to him that Wolff wrote to Lord Palmerston (then foreign secretary) suggesting that he should send 'not merely a charge d'affaires but a full ambassador' to Persia. Abbas Mirza also collected a large number of Turkoman chiefs together at his palace and made them promise not to harass Wolff on his onward journey to Bokhara; as a guarantee of their good faith, he announced that he was keeping two of the chiefs hostage until he had confirmation of Wolff's safe arrival. Wolff had the honour of being seated near to Abbas Mirza during this session but the embarrassment of being 'with his legs stretched out [. . .] for [he] was never able to learn to sit like an Eastern man [i.e. cross-legged]'.

All these introductions and safeguards seemed to be having some effect at last, because when Wolff reached Sarakhs (the next major settlement on his route) he was well received by the Turkomans, who lived in tents at the foot of the castle there, and who came out to welcome him as their guest and to ask for blessings from the 'holy man of England'. He heard them speculating among themselves that he must be 'the Prince Royal of England' because he had been observed in the presence of Abbas Mirza 'sitting with his legs stretched out, while all the grand ministers of state and others were standing'. As so often, Wolff's disabilities had worked out to his advantage. He spent several weeks at Sarakhs, preaching to the Jews and the Turkomans. He also did what he could to make himself useful in other ways. When one Turkoman told him his wife had just died and asked him what he could do 'by which a woman may be induced to fall in love with me', Wolff quickly remembered that he had just heard of a woman whose fiancé had committed a breach of his promise to marry her, so Wolff suggested that the widower should approach the spurned lady with a proposal, which he promptly did 'and was married to that lady the next day'.

When he reached Merv, the next settlement, he found that he

was able to obtain the release of several Persian slaves by paying for them himself. But he was surprised to discover that many other Persian slaves preferred to remain there, because they said they were better treated than they would be as free men at home, and because they hoped to earn their right to live permanently in liberty among the Turkomans. It was also while he was at Merv that he consolidated and recorded his conclusions about the best way to preserve his own safety – conclusions that were to stand him in good stead on this and his subsequent journey to Bokhara. He realized, from what he saw at first hand all about him, that once someone had been accepted as a dervish or a holy fool they could get away with speaking to rulers and others with a frankness and even disrespect which would have led to fatal consequences for anyone else. Wolff realized that he was benefiting from this indulgence himself, and – with his usual disregard of humility – compared himself to the Prophet Elijah, and to John the Baptist calling his listeners on the desert banks of the river Jordan 'a generation of vipers' with impunity.

Pressing on from Merv, Wolff crossed the frozen Oxus on the ice and proceeded through Karakul, where he called on the governor, who he was surprised to find was a former Persian slave. The governor gave him a meal of greasy tea and roasted horse flesh, and also gave him some good advice: 'Friend, be cautious in Bokhara, because one word against our religion will make the people forget you are a guest, and they will put you to death; therefore, be cautious [. . .]'. Moving on, he had to cross another river (which he claims was the Oxus again, but may have been a tributary), and this time the ice had partly melted and he had to be taken over in a rowing boat; Wolff was always terrified by water and screamed as the boat edged its way through the ice, so his Tajik guides held their hands over his eyes so he should be spared the sight, and this calmed him down a little. They reached the walls of Bokhara at night, and before they could see the city, they heard 'a loud rapping noise, as of strokes upon wood', which was made by the night watchmen, and the chanting of Islamic verses. Wolff countered by calling out 'Blessed be Thou, Jesus Christ, my God and my Lord, who hast redeemed me from all evil!' They had arrived at the gates of the holy city, but Wolff did not seem to have the governor of Karakul's warnings at the front of his mind.

It is at this point that the first volume of Wolff's third-person dictated memoirs ends. The second volume starts with some shrewd observations by Alfred Gatty, his friend and editor. Gatty explains that Wolff was essentially an orator: he could dictate from memory, including names, quotations and biblical references, without a note, but his written work was 'remarkably muddled'. Wolff's was a mind 'which requires hearers to whet its consecutive attention'. Although by 1860 he was already an old man by the standards of his time, he would exhaust three or four secretaries at a sitting, before drawing breath. Those who might have doubted the sixty-five-year-old's claims to have survived naked in the desert were silenced by the reality of seeing him walking barefoot along stone passages in winter, sleeping with doors open to the foggy Yorkshire moors, and insisting on a cold bath every morning. Gatty also explains that Wolff was not insensitive: 'his first feeling is fear [. . .] yet no man has faced more appalling dangers'. His egotism was said to be unlike other people's egotism: 'a large congregation or audience will make him believe that he has preached like St Paul, or lectured like Plato'. Nor did he doubt that his autobiography would be much read and admired: 'It will be a standard book, like Robinson Crusoe', was his verdict on his own work.

Wolff was well aware when he reached Bokhara that he was not the first Englishman in living memory to do so: William Moorcroft was much in his mind. As soon as the vizier of Bokhara heard that Wolff was outside the gates, he sent a horse and an escort to bring him in to his palace. And the first thing the vizier said to him was that they had not killed Moorcroft at Bokhara, as had been widely reported. The vizier questioned him closely about his origins and nationality. When Wolff responded by declaring he was of Jewish descent, but a naturalized Englishman, 'suddenly a voice proceeded from the crowd of the Jews outside, which shouted – 'He is a liar! He is a Russian spy!'. But Wolff managed to silence the man by pointing out that the bibles he was carrying were printed in London and not in Russia. The vizier was convinced of Wolff's bona fides, and told him 'The king's [emir's] command is that you go wherever you like among the Jews, but you must not talk about religion with the Mussulmans'. No sooner had this command been conveyed, than Wolff started expounding St Paul's epistles to the Moslem vizier. His missionary spirit was irrepressible, and not confined to converting the lost tribes of Israel. However, he seemed to be forgiven for this, and the vizier on a later occasion told him he had permission to discuss the theological differences between Islam and Christianity; not surprisingly, Wolff jumped at the chance and a long debate ensued. Wolff was somewhat taken aback when he asked the vizier for the Islamic definition of purity in a man and was told it was 'a man who makes holy war against infidels'.

After a three-month stay, Wolff left Bokhara with the emir's consent in April 1832, heading for Kabul. On his way, he was repeatedly advised to say that he was a Moslem from Arabia, and that this would enable him to pass safely through the region.

However, Wolff refused to do this and said that as long as his companions did not betray him he would be able to look after himself without resorting to denying his faith. He was encouraged by the belief that 'Eastern people are able to keep secrets in the most wonderful way', and he quotes as evidence of this the 'late conspiracy of the sepoys in India' – that is the Indian Mutiny (or, as it is now called there, the First Independence War) which had taken place just three years before he was dictating his memoirs. He was as good as his word: when he reached Mazar-i-Sharif in Afghanistan and the local governor started interrogating him about his origins and beliefs, he put up such a bewildering performance – talking in the same breath about the sons of Noah and steam ships in Malta harbour – that the governor declared that 'this man is too learned for me'; Wolff went on to record that although the governor 'did not understand a single word of it' he nonetheless 'walked away quite satisfied'. Wolff had not needed to tell any lies, let alone renounce his beliefs; he had merely bluffed, obfuscated and bored his way out of difficulty as so often before.

Wolff was now venturing into the domains of Murad Beg, the ruthless, European-hating ruler of Kunduz who had caused so much trouble and alarm to Moorcroft seven years earlier. Wolff (who had read Moorcroft's account of his adventures) 'kept himself quietly in a caravanserai' and pressed on as quickly as possible to the Hindu Kush, which he found so beautiful that 'it reminded the beholder of paradise'. But it turned out to be very different from paradise.

Soon he fell into the hands of some extremist Moslems – the mullahs of Doab – who refused to recognize him as a pilgrim and said that he must either declare publicly that Allah was the only God and Mahomet his prophet or they would 'sew you up in a dead donkey, burn you alive and make sausages of you'. Wolff – true to form – promptly declared, 'There is nothing but God, and Jesus the Son of God.' He then sat down and wrote a letter to Lord William Bentinck (the governor-general of India) explaining that when his letter arrived, he would undoubtedly be dead and could the governor-general please pay off his servants and 'write the whole account to my wife, Lady Georgiana'. (Incidentally, no message of farewell was sent to her.) It was at this juncture that the exchange occurred which is quoted at the beginning of this chapter. One of the factors that persuaded the mullahs of Doab not to kill him outright, but merely to rob him of everything he had (including his clothes) was that he claimed the right to be sent to Murad Beg, the dreaded ruler of Kunduz. Wolff takes up the tale:

> When they heard the name of Muhammad Moorad Beyk [Murad Beg], they actually began to tremble, and asked Wolff, 'Do you know him?' As Wolff could not say that he knew him, he replied, 'This you will have to find out.' They said, 'Then you must purchase your blood with all you have.' Wolff answered, 'This I will do. For I am a dervish, and do not mind either money, clothing or anything.'

And pursue his journey he did. His servants, who went on with him, were lost in admiration for his nerve and luck, and offered up their own Islamic prayer for his safekeeping. The governor of the next settlement he passed through was too poor to provide him with clothes, but sent him on with a letter describing him as an English ambassador who should be protected. Wolff knew this lacked credibility, and would have preferred to have been called an English dervish. As was to be expected, the next local governor along his route read the letter and exploded – 'What! A ragamuffin like you, without clothing! Do you want to make me believe you are an ambassador!' And he promptly ordered his staff to turn him out and send him packing on his way.

But his luck took another turn for the better as he approached Kabul. He had sent messages ahead, and was greeted as he reached the outskirts of the capital by mounted messengers who brought a letter to him from a Lieutenant Burnes (the future Sir Alexander 'Bokhara' Burnes) who had by good chance arrived at Kabul the previous day on his famous journey from India to Bokhara.[2] Burnes had been asked by Lord and Lady William Bentinck to look out for Wolff, as they knew he was on his way and rightly guessed he might be in serious peril. Greatly to Wolff's relief, a set of 'beautiful Afghan suits' was also sent to him, so he need no longer look like Adam in the garden of Eden. Dost Mohammad, the king of Afghanistan, invited Burnes and Wolff to a joint audience. Burnes gave a good account of himself, describing the system of government in England and India. When it came to Wolff's turn to speak, the conversation predictably became theological, and a mullah had to be called in to cope with Wolff's rantings until eventually Burnes managed to shut him up. Later Wolff tried to interest Burnes in his concept of an afterlife in which man would return to his natural state and 'eat of all manner of fruits'; Burnes on return to India reported Wolff as having told the king of Afghanistan that heaven consisted of a lot of vegetarians running around with no clothes on! There can have been little common ground between

---

2. For an account of Burnes's epic journey, see the author's book *Shooting Leave* (2009).

the highly motivated and ambitious Indian army officer and the self-styled holy fool from Bavaria.

After thirty days in Kabul, Wolff went on by river, on a boat consisting of skins stretched over a wooden frame – which must have terrified this aquaphobic traveller – first to Jalalabad and on to Peshawar. This important crossroad, then in Afghanistan and now in Pakistan, was then governed by a brother of the king of Afghanistan. This ruler asked Wolff to tell the governor-general of India that 'he would always be ready to serve the English nation' and that he wanted protection against the ruler of the Punjab and others. So once again Wolff was involved in political dialogue, whether he liked it or not. On grounds of principle however, he declined to take a political agent from Afghanistan with him through the Punjab and on to India; he thought this would have abused the hospitality of the Punjabis and was incompatible with his missionary role.

However much fun Burnes might have had in India at Wolff's expense, he tried to do him one good service in Kabul. Burnes warned Wolff to have nothing to do with one particular resident of Peshawar, whom he described as a total scoundrel. Consequently, when this dubious character called on him in Peshawar, Wolff 'took him by the shoulders and ejected him from his room'. He was not to know that the same man would be responsible for the murder of Stoddart and Conolly in Bokhara a decade later, and that Wolff himself would be entirely in his power when he returned to Bokhara on his second – as yet unanticipated – mission.

When Wolff passed through the Khyber Pass he found the scenery 'most romantic' and – as in the Hindu Kush – thought it must have been the site of the Garden of Eden or be paradise. He was less enthusiastic about crossing the Indus River by a suspension bridge on the back of an elephant to reach Attock, but when he got there he had a very warm welcome. His legend as a holy man with a gift for survival had preceded him. Ranjit Singh, 'the mighty conqueror of the Punjab', sent 'twenty pots of sweetmeats of all kinds, and linen to make twenty shirts [. . .] to the Padre of England'. Among a pile of letters for him were ones from the governor-general of India and from Lady William Bentinck. The former congratulated him on his safe arrival, and the latter very helpfully reminded him that, although there was a strict rule against British officials receiving valuable presents from native rulers, this did not apply to him as he was a private individual and was free to accept anything he was offered. As the sweetmeats and the linen had also been accompanied by a substantial monetary gift, this was welcome news to one who – however much he despised money – was from time to time dependent on it.

One of the letters was a friendly one from Ranjit Singh himself (who was absent in Amritsar) and Wolff felt it necessary to respond to this with one of his usual dissertations about the heavenly Jerusalem and the uniquely saving grace of Jesus Christ. When Lord William Bentinck saw a copy of this letter he went into his wife's room 'with a long face' and said that they must get Wolff to travel on through the Punjab just as fast as he could, since his militantly evangelical and provocative letter was all too likely to excite a revolution there. But it seems that Ranjit Singh did not take Wolff's letter amiss; he did however object when the irrepressible Wolff started putting up posters in the streets of Lahore 'calling on the nations to turn to Christ', and he wrote to Wolff saying that 'such words must neither be said nor heard'. Once again, he had overstepped the mark but got away with it.

It was not until he reached Amritsar that Wolff actually came face to face with Ranjit Singh. Hearing that he was invited to an audience with the great warrior, Wolff decided to tidy himself up by shaving off his beard, but he was advised not to do so as 'Ranjit Singh was very fond of people with fine beards'. So he left his beard – 'reddish in hue and a foot long' – and was told he looked like a lion. An elephant was sent to convey him to the royal palace. When Wolff found a circle of learned men and scribes surrounding the Sikh ruler, he tactlessly inquired whether they were all Moslems; this he soon realized was 'as it would have been in England to ask in the House of Lords whether all the peers were gypsies'. Again, no offence was taken, and Ranjit Singh 'laughed loud – Ha! Ha! Ha!'

But the short-sighted Wolff at least avoided an even worse faux pas when he nearly asked the extremely short Ranjit Singh 'whether he was one of the great king's little boys?'; just in time, he drew his chair nearer to the ruler and observed he had an immense beard and was blind in one eye. He had no compunction however in telling Ranjit Singh, who had brought on some dancing girls to entertain his guest, that 'as an English Fakir, he did not approve of seeing the girls dancing'. The ruler next tried him with a strong alcoholic drink, but he declined this too. Ranjit Singh, who had proved such a sinister and terrifying figure to Moorcroft, was obviously amused by Wolff but determined to catch him out. According to Wolff's memoirs, he next tested him with theological arguments:

> Ranjit Singh said [. . .] 'Do you teach that we should not be afraid of anything?' Wolff said 'Yes.' [. . .] 'Then why were you so afraid when you crossed the Indus over the suspension-bridge on an elephant?' (for every word and

movement of Wolff had been reported to the king). Wolff replied, 'Here Your Majesty has certainly caught me; and all I can answer is, that I am weak, and I have daily need to pray that God will show His power in my weakness.' Ranjit Singh said, 'Now, I call this candour and uprightness; but answer me one thing. You say you travel about for the sake of religion; why, then, do you not preach to the English in Hindostan, who have no religion at all?'

The religion debate continued and it was at this point that Ranjit Singh made his remark about his coming 'nigh unto God by making an alliance with England, in order to keep out the Russians from India'. Wolff had not only survived his ordeal, but done well. He went home to his lodgings with relief and cut off his beard to celebrate. After he left Amritsar, he was disturbed to be summoned back by Ranjit Singh, though apparently only for a further theological discussion. The moment the maharajah saw Wolff, he declared 'Ho! Ho! Ho! Where have you left your beard?' Wolff replied that he had left it where he had shaved, in the house of the maharajah's general, to which the maharajah – who clearly really was fond of beards – responded, 'I shall cut off his nose, the first day I see the fellow.'

Having eventually got away from Amritsar, it was not long before Wolff reached Ludhiana, then the northernmost frontier of British India. Here he was welcomed by a group of British officers and shouted out 'I am safe! After so many trials and adventures, I am safe!' For the first time for eighteen months, he now saw again a normal British life. He was invited to preach to the British community, and chose 'visions' as his theme. He recounted a vision he had himself had when St Paul had appeared and said to him 'and now thou shalt also have a crown'. The sermon was obviously a success – or at least he thought it was – because he went to repeat the story of his vision when he reached Simla 'to Lord William Bentinck in his drawing room [. . .] also all over India'. Wolff was invited to stay with the governor-general and his wife at Simla, and he recounts in detail the many conversations they had. He made the case for sending a British ambassador to Bokhara, but Lord William Bentinck said he would have to consider the effect this would have on relations with other neighbouring countries such as Persia and Russia. However, for most of his time in Simla, when he was not preaching, he was teased in a good-natured way by Lady William Bentinck and the governor-general's staff: they had all concluded that though he was not 'cracked' (as they put it) he was something between a ragamuffin-explorer, a chaplain and a court jester.

Wolff continued his travels to Kashmir and then returned to India, visiting Delhi and most of the main cities of the subcontinent. Summing up his Asian travels in his memoirs, he stresses how many Jews he converted to Christianity (this had, after all, been the professed motive of his travels) and how he thought the British were losing credibility in Central Asia by appearing frightened of the Russian threat. Meanwhile, after returning briefly to Malta and re-meeting with his long-suffering wife, he was to set out on other travels – to Abyssinia, Arabia, Yemen, St Helena and even New York – before coming to rest with his wife in England in 1838. By now he was fully ordained and eligible to settle down in an English vicarage but, as his old friend Henry Drummond wrote to him, 'you are as fit for a parish priest as I am for a dancing-master'. When eventually he accepted a curacy in Yorkshire, his predecessor preached a farewell sermon on the theme 'After me ravening wolves will come to devour the flock'. But however remote and humble Wolff's appointment, he was already – that rare phenomenon in Victorian England – a celebrity. The Archbishop of York paid him 'the greatest attention', and the Marquis of Anglesey (the famous cavalry commander who had lost his leg at Waterloo) invited him to dinner and insisted that the gentlemen followed the ladies promptly out after dinner 'since we must not deprive the ladies of his [Wolff's] interesting conversation'.

Lady Georgiana and her aristocratic background doubtless contributed to the acceptability of Wolff. Most people who knew Wolff at the time, or have written about him since, have expressed surprise at Lady Georgiana having ever agreed to marry him. She was by all accounts a good-looking woman of private means and exceptionally well connected, being the daughter of the Earl of Orford and descended from Sir Robert Walpole, the first prime minister of the United Kingdom; he was short, fat, vain, argumentative, and with the manners and upbringing of a very different caste. It says something for her lack of prejudice that she could see the sterling qualities in him. Wolff himself, of course, always maintained that he was a success with the ladies, but more – one imagines – as a curiosity than as a suitor. His wife's connections undoubtedly opened many doors to him in British diplomatic establishments on his travels. The marriage, though subject to long periods of absence, was a happy and loving one, and the formality of some (but not all) of his letters to her reflect more the conventions of the period than any lack of affection. They had a son, who became Sir Henry Drummond Wolff and had a distinguished diplomatic career. But now the marriage was about to undergo its most testing experience.

Quite suddenly in early 1843 this life of rural parish duties and high society invitations was brought to an unexpected close by a piece of news from Central Asia: Colonel Stoddart and Captain Conolly were reported to be in mortal danger – or possibly even already murdered – in Bokhara. Wolff immediately saw a role for himself in rescuing them, or at least discovering their fate. In this decision he was influenced by the fact that again and again in his chequered career of outlandish travel he had been rescued by military men when he was in extremis. In his memoirs he lists such occasions in three very long paragraphs, concluding: 'Now I am going to Bokhara to try to pay back a debt of gratitude which I owe to British officers'. Lord Aberdeen (the foreign secretary) told Wolff that the government was privately convinced that Stoddart and Conolly had already been put to death, and that 'they [the government] could not take on themselves the responsibility of sending Wolff on so dangerous a mission, as he would be exposed to a similar fate'. However, if Wolff was determined on going, Aberdeen said that the government would give him 'every recommendation he could require'; he would, in fact, have moral but not practical support and could not claim to be representing Her Majesty's Government. However, the lack of government funds was compensated for by the fact that various wealthy friends offered to finance the expedition; and Wolff, never one to suffer from reticence, took up the foreign secretary's offer of 'recommendations' by requesting letters from the sultan of Turkey to the potentates along his route, and a personal introduction to the shah of Persia when he passed through that country.

He also managed to obtain a free passage on a British ship

from Southampton, where he was seen off by Lady Georgiana, to Constantinople; he had hardly set sail before he was talking earnestly to the ship's captain 'about the coming of the Lord', and noting that many of the other passengers, including 'a fat Methodist woman' were 'canting and whining' about everything. He himself was gratified to be greeted with respect by the governors of Gibraltar and Malta, and when he reached Athens was presented to the king and queen of Greece by the British ambassador. The king referred to his trip as 'a great journey for a benevolent purpose'. When he reached Constantinople, the VIP treatment continued: Sir Stratford Canning, the British ambassador who was to play such an important part in the lead up to the Crimean War a few years later, invited him to dinner and to preach at the English chapel – possibly not expecting him to launch into a series of six major theological dissertations.

Lady Canning adopted a motherly attitude towards Wolff, sorting out his luggage and buying him flannel shirts to keep him from catching cold on the steppes of Central Asia. The Turkish foreign minister told Wolff, 'I feel the highest regard for you, and, as proof of it, I offer you a pinch of snuff from my snuff-box.' At a rather more practical level, the sultan gave him handwritten letters to the emirs of Bokhara, Khiva and Khokand, which Lady Canning sewed up for him in his coat so they should not get lost or stolen. Sir Stratford gave him a compass and telescope. Altogether, he set off not only heartened by universal messages of goodwill, but also provided with some useful introductions and equipment. His first stage was by sea along the Black Sea coast to Trebizond, and he was brought up with an emotional jolt on finding the signature of Arthur Conolly – who had taken the same route only a year or two before – in the passenger book.

Now his second dangerous overland journey to Bokhara was beginning in earnest. Wolff was soon crossing through eastern Turkey and into Persia in mid-winter, with snow so deep that the horses could scarcely wade through it. His escort and introductions ensured him shelter along the way, and Lady Canning's flannels kept him from freezing. He was now traversing the same country that he had crossed more than a decade before when he had been captured, stripped and chained up, before being rescued by the Persian officer – Mohammed Khan Kerahe – who, after liberating him, had then pocketed all the money that had been taken from Wolff by his assailants. By a strange quirk of fate, he was taken to see this same man, who was now himself chained up and in prison, having earlier fallen out with Abbas Mirza. Mohammed Khan said to Wolff, 'That time you saw me as a great man, now you see me a little man [. . .] one must have patience in this world.' Wolff noted in his memoirs that he thought his former saviour 'showed far greater [strength of] mind in his prison than Napoleon I did while in exile upon the island of St Helena'.

When he reached Tehran, Wolff was well received by the British envoy who told him that, from all the reports he had heard, 'he, in his own mind, had not the slightest doubt that both [Stoddart and Conolly] had been killed'. Although privately Wolff had reached the same conclusion, he felt that he could not turn about and go home at this point, or people would think 'that the whole of his attempt to go to Bokhara had been a piece of humbug, and was the work of a braggart'. He therefore kept quiet about his private opinion. Later, he donned his full canonicals, 'his doctor's hood over his gown' and was taken by the ambassador to an audience with the shah, who said he admired Wolff's 'philanthropy', and the conversation went so well that 'Wolff actually forgot himself and interrupted His Majesty while he was talking'. At this, the ambassador 'gave him a push' to shut him up; Wolff could never be relied upon to behave diplomatically.

Wolff was distinctly nervous about the next stage of his journey, through Khorasan. It was here that on his previous trip 'they stripped me, and tied me to the horse's tail [. . .] put me in a dungeon [. . .] and offered me for sale for £2. 10s.' He was afraid that he would 'again meet with dreadful hindrances in that horrible country'. But in the event, he found things much changed for the better in Khorasan. Whereas when he first went there 'the name of Englishman was scarcely known [. . .] now, the name of an Englishman was actually a passport'. He attributed this change to the First Afghan War which, although it started so badly with the massacre of General Elphinstone's army, had ended with the British reoccupying Kabul in late 1842 and establishing a mastery (albeit short-lived) of the region; a year later, when Wolff was passing through the region, British prestige was therefore on a high; he could get as much money as he wanted on credit.

When he arrived at Meshed (the capital of Khorasan) he was disturbed to find that all the surviving Jewish community had not become Christians, as he hoped they would, but had adopted the faith of Islam; this had followed a massacre of Jews, resulting from one of them having killed a dog in a manner that was considered 'in derision of Islam'. The local governor was concerned on hearing he was heading for Bokhara, where he said the Marwee tribe were very plentiful and were 'the worst of people but very rich, and of great influence with the King of Bokhara'. The governor said the best tactic was to take an escort of 'nine rascals of the Marwee tribe [. . .] and if they don't behave well, I will burn their wives and children who remain in my hands'. It was not a statement which had any great appeal to the Christian-principled Wolff, but he concluded that he was in the governor's hands and had better go along with his proposal of providing the nine rascals.

From Meshed, he pressed on through Sarakhs to Merv, where the khan assured him that he knew all about Stoddart and Conolly and they were certainly dead. The khan said he personally did not dare to go to Bokhara because the emir 'had lost all fear of God [Allah]'. Various eminent Jews in Merv also came forward and told Wolff all about Stoddart's arrogant behaviour in Bokhara and of their conviction that he and Conolly had been executed; they gave graphic details of how Stoddart had retracted his conversion to Islam and of how Conolly had said, 'I am a believer in the Lord Jesus Christ – here is my head!'; they told Wolff there was nothing more to be discovered and begged him not to go there. But Wolff was adamant: 'I must ascertain all the circumstances of their death, and to Bokhara I will go', he said.

As he got nearer to Bokhara, things did not get better. The governor of Karakol – which was within the jurisdiction of the Emir of Bokhara and only some thirty miles from the capital – told Wolff – 'The moment you see horsemen come out from Bokhara, you will observe that some come with baskets; these baskets will contain bandages with which you will be blindfolded, and chains with which you will be chained, and knives with which you will be slaughtered.' And sure enough, as predicted, when he approached the city some horsemen with baskets were seen approaching and calling out 'Art thou Joseph Wolff?' At this, his servants dropped back, pretending they had nothing to do with him. But when the horsemen caught up with him, they opened their baskets and, instead of chains and knives, they turned out to be full of pomegranates, melons, cherries and roasted horse-flesh – all presents from the emir. On seeing this, his servants rejoined him, one of them declaring, 'I am Wolff's servant; I must have a share of that.' His servants then started telling the chamberlain who had been sent out to meet Wolff that the latter was a person of immense importance: 'The Grand Vizier of England never sits down in his presence', and so on. Wolff sensibly told his people 'not to tell lies, and that on arrival in Bokhara he would speak for himself'.

It was April 1844 when Wolff entered the holy city for the second time, and the streets were lined with crowds shouting messages of welcome. The master of ceremonies asked Wolff if he would submit to the usual etiquette when presented to the emir and would bow and say 'Asylum of the world! Peace to the King!' three times. Wolff replied that there was no problem: he was ready to say this thirty times. So he was granted an audience the following day, and, dressed in his usual full canonicals and shovel hat, carried out the appropriate rituals. The emir then invited him to come closer, so that he could have a better look at him. Having done so, the emir declared: 'Thou eccentric man! Thou star with a tail! Neither like a Jew, nor a Christian, nor a Hindoo, nor like a Russian, nor like an Uzbeck [. . .]'

He went on to explain that he had indeed executed Stoddart and Conolly: Stoddart had not paid him proper respect, and 'Conolly had had a long nose (i.e. was very proud)'. The emir claimed that when he had told Conolly that 'you Englishmen come into a country in a stealthy manner, and take it', Conolly had replied that they did not come in stealthy manner but went in openly as they had done at Kabul. Wolff responded by saying that neither Stoddart nor Conolly had probably understood the

customs and etiquette of Bokhara, and their mistakes were
unintentional. While all this polite badinage and pantomime was
going on, Wolff reminded himself of the true nature of the man
he was talking to, of how he had murdered his brothers and his
father as well as anyone who had seemed the remotest threat to
him, and how he had made free with the wives of his citizens
and disregarded all the injunctions not only of Christendom but
of Islam too. Though relations had opened reasonably well for

him, Wolff did not underestimate the danger in which he still stood.

When later he had an audience with the minister for foreign affairs, Wolff tried to persuade him that it would be a mistake to make an enemy of England, a world power which ruled over India, and that there was a real risk that his countrymen would demand war with Bokhara if more Englishmen were killed. The minister responded by asking how far England was from Bokhara. At this point his rascally Marwee guide from Merv unhelpfully piped up and said that England was 'six months away', and therefore no real threat. Wolff corrected this impression, and was then asked what was the real purpose of his journey. He explained that he had come to find out the fate of 'his friends' Stoddart and Conolly and, if they were dead (the emir had already admitted as much), to request that an ambassador should be sent back with him to repair relations between England and Bokhara. Wolff calculated that if he did not offer some prospect of reconciliation, then he might well share Conolly's fate; also, he thought a Bokharan companion on his return journey would greatly ease the process both of getting away and of crossing Central Asia. He also had an audience with the grand vizier, who asked him what his red academic hood signified, and he rather provocatively replied 'the red colour indicated Wolff was ready to die for his faith'.

After all these meetings, Wolff found that, far from things being easier, his condition became more confined. He was not allowed out of his quarters, and he was watched day and night by the royal chamberlains. The emir was obviously puzzled and unconvinced about his motives, and Wolff was subsequently told that when he had left the emir the latter had said: 'I have in my empire two hundred thousand slaves, and no soul ever came from Persia to ask after any one of them: and here I have killed a few Englishmen, and Joseph Wolff comes with a Bible in his hand, and enters my capital without a sword, and without a gun, and demands those two Englishmen!'

The emir had even sent for Wolff to enquire wistfully whether he was able to raise the dead, because he wished he could 'awake Stoddart and Conolly'. He also sent to ask him – as a trap to see if he was genuine – the names of the grand viziers of England; Wolff told him the name of the prime minister – Sir Robert Peel – and a few other senior ministers; he was then sent for and told he was a liar, because Stoddart and Conolly had both independently given different names, notably that of Lord Melbourne. Wolff then tried to explain the democratic process by which prime ministers (grand viziers) were changed from time to time, but the emir persisted in imagining that Lord Melbourne and others had had their heads cut off by Queen Victoria. Constitutional monarchy was not a concept readily understood in Bokhara.

It was at this stage of his detention at Bokhara that Wolff became involved with a particularly unsavoury character called Abdul Samut Khan, a Persian known as the Nayeb, who was in command of the emir's artillery and with whom Wolff had quarrelled some years before at Peshawar. The Nayeb played a cat and mouse game with Wolff, continually promising that he was about to be free to leave the city and at the same time continually demanding more letters of credit from Wolff. He claimed to have befriended Stoddart and Conolly, but Wolff was unconvinced, and when he told him so the Nayeb apparently confessed with relish that he had indeed been instrumental in the murder of the two Englishmen. At one point, the Nayeb even suggested to Wolff that if the British government promised him enough money he would invite the king (emir) to sit on a special throne and then blow him up. Wolff very properly replied that no British government would have any hand in such a scheme as they considered kings to be 'the shadow of God'. At the same time, the pattern of royal favour followed by distrust and ever closer confinement was becoming all too reminiscent of the treatment of Stoddart. The only hope of his safe departure seemed to lie in the arrival of a Persian ambassador who pleaded his cause.

As the supervision of Wolff became ever more stringent, with the emir's agents even sleeping in his room, the Persian ambassador thought it necessary to arrange for one of his own servants also to sleep in Wolff's room 'in order that he might not be assassinated'. Meanwhile, Wolff devised an ingenious method of communicating without these ever-present spies understanding what was going on. He invited various Jews to visit him and, although they were only allowed to converse in Persian, so that the emir's agents knew everything that was being said, Wolff got permission to read aloud to his visitors from the scriptures in Hebrew, which they did not understand. Then – while pretending he was reading – he introduced questions and instructions to his listeners. The following day the same Jews ('who are no fools, in whatever country they may be', Wolff comments) returned and, in a reading tone of voice, explained to him: 'The King of this country is not by far so wicked a scoundrel as that horrid Persian [the Nayeb] outside the town, who was the instigator of the murder of your countrymen. Ephraim, a Jew, who came here to assist your countrymen, when that villain informed the King of it, was beheaded. And, Wolff, be on your guard!' Conversations of this sort went on in secret for some three months.

All the time the outlook was getting worse. At one point the emir sent a peremptory demand to Wolff that he should immediately renounce his Christian faith. Wolf replied 'Never! Never! Never!', and when it was suggested to him that he should couch his answer in more polite terms he merely said, in that case, 'No! No! No!'. A few hours after this exchange of messages, the state executioner was sent to see Wolff and told him that he was going to suffer the same fate as Stoddart and Conolly. Wolff wrote a farewell message to his wife on the fly sheet of his bible, which read 'My dearest Georgiana, I have loved you unto death. Your affectionate husband, J. Wolff'. He then threw away the opium he had always carried with him 'so that in case his throat was cut he might not feel the pain' – apparently resolving to spare himself nothing in his martyrdom.

But rescue was at hand. The Persian ambassador delivered a letter from the shah, which persuaded the emir to make a present to him of Wolff. The snag was that the intermediary to effect his release was none other than the scoundrelly Nayeb, who promptly demanded a ransom fee of 3,000 ducats, and insisted on him writing an IOU on the spot. Wolff responded by writing in English: 'In the garden of the infamous Abdul Samut Khan [the Nayeb], surrounded by his banditti, and compelled by him, I write that he forced from me a note of hand for six thousand tillahs. Joseph Wolff, Prisoner.'

Not everyone was pleased at the prospect of Wolff being able to leave Bokhara. One Afghan said that, if left to his own devices, he would have made away with Wolff with his javelin. When told that this would have been wrong as Wolff was a holy dervish, he replied: 'I know these English dervishes. They go into a country, spy out mountains and valleys, seas and rivers; find out a convenient adit; and then go home, inform a gentleman there – a chief, who has the name of Company, who sends soldiers, and then takes a country'. The East India Company may not have been a person, but its reputation as a conqueror had spread throughout Central Asia.

Even one of his own servants – encouraged by the odious Nayeb – turned against him, telling him that he was going to be killed by the emir and demanding, with threats against his life, a present of 2,000 tillahs and a letter of recommendation to the British ambassador at Tehran. Wolff, who was normally long-suffering, lost his control at this and 'took a stick and gave him such a beating as he never gave to anyone in his life'. He commented in his memoirs that it was just as well that the servant in question was a Sunni and not a Shia Muslim and so had no local friends to come to his help.

In the end, despite the machinations of the Nayeb and of his threatening servant, Wolff got the final consent of the emir for his departure, and also agreement that he should be accompanied by a potential Bokharan ambassador to the Queen of England. The emir declared that while Stoddart and Conolly had 'excited the neighbouring countries to war against him' (a completely false accusation), Wolff had proved himself 'to be a man of understanding and knowledge'.

But his departure was not the end of his dangers: the malicious Nayeb had hired ten professional assassins to travel with the caravan on which Wolff was leaving and to murder him when they were well clear of Bokhara. The ambassador-designate heard of this plot, and summoned the caravan together and told them roundly that it was the duty of all true Muslims to protect the Englishman who was under his care. When they crossed the frontier into Persia, the suspected assassins were rounded up and this particular danger appeared to have passed. Wolff was also glad to reach a more ordered country than that of the 'lawless tribes' through whom he had been wending his way; he concluded from these experiences that 'there cannot be worse despotism than the despotism of a mob [. . . he] would always prefer to live under one tyrant than under many!'

Wolff later learnt with some satisfaction that the nefarious Nayeb had subsequently got his just deserts: his intrigues had extended to plots against the emir who, on hearing of this, 'did take an axe, and actually cut him in two with his own hands'. Much later and less happy was the news of the fate of the ambassador-designate; the latter was to prove unacceptable to Queen Victoria, who 'would not receive the ambassador of an assassin' [i.e. of one who had killed two of her officers]; so the unhappy man had no alternative than to return as a failure to Bokhara 'where the King cut off his head'. With the realization of how much slaughter was still going on at the court of Bokhara, Wolff appreciated all the more his miraculous escape.

The last pages of his memoirs are given over to telling of his warm welcome by his wife and others on his return to England. He still suffered from some physical problems – a tape worm had to be removed – from his outlandish travels. He enjoyed the access to the great and good which his audacious and high-minded mission had won for him; he was lost in admiration on encountering Sir Walter Scott, 'every one of whose writings he has since read aloud'; he spent nine days staying with Lord Tennyson, 'and heard him read his songs'; he made the acquaintance of William Gladstone – and judged the political leader to be 'a religious man of enlarged principles'; and so on. Once more, anecdotes of prelates and peers fill the pages of his book. But he eventually settled in an Anglican parish in the west country and lived for nearly another twenty years of long walks and cold baths.

Wolff was not like other British adventurers confronting tsarist Russia. No one could have accused him of being a warrior in the Great Game; his enemy was not the tsar but the Devil. He was prepared to accept hospitality from Russians and even to preach the gospel (*his* gospel) to them; but by his provocative activities he defied St Petersburg's domination of the steppes and of the emirates in that no-man's land between the tsar's and the viceroy's empires. His private-enterprise – indeed maverick – mission to rescue Stoddart and Conolly was promoted in a pamphlet that was highly critical of the former ineffectiveness of the British Foreign Office; he was not, as he sometimes supposed, some latter-day St Paul preaching at Ephesus, but neither was he some precursor of Lord Curzon speaking for the British Empire. He was to be remembered long after 'the tumult and the shouting dies; the Captains and the Kings depart'. He was above all himself: a holy fool, with the tenacity of a Jew, the proselytizing fervour of a Victorian Christian, and the courage of an Englishman.

Chapter 8

James Stanislaus Bell: The Cautious Merchant Adventurer

'A merchant shall hardly keep himself from doing wrong'
– Book of Ecclesiasticus

James Bell, a friend of David Urquhart and featuring in James Longworth's account of travels in Circassia, owned and was in charge of the *Vixen* when she was captured by the Russians. His experiences mirrored and overlapped with Longworth's, but show a different angle on the events. Having spent over two years in the region, he perceived the resistance movement in greater depth than any of his compatriots.

In the preface to his two-volume account of his experiences (*Journal of Residence in Circassia during the years 1837, 1838 and 1839*, published 1840) he explained how he had heard at first hand the stories of families reduced to misery by the Russian occupation, and how he 'freely took part in the councils of the natives [...] counselling them as to the particular species of warfare which seemed best suited to the troops they could bring into the field, and most likely to defeat the tactics of their enemies'. He felt that his efforts entitled him to take some credit for the military successes of the partisans – the capture of almost all the Russian forts – which had started before he left. But unlike Longworth and Knight, he was careful to keep out of the conflict himself.

As with the other English adventurers, he had to run the gauntlet of the Russian blockade before he even got there. To increase their chances of out-sailing their pursuers, the Turkish crew threw overboard the heavy gun-carriage they were smuggling in, but declined to jettison their own commercial cargo. At one point the Turkish crew discussed 'striking the sails in token of submission', but one of the Circassians on board drew his dagger and threatened to stab the Turk if there were any more talk of surrender. Bell himself went below decks to prepare to ditch his more compromising possessions: barrels of gunpowder and letters revealing his intentions. He also took his turn at the oars. When finally they approached the coastline on which they planned to land, they were welcomed by hordes of natives running down the hills and across the beaches to help them land and show the pursuing Russian ship that the visitors were now 'under their protection'. The Russian brig, after a few desultory shots, headed back to sea.

After he had joined up with the native resistance forces and eventually met with James Longworth, he too was much impressed with their leader Tougouse – the Wolf. They were presented with such useful gifts as 'an excellent coat of chain mail [. . .] a lively white charger [. . .] and a sabre, the scabbard of which was embroidered with silver lace'. They heard tales of a recent raid across the Kuban river, when the melting snow had raised the waters so high that the raiders had to leave their powder and firearms on their own side of the river and go across armed only with their sabres. Even so, they had managed to scare the Russian soldiers, who were gathering in the harvest near their forts, so badly that the Russians fled back into the forts, leaving their scythes, 'about two hundred of which the Circassians brought off in triumph'. Meanwhile there were the usual rumours of a British fleet – 'twenty men-of-war and two steamers all bearing red flags' – being about to come to the rescue of the insurgents; but as always, the rumours turned out to be false, and Bell found himself trying to persuade the highlanders to adopt a more effective method of observation and communication – beacons on the hilltops rather than the random discharge of musket fire, which all too often was misinterpreted.

One incident which Bell describes in detail illustrates the deviousness of both the insurgents and their Russian opponents. A small three-masted Russian vessel sent a boat ashore and explained to the Circassians on the beach that the crew had been living on nothing but black bread for the past five months and they wanted to buy or barter for meat and eggs. The Circassians replied that they could not give them these provisions until 'they had got permission of the two Englishmen', but if they cared to come ashore the next day they were sure they could provide what they wanted. The insurgents then laid a careful trap to ambush the Russians when they landed the following day. It was not quite careful enough: some of those lying in ambush fired too soon and the Russians withdrew in short order to their rowing boat, but not before the ambushers had managed to kill or wound all but one of the Russians on board. Bell was very upset by this incident: he had tried to intervene to stop his friends behaving in such a duplicitous and murderous way, but he had arrived too late to do so. However, he subsequently became convinced that the Russians too were playing tricks, and had just wanted an excuse to make contact with their opponents – probably to find out the whereabouts of the Englishmen. The discovery of poles and boards marking a path on the shore to where Bell was staying caused concern: extra sentries were posted.

It was not surprising that the Russians were disturbed by the presence of Longworth and Bell among the Circassians. Shortly after their meeting up together, they presented the insurgents with some 1,400 lbs of lead (for bullets) that they had brought into the country with them. About a third of this was divided among the warriors of the southern tribes, and the rest 'divided with scrupulous impartiality' among the inhabitants of other warring regions. But the casualties inflicted by all these bullets were insignificant – according to a captured Russian officer – beside the loss of personnel brought about by desertion, death and disease among the garrisons of the forts, where Bell was able to confirm from first-hand accounts that the conditions were appalling.

When he was invited to attend councils of the elders, Bell never missed an opportunity to emphasize that the tribesmen should take advantage of the low Russian morale to campaign more actively against them, and to encourage foreign support for their resistance. He said that 'since they appeared to think our presence so beneficial, and promised to take more active measures shortly, we should comply with their request, and remain among them for the present'. Soon after this conference, Bell learnt that a Russian cavalry officer had deserted from Anapa because of 'the degraded situation he found himself reduced to (on account of a duel with his colonel) and his despair of being able to improve it'; it was possibly this source who disclosed that '4,000 of that army are already *hors de combat*'. Some deserters described their treatment in Tsar Nicholas's army as 'worse than that of dogs in Europe'.

Bell's urging to action seemed to bear some fruit. In September 1837 he reported in a letter home that 'a very valiant nobleman crossed the Kuban a few days ago, with a small party who swam the river during the night, towing after them a small boat containing their arms'. They were quickly surrounded by the enemy on the far side and their leader was fatally wounded before he could regain the southern bank. Bell was invited to his funeral – a very military affair – no doubt to remind him of how his promptings to action had been acted upon.

Meanwhile Bell's own morale was not helped by the arrival of letters from England reporting 'the disastrous decision come to by our government in regard of the capture of the *Vixen*'. It seemed to Bell that his own government had acquiesced in the Russian claim to have negotiated treaty rights over the Caucasus from the Ottoman Empire and was not intending to take any vigorous diplomatic action to obtain compensation for the seizure of the *Vixen*. This was a financial blow to Bell, but he felt even more bitter about the loss of 'the spirit of honour which once animated [British] counsels'. He decided to say nothing about this to his Caucasian hosts, as he feared that news of the half-hearted attitude of his own country would discourage them.

This fear was however counter-balanced by an encounter with Nadir Bey, aka Mr Knight – brought to meet him by Longworth – who 'seemed to travel for the excitement of adventure' and to share their commitment to the cause of independence. To enhance the impact of Mr Knight's arrival, and to dispel any fears that he might be a Russian spy, Longworth and Bell agreed that he should 'assume the ambassadorial character' which his hosts were so anxious to force on him; the fact that he brought the news of the death of King William IV gave some credence to his role as an official representative of England. Even more convincing was Nadir Bey's appearance in the uniform of the Royal Company of Scottish Archers (the king's bodyguard in Scotland) replete with an eagle-feathered hat.

It is to Bell that we owe evidence of the Russians' duplicity towards the Caucasian chiefs. He describes in letters home how some of these chiefs were lured 'to a conference' on Russian soil, and then detained there as hostages for the good behaviour of their tribesmen. He also recounts remarkable tales of escape by some of the Circassians captured while on operations – filing off fetters, digging holes through dungeon walls, fighting off Cossacks with planks of wood, swimming rivers across frontiers – which made him feel that his own non-belligerent status left him open to the criticism of wimpishness.

This impression was enhanced by the obvious willingness of fellow compatriots Longworth and Knight 'to join in the first regular enterprise against the Russians'. Bell's reputation was restored to some extent by his practice of medicine (sometimes little more than urging less hard drinking on a people who were naturally abstemious but had caught bad habits from their Russian invaders), and by his obviously genuine enthusiasm for his 'searching for fossils, plants, etc.'. But the incident that did most to establish his credentials among his hosts was his prediction of an eclipse of the moon. His forecast regarding this was widely disseminated among the tribes, together with a reassurance that they should not view the phenomenon as an evil omen – as they would otherwise have been inclined to do. When the forecast proved true, no amount of explanation of calculations could dissuade the tribesmen from a belief in his supernatural powers.

Another factor that distinguishes Bell from his compatriots in the Caucasus is his awareness of many of the failings of those tribesmen in whom Longworth could see little fault. Some of them were devious to the point of disloyalty, others were greedy in their soliciting of gifts, while some indulged in extreme and antiquated forms of Islamic practice: marriage within a 'fraternity' (which might be several thousand people strong) was looked upon as incest and punishable by drowning.

It is enlightening to read Bell's account of the Kuban river-crossing raid, carried out in conditions of melting ice, which is described in such detail by Longworth. The basic facts are corroborated by Bell's account, but he does not share Longworth's somewhat gung-ho attitude to the whole enterprise. There are references to 'the impropriety of the attempt' and to its 'impracticality becoming but too palpable' and to the risk of 'a useless sacrifice of lives'. This is the language of a rational spectator rather than of a committed participant.

His lack of military dash did not however modify the Russians' venom against him. He had long known that the governor of their fort at Anapa was anxious to capture him; he later learnt that the governor's superior officer – Baron Rosen, commander-in-chief of the imperial army in the Caucasus – had urged the Circassians to 'cut these English to pieces'. The baron went on to tell his interlocutors that if they put the Englishmen to death and pretended that the Russians had done it, they would see that the British did not intervene in any way, because the tsar treated the British government 'as a child, making it do whatever we think proper'. Shortly after this event, a messenger who took a letter to the Russians reported that the Russian general had offered to give anyone who would deliver Bell into their hands 2,000 silver roubles, and for Bell's dragoman (interpreter/guide) half that amount; Bell wryly commented 'we have thus now – my man and I – some idea of our market value'. The Russian general had added that, if the Circassians feared he would not keep his word, he was ready to pay them in advance on trust – a statement that said something about both their keenness to secure Bell and the relative trust of each side in the other's word.

Even if he felt mostly safe from murder by his Circassian hosts, Bell was never very far from being captured by the Russians. On one occasion he had to give up his relatively comfortable billet to make room for a wounded rebel soldier. And on another occasion – 24 April 1838 – he witnessed a major battle when a Russian ship landed a substantial force, including artillery, on the coast of Abkhazia (just south of Circassia on the Black Sea shore). The tribesmen rushed among the Russians 'sabre in hand' cutting down about 150 of them and carrying off twenty prisoners and three cannons. But Bell comments that the rebels' losses amounted to twice that number and included a large proportion of chiefs and nobles. The captured cannons had to be abandoned as they proved too heavy to propel over the rough ground. Once consolidated ashore, the Russians had set about cutting down the surrounding forest and establishing a permanent fort. In all, Bell comments that the encounter with the intruders had 'proved as usual little else than a sacrifice of the bravest and the best'. The merchant in him was forever totting up the cost.

Sometimes his spectator status was resented by those who were risking or sacrificing their own lives while Bell remained –

in their view – a voyeur 'enjoying the disasters of [their] countrymen'. While battle often raged around him, Bell generally 'judged it best in the circumstances to sit still and look indifferent (inspecting, however, at the same time, the trigger of my pistol)'; this sort of conduct generated so much anger on one occasion that a passing horsemen told his Polish servant that 'had [Bell] not been the guest of Hassan Bey [a local chief] he would have shot me'. Bell concluded from the incident that he must be cautious, since, in the absence of any positive British support, some of the rebels were viewing him with increasing suspicion. Nonetheless he was still invited to help draft a reply to a Russian ultimatum, and the invective against England in this Russian communication went some way towards restoring him to his hosts' goodwill.

Indeed, it was unjust of Bell's hosts to imagine that he took any pleasure in their discomfiture. In his letters he reports with enthusiasm those of their successes where he calculates that the risks were not foolhardy. He recounts in May 1838 how a body of Abkhazians lay in ambush on the verge of a forest and attacked a Russian force as it was attempting to cross a fast-flowing river: 'a great proportion was drowned [. . .] and of the whole detachment but a very few escaped [. . .] the evil doings [of their leader] will – thank God! – be suspended for a time, for he was wounded in the leg'.

Bell goes on to express the hope that this will be the prelude to further concerted attacks upon the invaders, and his hopes were fulfilled when the Circassians captured a small fort near Anapa and carried off its garrison, ammunition and another three guns. Such guns could be a decisive factor in reducing the mud and wood Russian fortifications ('sod-forts' as they were known) to a rubble that could be easily overrun by the

sabre-wielding tribesmen, Bell notes. When shortly afterwards several ships from the Russian Black Sea fleet were wrecked by a storm off the Circassian coast, and their crews mostly drowned or captured, together with yet more cannons, Bell describes the affair with obvious satisfaction. A calculating observer Bell might have been, but not an impartial one.

Just how careful it was necessary to be, to avoid being mistaken for a Russian sympathizer, was illustrated by the fate of a Sardinian ship captain who set out for the Caucasian coast with a cargo of goods for sale. Although he had been before on similar missions, on the occasion in question a report was spread around that the captain was a Russian secret agent, and so his ship was boarded, he and his second-in-command were killed, the crew made prisoner and sold into slavery to the Turks, and the cargo divided among the captors. Despite the fact that this event occurred some years before Bell's visit, it nonetheless haunted him: a false rumour about a foreigner could easily prove fatal.

If Russian spies were thought to be everywhere, Russian deserters were even more in evidence. One such, a Tartar from Kazan, was considered by the brother-in-law of Bell's protector, Hassan Bey, to have deserved well of his new patrons, who consequently purchased for him a young serf girl to be his bride. However, the lady in question did not fancy being married to a Tartar, particularly not one who had Mongol features and who was more than twenty years older than her. The girl – who was reputed to be beautiful as well as very young – roundly declared that she would only marry one of her own countrymen. When Hassan Bey's brother-in-law insisted, she promptly hanged herself, and not long after her brother stabbed the offending brother-in-law. Bell's sympathies were wholly with the stabber rather than the stabbed, despite his connection with the latter. Indeed, he found that this whole incident fuelled his reservations about the Circassians, and he commented in his letters that they reduced their serfs 'to the level of cattle, which must propagate for the benefit of their master'.

Whatever his reservations about his hosts, and whatever his shock at what he saw as some of the more unacceptable facets of extremist Islamic behaviour, Bell was far more shocked at the arrogance of their Russian invaders. Being used as a scribe for some of the correspondence with the Russian general meant that he saw the text of the threatening Russian missives dispatched to the rebel leaders. One such read: 'There are but two powers, God in heaven, and the Emperor [tsar] upon earth! Do you not know that if the heavens should fall, Russia has power enough to support them on her bayonets?'. Reading this, Bell for once explodes in his letters: 'Powers Eternal! Such names mingled!'

It was not only at sea that the Russians were experiencing setbacks. When the tsar's troops tried to rescue some of the material from their ships which had been wrecked in storms on the coast, they were chased back to their forts with heavy losses. Frequently only a small proportion of the sortie parties got safely home. The tribesmen then looted the shipwrecks themselves and carried off all the metal goods they could find, with the intention not of beating swords into ploughshares, but of doing just the reverse: iron bolts were beaten into knives, water tanks transformed into axes 'and other necessities'. Bell kept passing these looting parties on the beaches and they told him what they were up to. The beaches were often within range of the cannon from the forts, so Bell and his companions had to keep 'close under the foliage of the bank to prevent being fired at'. There were also some Russian corpses still on the beach, and Bell – knowing how much importance his hosts attached to the retrieval of their own dead – suggested an exchange of bodies with the Russians.

Bell was safer however, even on the beaches, when he had a Circassian escort. When alone, quite unarmed except for a walking stick, he was detained by tribesmen on one occasion under suspicion of being a Russian deserter (who could be captured and sold to the Turks) or a spy (who should be shot). When a body-search revealed that Bell had no hidden pistols, they thought this even more strange, and had he not been recognized by one of his 'protectors' it might have ended up badly for him.

But one thing that annoyed Bell far more than his being searched and detained was the interception of his letters back to Constantinople, with all his innermost thoughts and reflections on what was happening in the Caucasus. This came about because 'a discarded domestic of David Urquhart's [...] had latterly been converted into a Russian hireling or spy' and had shared a room at Sinop on the Turkish coast with the courier who had been carrying Bell's confidential correspondence. During the night he had extracted Bell's letters and substituted for them other papers and then resealed the packet. So the courier was quite unaware that what had been entrusted to him had been purloined, until he reached Constantinople and the blank papers were discovered. Bell, on hearing of this and being told that the Russian consul was in possession of his private letters, once more exploded in wrath: 'The tricks and petty plottings of these imperial functionaries would really almost degrade the meanest-of-all-possible of pettifogging attorneys or brokers'. It was not made better for Bell by hearing that the discharged servant who had stolen his letters had been rewarded with a post in the Russian diplomatic service. Greater British involvement in the region – a consul at Sinop for instance – seemed to Bell to be called for urgently.

In contrast to this Russian duplicity, Bell records the honesty of the Circassians among whom he was living. He explains in his letters how for four months he slept out of doors under a great pear tree in an orchard, or on a platform erected for him by his host Hassan Bey, overlooking a valley running down to the coast where so much military action was taking place. On this platform, which served as bed and residence in one, Bell was accustomed to leaving his valuables – 'my watch, silver snuff-box, silver-mounted dagger, knives, etc [...] quite un-protected'. He says that although his retreat was widely known throughout the neighbourhood, he never missed a single article. More importantly, no one betrayed his whereabouts to the Russians although, as he had already discovered from the Russian general's remarks, 'my person also is of no little value'. Part of the reason why he and his hideout were so well known was that people were always dropping in to ask for favours; usually these were either in the form of requests for 'a flint or a few charges of powder and balls' before some raid, or else for medical prescriptions or advice. In respect of the latter, Bell was continually amazed at the way in which wounded tribesmen, instead of being left to rest and recuperate in quiet and whatever comfort was available, would instead find their tents or huts were the centre of the noisiest activity – it being considered that a rowdy party was the most heartening and restorative experience that could be afforded them.

Like Longworth, Bell was aware of the tsar's visit to the Caucasus in the autumn of 1837. Bell also learnt about the changes made in the Russian military command as a result of the tsar's disappointment at the way the campaign was being conducted. Marshal Rosen, the governor of the province, and General Williamanoff, the military commander, were both dismissed from their posts and downgraded. The invading force was strengthened and the spring offensive the following year was brought forward to allow for a longer campaign.

This surge in troops was attended by a measure of success. In particular, threats to devastate one of the regions to the east of that in which Bell was operating resulted in the tribesmen handing back to the invaders some seventy Russian refugees – many of them Poles – who had converted to Islam and professed to be anxious to go on pilgrimage to Mecca. The unforgiving Tsar Nicholas I had all these 'deserters' sent to Siberia for an indefinite period of hard labour. However the act of having handed them back was viewed as 'perfidious' and upset the unity and solidarity of the resistance movement.

The intelligence reaching the new Russian commanders also seemed to be improving. When a large-scale gathering of the clans was organized to launch an assault on one of the Russian forts – an operation at which Bell planned to be a witness but not a participant – the assailants discovered that the enemy were completely on their guard 'no doubt through treachery' and great fires had been kept blazing around the walls all night and a corps of infantry already standing to arms to repel the attackers. But although the planned assault was frustrated, other lesser attacks continued, particularly focused on the supply columns between the Russian forts. Bell, although keeping his distance as always from the melees, was close enough to witness some scenes of remarkable audacity: the more dashing of the young tribesmen when confronted with discharges of musketry and artillery 'never fired a shot themselves, but drawing their sabres, rushed amid the ranks wherever they could find openings'. It was a point of honour among them to leave no part of their gear behind in enemy hands: 'to lose one's bonnet is as great disgrace here now as it was anciently to leave behind one's shield'. One youth is singled out for special praise by Bell because, when his horse was shot from under him, he 'kept the bayonetted Russians around him at bay with his sabre' until he had unstrapped his saddle and cut his way out carrying off this vital piece of his equipment.

Bravery was more in evidence than discipline among the tribesmen. Bell records how when the ramparts of one Russian fort was scaled without ladders, and the occupants all killed or held prisoner, the position had to be abandoned because they found that their fellow tribesmen 'who had been placed at the port-holes of the [Russian] guns commanding the fosse, to pistol the gunners whenever they presented themselves, neglected that important duty, and thoughtlessly joined the scaling party'. Consequently when the Russian gunners reappeared they turned their guns on the massed Circassians in the fosse and mowed them down with the dreaded grapeshot.

For a considerable time now, Bell had been the sole Englishman with the insurgents as Longworth and Knight had

departed some months before. By October 1839 he had therefore decided that 'the time is arrived for my again running the gauntlet in departing in one of those crank-looking Turkish crafts'. When the winds turned favourable, he and several shipmates assembled in a little creek which was concealed from view. It was agreed that the danger from the Russian coastal patrol ships in smooth conditions was greater than that of setting out in rough weather. Indeed, the frequency of sightings of Russian warships convinced Bell that he was the object of this special vigilance: the Russians had probably learnt of his intended departure and saw this as a last chance of seizing him.

There were various false starts: no sooner had a favourable wind induced them to foregather in the creek, than they saw 'an old acquaintance – the three-masted cutter I was formerly chased by'. The decision of when to set sail was complicated by the fact that the greedy skipper of Bell's ship had signed up far too many passengers in the hope of making more money on the dangerous run to Turkey, and he was now afraid that if he delayed they might defect to another vessel. Bell went down to the creek with his baggage and a debate ensued about whether or not to sail; the captain was so keen to set out before he lost his lucrative passengers that, when confronted with the threat of the Russian cruisers, resorted to the mantra that 'Their fate would be decided by the Will of God' so they might as well sail. This placed Bell – an unbeliever – in an awkward position, but he argued that although it was true that everything depended on the will of God, that did not absolve the captain from taking the best decision he could in all the circumstances. Finally, a postponement was decided upon, until the coast was clearer.

When eventually Bell got a message that the weather and absence of blockading ships made it possible to get away, it was a frantic rush to collect his kit, check the coastline from the lookout point, and ride down to the creek before sunset: 'the bustle was mingled up with embracings, protestations of friendship, last speeches and injunctions'. And when they did get out to sea after all the favourable wind petered out and they twice had to resort to the oars to distance themselves from intercepting vessels. All this was compensated for by a sun-lit glimpse of Mount Elbruz (revealing the cleft in its summit allegedly made by the keel of Noah's ark); Bell reflected in self-congratulatory mood 'the guardian spirit of the land has thus deigned to reward my humble endeavours for its benefit'.

Even when they reached the Turkish coast, their troubles were not over. They were told they would have to stand off shore for eighteen days of quarantine, and some of the Circassians on board – hungry, cold and fearing Russian boarding parties –

threatened to make a forced landing and 'rather to perish sabre in hand than submit to such treatment'. Bell managed to calm them until he had sent a message ashore and arranged for them to be allowed to proceed on to Sinop; even there, the Russian consul (there was still no British representation) managed to delay their landing for a further four days. And lest he should be in any doubt about the nature of the risks that he had been running, Bell was confronted ashore by reports that orders had been issued to the commanders of all the Russian ships involved in the blockade to the effect that whatever ship captured Bell 'should immediately hang me' on the orders of the tsar himself. Bell used all his influence, that an Englishman commanded as of right, to settle old scores and protect his shipmates: he wrote to the local pasha pointing out that the obstructive Russian consul was in fact 'a servant who had been turned out of the establishment of an English gentleman for disreputable conduct' and that such an appointment was an insult to the pasha and to his sultan. He also secured the release of the captain of his vessel who had been arrested – again after Russian pressure – for running the blockade.

James Stanislaus Bell was an unlikely player in the Great Game: a civilian, an unauthorized agent, and a cautious character. Bell was no warrior. But he was a merchant adventurer who – in the wider interest of British trade with Turkey and the Caucasus as well as in his own purely personal interests – had firstly been prepared to suffer the loss of his ship the *Vixen* to try to force the British government's hand, and then had been prepared to live for nearly three years among the warlike guerrilla tribes of Circassia and do all in his power to encourage the tribal leaders to pursue their independence struggle against the tsar's occupying army.

He did not hazard himself in the front line as some of his compatriots did, but he was a source not only of encouragement and advice, but also of practical supplies of powder, shot and medicine. And he did all this not only without any prompting from home, but rather in the face of his own government's (Lord Palmerston's) disinclination to upset the court in St Petersburg – the court of a former ally and an emerging European power. But Bell, although by profession and inclination a merchant rather than a warrior, was not unaware of the political and military threat from Russia not only to British trade with Persia, Turkey and other eastern markets, but also to the security of the frontiers of British India. In the concluding pages of his published letters home, he declares 'the Muscovite is in full career for Herat [the Afghan city viewed as the gateway to India] ... having secured a clear field for this enterprise by destroying our influence in Persia'.

Chapter 9

Arminius Vambery: The 'English' Dervish

'Sir, so you had a good walk across Central Asia.'
– Lord Palmerston to Arminius Vambery in 1864

'In the name of Allah, I swear you are an Englishman!'

So spoke the sixteen-year-old prince-governor of Herat, pointing an accusing finger at a newly arrived and somewhat pale-skinned dervish pilgrim from Turkey known as hadji Reshid. It was a serious accusation. The year was 1863 and no European had been bold or rash enough to visit this Central Asian oasis within living memory. The Afghans had recaptured it from the Emir of Bokhara only a matter of weeks before, and the young prince was a son of the King of Afghanistan. Both king and prince were known to be deeply suspicious of Europeans, and especially of the English and the Russians, who were thought to have predatory intentions towards this no-man's-land between Russia and India.

So when he followed up his remark – like a clever child who has made a new discovery – by saying 'Tell me, you really are an Englishman in disguise are you not?', it was an anxious moment. Hadji Rashid laughed it off, saying, 'Have done, Sire!' and reminding him that those who mistook a believer for an infidel were themselves unbelievers. In truth, any Russian or

Englishman discovered at Herat would have been in danger of his life, but any who had been so monstrously blasphemous as to disguise himself as a hadji and a holy man of Islam, when in fact he was a Christian infidel, would have been in danger of meeting a very grisly death indeed.

The hadji in question was not in fact a hadji, nor a dervish, nor a Turk, nor an Englishman; he was a Hungarian named Arminius Vambery, but he aspired to be an Englishman. He spoke English and when his adventurous travels were over he returned to England and shared his experiences with London society. In addition, he was every bit as dangerous to the independence of Herat and Afghanistan as any born Englishman could have been. In fact he was to warn the British government in explicit terms about the dangers of leaving a vacuum in this quarter of Central Asia. How he came to be there, however, is an intriguing story.

Born in Hungary in 1832, Vambery had early in his life shown an aptitude for languages and an enthusiasm for all things oriental. He had settled in Constantinople and become to all outward appearances a Turk; he shunned European society, European clothes, European food, European languages and the European quarter of the city. In particular, he was obsessed with all the ramifications of Islamic life and doctrine. He longed to visit those spiritual havens of Islamic learning and tradition which were to be found in Central Asia at Bokhara, Khiva and elsewhere. The fact that no European had ventured into this wild haunt of Turkoman slave-traders for almost twenty years (since Dr Wolff had set out from England to determine the fate of Stoddart and Conolly) acted as a further incentive to the adventure-seeker. Another inducement was the political import-ance of the region: with the Russians advancing year on year across the steppes, and with one khanate and emirate after another shortly to fall to them, Vambery felt that there was no time to lose in finding information about what was going on, and transmitting that to the party most interested – Britain with its Indian empire. But whatever the incentives and inducements, the most important thing was to find a way of getting there and getting back alive.

It was with this in mind that Vambery moved from Constantinople to Tehran. Here in Persia he based himself in the Turkish embassy and, in view of his long residence and excellent connections, received the support and help of the Turkish ambassador. The ambassador also made a practice of befriending Islamic pilgrims who passed through Persia on their way to or from Mecca. Many of these were Tartar dervishes, and Vambery found in them, for the first time, a group of people who shared his obsession with travelling to the Islamic holy places of Central Asia. Word spread through the caravanserais of Persia that here at the Turkish embassy in Tehran was a man who understood and sympathized with dervish pilgrims. There was speculation that he might well be a dervish himself, so convincing was his knowledge of all things Islamic and his command of Turkish and other languages.

Vambery saw his chance in March 1863 when a group of pilgrims from Chinese Tartary called at the embassy: 'barbarous as they seemed, wretched as was their clothing, I was yet able to discover in them something of nobility', he later wrote. Their leader wore a green robe over his ragged dress and topped it all with a colossal white turban, and 'by his fiery glance and quick eye, showed his superiority'. These pilgrims were the chiefs of a small caravan group, numbering some two dozen souls in all. They were homeward bound to Khokand and Kashgar, and would therefore be travelling through all that part of Central

Asia which Vambery had for so long wished to reach. After an hour of talking to them, an idea struck him: 'What if I journeyed with these pilgrims to Central Asia? As natives, they might prove my best Mentors: besides, they already know me as the Dervish Reshid Efendi [. . .]'

He calculated that they had good connections in Bokhara. While memories of Stoddart and Conolly were still alive this was undoubtedly the most frightening of his possible destinations. But one problem was that he knew such oriental pilgrims would never believe he was motivated by genuine geographical curiosity: 'they would consider it ridiculous, perhaps even suspicious'. So he had to persuade them that his motive was purely religious, that: 'I had long silently, but earnestly, desired to visit Turkestan, not merely to see the only source of Islamite virtue that still remained undefiled, but to behold the saints of Khiva, Bokhara and Samarcand'. Not a word should ever be uttered about his political and quasi-military concerns about Russian expansion into the region.

He said he had been waiting a whole year in Persia in the hope of finding just such a group of dedicated pilgrims as themselves with whom he could travel in fulfilment of his pious ambitions. His listeners were totally persuaded of his sincerity and, by now being convinced that he was indeed a dervish, they said it gave them 'infinite pleasure that he should regard them as worthy of the friendship that the undertaking of so distant and perilous a journey in their company implied'. He had been accepted.

His future travelling companions immediately started warning him of the dangers: there would be periods when, for weeks at a time, they would be with 'no house, no bread, not even a drop of water to drink'. Besides the risk of being killed or taken prisoner and sold into slavery, there was also the risk of being buried alive in sand storms. 'Ponder well, Efendi, the step! You may have occasion later to rue it.' They also wondered how he would manage the return journey without them. He persuaded them that such material considerations did not weigh with him: 'I must hasten away from this horrid kingdom of Error', he said. Eventually, to seal the deal, the leader of the dervish caravan embraced and kissed him, which forced Vambery to confess, 'I had, it is true, some feeling of aversion to struggle against. I did not like such close contact with those clothes and bodies impregnated with all kinds of odours'.

When Vambery told his Turkish patrons and friends of his decision, they declared he was a lunatic to journey to a region from which few had ever returned. Especially, they said, he was mad to go with a group of dodgy characters 'who for the smallest coin would destroy me'. Despite all these forebodings, it was decided that the expedition would set out within a week: Vambery did not want his credentials to be exposed to too long study – nor did he want his own nerve to give way. He asked for advice on what he should take with him, and was told to shave his head and to exchange his Turkish-European costume for Bokharan dress; he should also 'dispense with bedclothes, linen, and all such articles of luxury'. His anxiety about the trip was not diminished by visiting his potential fellow travellers at their caravanserai and finding them in two small cells – one with ten occupants, the other with fourteen. 'They seemed to me dens filled with filth and misery.'

But rather than dwell on these awaited discomforts, Vambery got down to discussing the route they should take. There were basically two alternatives: the first – via Meshed, Merv and Bokhara – was the shortest, but involved passing through the Tekke tribes, 'the most savage of all the Turkomans, who spare no man, and who would not hesitate to sell into slavery the Prophet himself, did he fall into their hands'. The second route passed through the country of the Yomut Turkomans, who were considered an honest and hospitable people, and then passed through Khiva; the trouble with this route was that it involved a passage of forty stations through the desert, without a single spring of drinking water. Considerable debate followed, at the conclusion of which it was decided that 'It is better to battle against the wickedness of the elements than against that of man [. . .] God is gracious, we are on His way [. . .] He will certainly not abandon us'. Beards were stroked and everyone acclaimed 'Amen'.

Vambery was told to be ready in two days' time. He spent those two days having last-minute doubts: even if he were brave enough to face the risks, was he physically strong enough to survive the hardships? One thing that bothered him especially was that he had been lame since birth: would he tire too soon if forced to walk long stretches? Vambery was not a man to go back on his resolve: he decided he and his companions would just have to put up with his lameness. The call of the khanates was not to be denied.

Having left Tehran, the first obstacle was the Elburz range of mountains along the southern shores of the Caspian Sea. It was uncomfortably hot during the day, and mercilessly cold at night. Despite his lameness, Vambery found he needed to dismount from his horse and walk for longish periods in the early mornings to keep his circulation going. What luggage they had was carried on the horses. Their night quarters were in villages surrounded by forests of boxwood.[1] When the villagers went out

---

1. When the author crossed the Elburz mountains in the course of the journey recounted in *The Trail of Tamerlane* (1980), his muleteer-guide assumed that his luggage included a tent. When informed it did not, he managed to find overnight shelter under the roof of a brigand-like family whose reaction to his arrival was more hostile than welcoming.

to collect spring water to make tea, there was a sudden alarm: undefined wild animals had been seen loitering round the spring, and leaping into the forest at their approach. Vambery seized a rusty sword and set off into the trees, only to discover – fortunately at a good distance off – 'two splendid tigers, whose beautifully-striped forms made themselves visible occasionally from the thickets'. A more menacing presence was that of the jackals who infested their camp and against which Vambery 'was obliged, in self-defense, to use both hands and feet to prevent their making off with bread-sack or a shoe'.

After some difficulties, mostly caused by suspicions about the provenance of Vambery, they managed to embark on their crossing of the Caspian in a boat made out of a hollowed tree-trunk. The passengers were packed in two rows alongside each other 'like salted herrings' so that the centre of the boat was free for the passage of the crew. At night, Vambery's neighbouring passengers fell on top of him snoring, but he felt he could not wake them, as to do so 'would have been a heinous sin, to be atoned by never-ending suffering'. Fortunately a favourable wind carried them quickly across the water to the Turkoman coast of the Caspian and Vambery felt for the first time that Persia was behind him and there was no looking back. Even here, he was observed to be different from the other pilgrims and given special treatment by a Turkoman chief who assumed he was Turkish. Convenient as it was to be given preferential treatment – a place in a more comfortable tent – it was nonetheless disturbing to be so consistently spotted as the odd man out and it made him nervous.

As they sailed further up the Caspian coast, they reached the southernmost extremity of the tsar's domains. Vambery noted that there were three Russian warships patrolling these waters, to prevent Turkoman pirates from harassing shipping along the Caspian coast. While Vambery could see the need for this, he later commented in his book that the Russians were exploiting their control of the coastal shipping to 'establish friendly relations with one tribe so as to make use of it against another'. One local khan was known to act as a spy on behalf of the Russians and give advance notice to the latter of intended raids; however, he had at an early age succumbed to the charms of 'Russian brandy' (vodka) and had become such a confirmed alcoholic that he no longer functioned and his sons 'were very careful not to give intelligence to the Russians of any projected marauding exped-ition'. Vambery was already alert to such evidence of the Russians employing their policing activities to gain political influence.

The same khan made a practice of receiving all pilgrims on their way through his port, but Vambery was very relieved that they were obliged to anchor off shore and so not be exposed to a meeting with him, as he was sure that the khan's experience of European countenances would have enabled him easily to expose Vambery as something very different from what he purported to be. The ship was due to be inspected by the Russian authorities the next day, and Vambery was anxious that as his complexion 'was not yet brought to an Asiatic hue' he might be detected. He did not fear any inhumane treatment at Russian hands, but rather that they would 'dissuade me from persisting in my adventure'. So when the Russians approached he adopted a 'stooping and half-lying position' which he hoped would conceal his neck, which was particularly white. It was a close run thing. One of the Russian naval officers scanning the group of pilgrims remarked, 'See how white that hadji is'. But he did not pursue his comment further.

When they got clear of the Russian port and set off overland, one of the other pilgrims coached him in how to throw off his Turkish manners and appear to be a more oriental pilgrim. None of their party ever suspected him of being more closely European than his professed identity as an Islamic Turk. Sometimes they stayed for lengthy periods based in one place, and Vambery was able to accompany local chiefs on local missions, learning more all the time about his surroundings. Occasionally such missions were prolonged by the need to 'keep clear of hundreds of wild boars which were roaming about' or other natural hazards. As he coped with all this, he was gradually becoming part of the scene. He was even able – with the use of his compass – to help them orientate a mosque correctly towards Mecca. He also found that, since as a dervish he was expected to spend many hours in contemplation and reverie, he was able to sit slumped listening to the endless political talk about their raids and their relations with all their neighbours – Russians, Persians, Khivans and others – without being expected to contribute to the talk. Vambery was successfully immersing himself in the Turkoman world and gaining insights that no previous traveller had achieved.

Before long, Vambery and his travelling companions were impatient to move on. One of the most unpleasant aspects of their life as guests of the Turkomans was having to witness their cruelty towards their Persian slaves, many of them young lads who had been captured at sea or on land and were being held – shackled day and night – in the hope of raising a ransom for their release. Those who were too poor to command a ransom were sold off in the slave markets of Khiva for whatever they could fetch. Vambery was torn between trying to help and comfort them, and his fears that by doing so he might draw attention to himself as acting out of character.

The pilgrim group set about negotiating the hire of camels, one between two pilgrims being the most they could afford. Vambery himself, who had sewn money into his ragged clothing and who had received donations from the Turkomans, could have afforded to hire his own camel, but he was strongly advised not to, as the covetousness of the nomadic tribes 'was sure to be excited by the slightest sign of affluence [...] a suspicion of wealth might convert the best friend into a foe'.

Vambery had two special reasons for wanting to depart so swiftly. He feared that as the weather got hotter the rain water still to be found in the desert would become scarcer. But more urgently, he once again feared that suspicion was growing about his dervish character: some of the Turkomans were already speculating that he was 'an envoy of the Sultan [...] who was bringing a thousand muskets with him and was engaging in a plot against Russia and Persia'. He reckoned that the discovery of his disguise 'might have involved a cruel, perhaps a life-long captivity'.

So it was very welcome news when they found that the Khan of Khiva, whose capital was to be their next destination, had sent a specially trusted and experienced caravan leader to collect two buffaloes from Astrabad and bring them back to Khiva. Buffalo milk had been recommended by his physician to the khan for his health, and now his caravan with the buffaloes was passing near by and they could join it for the next leg of their desert journey. For the first stage of their march towards the rendezvous with the caravan, Vambery was allocated a horse to ride rather than a camel. But a disaster nearly ensued; riding through tall rushes, they stumbled on a wild boar's lair and as his horse shied Vambery was thrown to the ground in the path of a charge by the mother of the young boars; he was only saved by one of the Turkomans riding between them with his lance and forcing the mother boar to retreat. It had been an unexpectedly narrow escape and he was congratulated on his luck by his fellow pilgrims because, as they reminded him, 'death by a wound from a wild boar would send even the most pious Moslem into [. . .] a hundred years' burning in purgatorial fire' to cleanse away the uncleanness of the porcine wound.

Meeting up with the large caravan from Khiva was not quite as straightforward as they had hoped. Several days were spent at Etrek, another Turkoman settlement which was renowned as a holding station for Persian slaves. All the repulsion which Vambery had felt earlier at the treatment of these captives was multiplied by witnessing the even harsher conditions here. One Persian girl, who had managed to change her status from that of a slave to that of a wife, was particularly harsh in her dealings with her compatriots in an effort to demonstrate how strong were her loyalties to her new Turkoman husband. When eventually they left Etrek they had to cross the river of that name, which was in flood, and spent much time trying to find the shallowest crossing point; the cargo on the camels got soaked and at one point Vambery thought he was going to have to swim for his life.

The good news was that having crossed the river 'the anxiously-awaited caravan came in sight', recognizable by having in its van three buffaloes (two cows and a bull) to supply milk to cure the Khan of Khiva. (It seemed that buffalo milk was a favoured remedy·for impotence.) Vambery attached much importance to making a good impression on the caravan leader, who would not only be their protector in the desert but would also open the way to a welcome in Khiva. He was therefore very disconcerted when he learnt that one of their party – an opium-addicted Afghan-born merchant who had recently attached himself to them – had denounced him as a European to the caravan leader and suggested that the rigours of the Khan of Khiva's torturers would reveal him for what he was.

This Afghan had some skill in spotting European features, because he had been brought up in Kandahar during the British occupation and had seen many Englishmen; he had also been compelled to leave Kandahar after committing various crimes, so he had no love for the British. He had more than once approached Vambery threatening to expose him if he were not bought off. For the moment, his malicious remarks were countered by the loyal protestations of his fellow pilgrims, but the Afghan could well prove a fatal enemy when they reached Khiva.

Some nights later, Vambery found himself drinking tea alongside the same Afghan, who was in an advanced state of drugged delusion; he found himself sorely tempted to slip one of the strychnine tablets he had been given before setting out (as a means of suicide if he ever found himself facing torture and death) into the Afghan's bowl of tea, and thus rid himself of his blackmailer and persecutor. But the combination of the beauty of the heavens and his own Christian conscience prevailed, and he let the tempting opportunity pass.

Meanwhile the caravan leader was busy urging his pilgrims to fill their water skins to the full and prepare themselves in every way for the impending desert crossing. When they finally set off, they numbered forty men, of whom twenty-six were unarmed pilgrims and most of the rest heavily armed Turkomans. Between them they had some eighty camels. They struck out on a direct line northwards, the shortest – but driest – route to Khiva. By day, they took their direction from the sun; by night, from the Pole star. The camels were roped together in single file and led by a man on foot. Progress was mostly at night, to avoid the heat of the day, and was slow because of the pace of the buffaloes. One of the cow buffaloes was heavily pregnant and later gave birth to a calf which did not live long in the arduous conditions of a desert crossing. Everyone was worried about the scarcity of water.

For Vambery, however, there were additional worries. He saw the caravan leader in deep conversation with the leading pilgrims, and when he tried to find out what was going on, he was told that the caravan leader 'was making many objections to my joining him on the journey to Khiva'. Chief among these objections was the fact that he looked suspicious (the Afghan's slanders had clearly not been forgotten) and that the Khan of Khiva was paranoid about visitors mapping the routes into his domains. The Khan had recently found two visitors gathering such information about the caravan tracks and had not only executed those who had passed information to them, but had also threatened to execute the caravan leader himself for bringing these spies into the khanate in his entourage. No wonder the caravan leader was nervous. He was considering dumping Vambery where they were, and letting him try to find his own way back.

The caravan leader was eventually persuaded that Vambery could stay with the party, provided – his friends said – he was prepared to be 'searched to see if thou hast any drawings or wooden pens (lead pencils), as the Frenghis [Europeans] generally have; and second that thou promise to take away with thee no secret notes respecting the hills and routes'. Otherwise he would be abandoned where he was. Vambery made a considerable scene about all this, declaring that when they reached Khiva they would learn how holy a man he was and what an affront such suspicions were. He appears to have got away with it. But it must have been an anxious moment for him, as he not only had money but other things concealed in his ragged clothes; in particular, he had some spare paper for writing notes leafed into his copy of the Koran which he always carried on a cord round his neck. The whole incident meant that he felt he could not now ask any questions as to the names of different places and landmarks; this was frustrating because 'however immense the desert, the nomads inhabiting the various oases have affixed a specific designation to every place, every hill and every valley, so that if exactly informed I might have marked each place on the map of Central Asia'. This had, after all, been one of his objectives in coming on the trip. Despite the inhibitions, he resorted to cunning methods – not disclosed in his book – of recording as much as he could. In fact, he was doing exactly what the Khan most wanted to prevent.

Meanwhile Vambery made himself as useful as possible. One night, while he was catching a brief few hours' sleep in his pannier basket on his camel, he was rudely woken by cries from those around him that they had lost their way – the clouds had covered the stars – and could he use his compass to put them on the right track again, which he did. When they had to dismount and walk on foot, sometimes for four hours at a stretch with his bad leg, he noticed that the caravan leader now sought out his company and went out of his way to be friendly, as if to make up for his former hostility and suspicion. The leader's nephew, who was also part of the caravan, did the same; he had not seen his young wife since the previous year (presumably because he had been travelling so much) and was anxious about her welfare and faithfulness; so he asked Vambery, whose character as a dervish he never doubted, 'to search in my Koran for a prognostic regarding his family'. Vambery was a bit taken aback by this request but recorded that he 'made the usual hocus focus, shut my eyes, and fortunately opened the book at a place where women were spoken of'. He then went on to extrapolate an encouraging meaning from the passage, and the nephew thanked him and 'I was delighted to find that I had won his friendship'. Vambery was pushing his luck and living dangerously by this sort of blasphemous play acting.

The caravan leader kept his own counsel about which route he would take for the next stage across the desert until the very last minute, because of fears that if any word leaked out from the caravan to some passing shepherd it would increase their chance of being ambushed. The pilgrims were warned not to speak loudly at night in case they gave their position away. No fires were lit at their stopping points. The pilgrims were urged to pray to Allah for safety, and that 'in the hour of danger we should not behave like women'. From time to time weapons were distributed, including to Vambery, who was pleased to find he was 'regarded as one having most heart [for a fight]'. At one moment he and the caravan leader thought they were indeed going to have a fight on their hands; they were exploring a cave when a wild figure clad only in a gazelle skin sprang out at them with a threatening lance in his hands; he turned out to be a half-mad refugee from a local vendetta, who had been haunting a desert well for years and trying to avoid any contact with other nomads who had a grievance against him.

Water was running out – and what dirty water they had was turning to mud with the jolting of the camels – so the leader chose the shortest route. Many of the party were suffering from acute dehydration. Some, including the leader, were thought to have concealed water with them, but no one dared mention their suspicions since 'any design upon a water-skin would be considered as a design upon the life of its owner'. Sometimes the camel chain broke in the dark of night time and individual animals got left behind; in those cases, a man would go back to look for the missing beast, and keep in touch with his companions by continually calling out to them; this worked well, unless the wind changed, and then there was a real risk of losing a man as well as a camel. On one occasion, the leader uncharacteristically fell asleep during a night march, and the camels walked into a salt morass, covered with a thick white crust in which their feet became entrapped. When the riders sprang down from their camels, they too became stuck. The leader – by now awake – shouted to everyone to remain where they were and, after three anxious hours, the dawn light enabled them to retrace their steps to firm ground. 'Had we only advanced a little further', Vambery concluded, 'a part or perhaps the whole caravan might have been swallowed up'. At one point the caravan leader insisted that they all dismounted and walked the final stage towards a desert shrine where they were expected to bellow out passages from the Koran; Vambery, with his lameness and his parched throat, found this particularly galling. But the leader's popularity was restored when, quite unexpectedly at a moment of maximum thirst and weariness, he revealed he had indeed been carrying a concealed supply of water – and shared it out among the pilgrims.

After several weeks of struggling through sand, suffering from thirst and the constant fear of attack, they reached the edge of the desert and the frontiers of the khanate of Khiva. Rain, freshwater pools and an escort of cavalry (at first mistaken for marauders) were a reward for their perseverance. While other pilgrims tried to smarten themselves up for their arrival, Vambery declined all offers of clean clothes and rejoiced in contemplating his face 'covered with a thick crust of dirt and sand'. He reckoned that the poorer and more dishevelled he looked, the likelier he was to avoid unwelcome attention. His excitement at seeing the minarets, fine meadows and lofty poplars of the capital was only mitigated by his apprehensions about his false role being detected: 'my nerves were all strung to the highest point'. The khan's reputation for 'at once making slaves of all strangers of doubtful character' was well known. As he passed through the welcoming crowds – such a large party of pilgrims had not arrived here for many years – he was mentally rehearsing ways 'to get the better of the watchful, and superstitious tyrant'.

His worst fears were quickly realized. No sooner had the khan's chamberlain (who acted as customs officer) addressed the normal questions to the leader of the caravan, than the malicious Afghan pressed forward and called out aloud 'We have brought

to Khiva three interesting quadrupeds and a no less interesting biped!'. The quadrupeds were, of course, the buffaloes; the biped – alas – was Vambery. All eyes immediately turned on him, and he heard whispers of 'spy', 'Westerner' and 'Russian'. The chamberlain ordered him to remain and addressed him in an exceedingly unpleasant way. But, once again, a combination of the support of his fellow pilgrims and his own ingenuity rescued him from his predicament. He had taken the trouble to refresh his memory about an eminent Khivan citizen who had been resident in Constantinople when he had been there; he now tracked down this former acquaintance to the Islamic college where he lived, and established his credentials with him as a Turkish dervish with whom – he claimed – he had common friends. He knew he had got away with it when the next day a messenger arrived from the khan, bringing a present and saying that the ruler had heard about hadji Rashid's arrival at his capital and was anxious to receive a blessing from such a pious visitor. Meanwhile the Afghan had been reviled for his regrettable outburst and unfounded accusations.

The prospect of a private audience with the khan was nonetheless a daunting one. He was accompanied to the palace by his former acquaintance who gave him some briefing about how to behave in the royal presence. He found the khan seated on a dais with his left arm supported on a velvet cushion and his right hand holding a golden sceptre. After giving a blessing to the khan, he retired a few paces and the official part of the ceremony was over. The khan then started to ask him questions. What was the object of his journey? How had he found the desert crossing, and the Turkomans? How long would he stay? Had he adequate funds? In reply to this last question, Vambery asserted, 'we Dervishes do not trouble ourselves with such trifles'; and he added a wish that the khan should live for a hundred and twenty years. He found that his answers seemed to give satisfaction, because the khan ordered that he should be given twenty ducats and a stout donkey. Vambery declined the ducats, saying that 'for a Dervish it was a sin to keep money', but then went on to specify that his donkey should please be a white one as that was what 'the holy commandment prescribed for pilgrimages'. (His self-confidence knew no limits!)

He returned to his lodgings through waving crowds and, only when he was at last safely in the privacy of his cell, did he feel he could congratulate himself on the fact that 'the Khan, who in appearance was so fearfully dissolute, and who presents in every feature of his countenance the real picture of an enervated, imbecile and savage tyrant, had behaved in a manner so unexceptionable'. He felt that he could now, with the khan's approval, visit whatever part of the territory he wished. And now that he was seen to be basking in the khan's favour, the inhabitants of Khiva vied with each other to entertain him in their houses; he was continually being confronted with large and disgusting meals of rice swimming in the fat of sheep's tails, and if he did not do justice to the meal, his hosts would speculate that it was extraordinary that someone 'so well versed in books, should have acquired only a half acquaintance with the requisites of polite breeding!'. Almost equally exhausting were the continual questions put to him by passers by, whenever he ventured out of his convent cell. Since they knew he came from Constantinople, many of the questions related to the Ottoman sultan. Was it true, for instance, that the sultan had all his meals forwarded to him from Mecca? And were they miraculously flown from Mecca to Constantinople in a few seconds of time? Vambery wryly thought to himself how very different in reality the sultan's worldly existence was from the divine vision imagined by his questioners: little did they know 'how much Chateau Lafitte and Margot garnished the sovereign's table' at the Porte.

Worse than any of these embarrassments however were the scenes that he was obliged to witness as he went around the capital. On one occasion he saw a party of captives – allegedly brigands who had attacked a caravan – being divided into those young enough to be worth selling in the slave markets, and those too old for any useful purpose. The latter had their eyes gouged out, the executioner wiping the blade of his knife on their beards. Since the khan was anxious to establish a reputation as a defender of Islamic law, a man who 'cast a look upon a thickly veiled lady' would be hanged, while the unfortunate lady who had attracted his attention would be buried in the ground up to her breasts, and then stoned to death. Such penalties usually followed a brief verdict of 'take him away' by the khan, who had been sitting in judgement. Vambery was uncomfortably aware that had his own performance at his audience been less convincing, he would doubtless have been subjected to the same verdict.

Gruesome sights were not confined to the fate of prisoners. One day he saw some magnificent silk robes being embroidered and on inquiry found they were being awarded to those who had brought home the heads of enemies severed in battle – the more the heads the grander the robe. The next day he saw the warriors returning to claim their awards; they were emptying sacks full of severed heads – as if they had been sacks of potatoes – at the feet of the vizier in the public square and receiving a receipt which they would later cash in for the appropriate robe. This was no city for squeamish sightseers.

But that was not the reason which persuaded Vambery it was time to move on. The pilgrims had been in the khanate for a month; great kindness had been shown to them; they had been laden with gifts (most of which Vambery rejected as became a true dervish); but now the weather was becoming ever hotter and they feared that if they delayed longer the further journey across desert and steppe to Bokhara would become unendurable. His Khivan friend tried so hard to persuade him not to go on and put himself at the mercy of the Emir of Bokhara, that Vambery had moments of wondering whether that friend had penetrated his disguise and realized just how great a risk he would be taking. But, having given a final blessing to the Khan of Khiva, he decided to go forward as planned. The pilgrims, owing to the generosity of the Khivans, were now better mounted than before: Vambery had the promised donkey to ride, and a camel to carry his frugal luggage. So many people came to see them off, and to follow them for the first mile or so requesting final benedictions, that Vambery's donkey eventually could stand no more of it and took off across the steppe at a crisp gallop, braying as it went.

It took them two days to cross the Oxus river, partly because the river was swollen and their ferry frequently was grounded on the sands, obliging some of the pilgrims to carry their own donkeys on their shoulders; and partly because the camels had to cross separately the following day. On the far bank of the Oxus, the countryside was relatively fertile: women offered the pilgrims drinks from their gourds; there were markets where Vambery even found other dervishes – though most of these were comatose through excessive opium consumption.

He waxes lyrical about the Oxus river 'rolling with a dull sound' by moonlight.[2] Although they felt safe here, the caravan leader was nervous about the approaches to Bokhara (six or eight days' ride away) since the emir was known to be on campaign with his army, and at such times the Tekke Turkomans (the most feared tribe) felt free to ambush caravans on their approach to the city. They were therefore very relieved when five horsemen, who galloped up to them at full speed during their midnight march, turned out to be Khivan merchants who had come from Bokhara and reported that the routes were now quite safe.

---

2. It seems more than likely that his romantic feelings about the Oxus owed something to Matthew Arnold's poem 'Sohrab and Rustum', which had been published less than ten years earlier and with which, as an ardent anglophile, he would have been familiar.

The feeling of security was short-lived. On the banks of the Oxus they came across two half-naked men who had been robbed of everything they had by an unusually large – 150-strong – band of Tekke Turkomans, and who urged them to fly or conceal themselves because 'in spite of you all being pilgrims, they will leave you behind in the desert without beasts or food'. The warning was enough to persuade the caravan leader – who had twice previously been waylaid and narrowly escaped with his life – to order an about turn. After a brief rest, and refilling of water skins, he then led the caravan off directly into the desert: the going would be harder but they were more likely to avoid the Tekke. A number of the pilgrims were so frightened of another desert crossing (it was now July, the hottest month) that they accepted a lift on a skiff returning down the river. Only fourteen of the original party remained with the caravan leader, among them Vambery, who decided in his own words, 'my life, indeed, is threatened everywhere – is everywhere on danger; forward, then, forward! Better to perish by the fury of the elements than by the racks of tyrants!'. With the dreaded Emir of Bokhara ahead of him, he could hardly have been sure he would avoid the latter fate.

There was good reason to dread the desert crossing that now ensued. First two of the camels died, obliging more of the party to walk. Then two of the pilgrims became so exhausted that they had to be strapped onto the backs of other camels, being unable to ride or sit and calling out continually and unavailingly for water. One of them died on the fourth day, his tongue having turned black from thirst. Every man was now intent on his own survival, and slept with his arm around his water bottle. Vambery commented: 'It is a horrible sight to see the father hide his store of water from the son, and brother from brother; each drop is life, and when men feel the torture of thirst, there is not, as in other dangers of life, any spirit of self-sacrifice, or any feeling of generosity'. He noticed that his own tongue was beginning to turn black, and drank off at a single draught half his remaining meagre horde of water. He was at the end of his tether, but nature had a further unpleasant surprise in store for them. It was the camels that first sensed that the dust wave that could be seen approaching them was in fact a full-blown sand storm; they lay down and tried to bury their heads in the sand; the pilgrims then entrenched themselves beside the camels; when the storm broke over them, it felt to Vambery as if 'the first particles that touched me seemed to burn like a rain of flakes of fire'. He reckoned that if they had encountered the sand storm when they were even six miles deeper into the desert, they would all have perished.

As it was, they managed to stagger out of the desert and Vambery, who was too weak to dismount without assistance, was laid on the ground with 'a fearful fire seeming to burn my entrails'. He passed out, and when he regained consciousness found that he was in a mud hut surrounded by people with long beards who turned out to be Persian slaves from Bokhara acting as shepherds on the fringe of the desert. The shepherds had been given only the meanest supply of bread and water, to ensure that they did not try to run away, but they generously shared what they had with the pilgrims.

When they reached a village on the outskirts of Bokhara they were told to wait until the customs officials came out to examine and note down all their possessions. As so often before, the official in question looked suspiciously at Vambery and – when his dervish status was confirmed by his companions – gave 'a shake of the head full of meaning'. From here the track into the capital was through gardens and lush cultivated fields and soon they could see the minarets, domes and towers of Bokhara. It was an exciting moment for the pilgrims: this was the city which in Islamic legend (as Moorcroft had noted forty years earlier) instead of basking in the light reflected down from heaven, itself threw light up to heaven. No wonder it was known as 'Bokhara Sherif' – Bokhara the Noble.

The pilgrims managed to reject the suggestion that they should stay in the customs house, where they would have been subjected to further inspections, and managed to secure accommodation in the Moslem college, which Vambery described as 'the chief nest of Islamite fanaticism'. Here he was treated with deference and given a spacious cell to himself, as became a dervish holy man. But he was quick to realize the nature of his accommodation was a somewhat two-edged asset. On the one hand, it was an address which in itself confirmed his status; on the other hand he was surrounded by clerics who would be quick to observe any deviation from the accepted practices and doctrines of Islam, and who would probably want to engage him in endless debate. This was made the more dangerous in his case by the fact that, not only was Bokhara a most perilous place for all strangers especially Europeans (as the experience of Stoddart and Conolly had confirmed), but it was also a place where 'the Government has carried the system of espionage to just as high a pitch of perfection as the population has attained pre-eminence in every kind of profligacy and wickedness'. There would be plenty of cunning people trying to catch him out and to gain credit by reporting him to the barbaric authorities.

One of his first expeditions out of the college was to the bazaar. Here he was concerned to find a large number of goods of Russian manufacture – including samovars in the tea bazaar –

providing evidence of increasing commercial penetration from the north. But he was also proud and pleased to see objects labelled as 'made in Birmingham' or 'made in Manchester', though he had to be careful not to so far forget himself as to show any give-away signs of pleasure or special interest in this. The bazaar was crowded with people from every corner of the khanates and emirates of Central Asia, as well as with Jews, Indians and Afghans. Most of the clothes in the bazaar were of local manufacture, and in bright colours and lively fashions. Vambery concluded that for the Tartar 'Bokhara is his Paris or London'.

But word of the customs officer's suspicions had reached the grand vizier (who in the absence of the emir was in charge) and Vambery was subjected to endless efforts to entrap him, usually by inviting him to talk about Europe to see if he revealed any insider knowledge of its languages and mode of living. Eventually he told these provocateurs that 'I quitted Constantinople to get away from these Europeans' and that he did not want to spoil his time in Bokhara the Noble by talking about these matters. Having drawn a blank in this direction, the grand vizier summoned him to a levee, which turned out to be 'a sort of examination, in which my incognito had to stand a running fire'. As on previous occasions, Vambery met the challenge by taking the initiative: he turned the interrogation onto his interrogators, asking them all sorts of esoteric theological questions. A lively debate ensued and he managed to 'get safely through this ordeal'.

After this he was left to lead a relatively quiet life in Bokhara for the remainder of his three-week stay. Although now feeling less at risk himself, he was nonetheless depressed by the extent to which all the inhabitants stood in continual dread of being reported for some misdemeanour: even – he recorded – when a husband and wife were alone together they would not dare mention the emir's name without adding 'may he live 120 years'! As a holy city, it failed to come up to expectations: the water and almost everything about the sacred capital seemed dirty, despite a local saying that cleanliness is derived from religion (the Islamic equivalent of 'cleanliness is next to godliness'). Also, the citizens were far less generous to pilgrims than the inhabitants of Khiva: he had to sell his donkey, and left much poorer than he had arrived. But he was certainly lucky that the sadistic former emir (the murderer of Conolly) had been succeeded by a gentler tyrant, whose quirky vindictiveness was usually directed against the powerful rather than the weak, hence he was known as 'the slayer of elephants and the protector of mice'. Vambery would hardly have qualified as a mouse however, had he been detected in his monstrous deceptions.

However intrigued Vambery might have been by Bokhara and its markets, his fellow pilgrims were anxious to press on to Samarkand. Their numbers were now reduced to two cart loads of people, and were going to diminish still further as his companions reached their homes. He found these primitive carts even more uncomfortable than camels; the passengers shook around until 'our heads were continually cannoning each other like balls on a billiard table'. Progress was slow as the driver – who came from Khokand – was unfamiliar with the route and frequently lost his way. But now they were travelling through cultivated land rather than desert and he noticed that every village market, however small, had its Russian samovar – dispensing tea and reminding the inhabitants of the culture of their powerful northern neighbour. Indeed, the samovars were the central point of much political discussion – an activity frowned upon in Bokhara but acceptable here.

Vambery, who had been disappointed in the decrepit appearance of Bokhara, was enchanted by his first distant views of
Samarkand, which he thought was larger and more impressive
than Tehran. Although on entering the famous caravan destination, 'the focus of the whole globe', he found it again rather
shabby, he nonetheless spent most of his eight days there visiting
all the celebrated sights, including the tomb of Tamerlane, and
describes them all in detail in his book. He also witnessed the
return of the triumphant emir (who ruled over Samarkand as
well as Bokhara) from his military campaign; he thought that his
retinue looked more like the chorus in an opera than a troop of
Tartar warriors.

The day after his return, the emir declared he wanted to see
hadji Rashid (Vambery) in a private audience. 'This was a blow,
because we all now suspected that something was going wrong.'
He spent a nervous hour being kept waiting, and then was ushered
into the royal presence. The emir remarked that he had heard that
Vambery had come to see the tombs of the saints of Turkestan,
and remarked 'Strange! And thou hast then no other motive in
coming hither from so distant a land?' Vambery said that was the
case; he had no other business in life than being a world pilgrim.
But the emir was still sceptical, and said, 'What, thou, with thy
lame foot, a world pilgrim! That is really astonishing.' Vambery
cleverly replied that the same lameness had applied to the emir's
illustrious ancestor – Tamerlane the Great – and it had not
prevented the latter from becoming a world conqueror. The
answer flattered and amused the emir, who dismissed him with a
present. It had been an uncomfortable audience, and he was
advised by his friends 'to quit Samarkand at all speed and gain as
rapidly as possible the further bank of the Oxus'.

The moment had now come for him to decide whether he was

going to press on further eastwards into China and possibly even into Tibet, or return via Herat (on the Afghan-Persian border) to Tehran. His friends all advised him against going further east: he would be leaving the realms of Islam and entering countries where his role as a dervish and Moslem holy man granted no prestige or protection. After much heart-searching, he decided enough was enough: he was only thirty-one, and 'what had not happened may still occur; better, perhaps, now, that I should return'. But parting from his companions was a sad event; two of the other pilgrims in particular had been kind to him throughout and supportive in all his difficult moments; he knew he would never see them again and felt bad about leaving them still under a complete illusion about his real personality and provenance. At his last sight of them, they were still standing 'with their hands raised to heaven, imploring Allah's blessing upon my far journey'.

Accompanied now by a smaller band of other pilgrims, his way ran through Karshi and Kerki, two Turkoman settlements still within the domain of the Emir of Bokhara, and he stopped in the former place long enough to buy a supply of cheap hunting knives, needles and glass beads – all of which he was assured he would be able to trade for more vital commodities such as bread on the next stage of his travels. He felt he cut a strange figure: a pilgrim loaded with wares like a travelling shop. When they again reached the swollen river Oxus, which – with a rare childhood recollection of Hungary – Vambery decided was twice as wide here as the Danube between Buda and Pest, they persuaded a ferryman to take them on the three-hour crossing without charging them. But the far bank, where he had hoped he would be safer than on Bokharan soil, held an unpleasant surprise.

They had no sooner landed than an official representing the local governor arrested him on suspicion of being a runaway Persian slave and confiscated all his possessions. Vambery made his usual scene and produced a passport which had the seal of the sultan of Turkey (a document which had got him out of more than one scrape before) demanding that it should be shown immediately to the governor himself. The combination of documentation and bluster did the trick, and he was sent on his way with apologies and a small bribe to persuade him to keep quiet about the incident.

At Kerki he had to wait several days for the chance of joining up with a much larger caravan – some 400 camels, 200 donkeys and a few horses – which was made up of a mixture of freed slaves and genuine pilgrims. While waiting, Vambery occupied himself by noting in detail the defensive potential of the town (doubtless already having in mind the paper he would write about the Russian threat to India from this direction). Once underway with the caravan, he was subjected to listening to endless horrendous stories told to him by the ex-slaves: stories about the 15,000 Tekke Turkomans who were continually prowling over the steppes and deserts to capture more human hostages, and about the devastation caused to family life for those required to try to raise the ransoms demanded. At another settlement they passed through, an officious vizier demanded such an extortionate tax on the caravan that their leader protested violently and a fight might have ensued had not the local khan intervened and sent them on their way. The caravan, now doubled in size, felt that only their numbers protected them from robbery by brigands or unscrupulous officials.

At another staging post – the settlement of Maymene – renowned for its horse markets, Vambery again found time to

218

study the defences in depth, making notes of the height and thickness of walls and towers. Here it was not he who was arrested for being a runaway slave, but several other members of the caravan who claimed to be from Turkey and needed Vambery's corroboration to confirm their status. It transpired these 'fellow pilgrims' had been captured by the Russians while fighting in the Caucasus, and transported like common criminals to Siberia where they had been employed felling trees in the forests round Tobolsk. Years had elapsed before they learnt to speak any Russian, but when they did they set about chatting up their guards and even managed to reach a degree of familiarity with them which allowed of vodka-drinking parties. One night when the guards had drunk a bit too much, the prisoners felled them with their axes and appropriated their weapons.

They then escaped and, living on grass and roots and whatever they could find or steal, managed to reach Central Asia and join up with the caravan, hoping eventually to get back to Turkey. Vambery vouched for them – although he thought them criminals – and they were released. The incident probably went some way to strengthening his anti-Russian sentiments.

Before they arrived in

what was now the territory of Afghanistan (Herat had only been captured from Bokhara very shortly before) they had to go through some narrow passes and over some precipitous one-foot-wide paths where a false step by man or camel would have resulted in falling into a ravine far below. Vambery had pictured to himself 'Afghanistan as a land already half organized, where, through long contact with Western influence, at least something of order and civilization had been introduced'. He had hoped to be able to shed his disguise as soon as he got there. But he was sorely disappointed. From the first contact with the customs officials, he realized that he was still amid 'all the inhumanity and barbarity [. . .] of Central Asia'. The only thing that slightly cheered him up was the appearance of an officer who had a 'genuine soldier-like bearing, and his uniform buttoned tight over his chest'. This at least reminded him of Europe. But rather disconcertingly, the officer in question thought Vambery also looked European, and tried to shake his hand in the English manner.

Despite being so recently a war zone, Herat lived up to its reputation as a fertile and rich plain. But the city itself showed all too clear evidence of the recent fighting. Everyone went everywhere heavily armed, not just with poniards but with swords, shields and pistols: to be well dressed was to be martial-looking. Many were still wearing English red military coats – probably trophies from the First Afghan War – which they declined to take off even when sleeping. The friction between the dominant Pathans and the underclass of Heratis was already all too evident.

Vambery himself was by now so impoverished that he was sleeping rough in the ruins and scraping together whatever he could to eat: no longer did the locals support a visiting dervish as at Khiva. He tried in vain to join various caravans bound for Meshed in Persia. Finally he decided that the one person who might help him on his way was the ruling prince – the sixteen-year-old boy who, in the absence of his father the king, was governing Herat. The young prince was usually so bored by granting audiences that he sat by the window in his palace and spent his time watching the guards drilling outside. When Vambery was admitted, he adopted his usual technique of boldly asserting his status as a dervish holy man: he stepped right up to the prince and seated himself between the prince and his grand vizier 'after having required the latter, a corpulent Afghan, to make room for me by a push with the foot'. It was then that the awkward exchange occurred – with the prince accusing him of being an Englishman – which was recounted at the opening of this chapter. After Vambery had successfully managed to treat this suggestion as a joke, the prince had 'sat down half ashamed' saying it was still the case that he had never seen a pilgrim looking like this one. At that point, Vambery produced his much-used passport from the Turkish sultan and dropped the names of various distinguished Afghans who had appeared at the Ottoman court during the time of his residence there. After this all was sweetness and light, and the prince gave him a small donation.

However he was still no nearer to getting away from Herat. And when word got around of the prince's suspicions that he was an Englishman, everyone wanted to stare at him and express their own view on the subject. The longer he stayed, the more his feelings became hostile towards the Afghans; he heard shocking stories of how they had behaved after their capture of the city a few weeks earlier; he heard nostalgic talk of the days when the British officer Major Todd had presided there; and he even was persuaded that the population 'long most for the intervention of the English'. Everything conspired to make him feel that only a British forward policy in the region could protect it from the Russian advance or the cruelty and corruption of its own rulers.

Eventually he managed to join a caravan of some 2,000 people, mostly Hezaris from Kabul, heading for Meshed and Persia. This was a trading caravan, unlike the earlier pilgrim ones with whom he had travelled; many of his companions were carrying cargos of indigo or skins. He managed to negotiate a seat on a lightly loaded mule, by promising to pay for the privilege when he reached Meshed and 'should no longer be in a state of destitution'. By doing this, he realized he was for the first time compromising his cover story: no real dervish pilgrim would be able confidently to call on funds the moment he reached a Persian city. But he did not dare completely to set aside his disguise, because he thought the more fanatical Afghans might 'avenge their insulted tenets on the spot'. But all the time his true provenance was the subject of speculation among the merchants: some thought he was a Turk but an increasing number now leant towards the idea that he really was an Englishman. As they approached the frontier, Vambery himself started setting aside the postures of humility and holy status that he had for so long adopted as a dervish, and began more and more to revert to 'the upright and independent deportment of a European'.

At Meshed Vambery was welcomed by Colonel Dolmagne, an English officer in the Persian service, who offered him the hospitality of his house for a month of recovery from the rigours of his travels. From Meshed onward his journey was totally relaxed. At Tehran, from where he had set out nearly a year before, he was made welcome by Mr Alison, the British Charge

d'Affaires, who arranged an audience for him with the shah, in the course of which he was decorated with the Order of the Lion and Sun. More importantly, Alison also paved the way for Vambery's warm reception in London.

The first thing Vambery wanted to do on arrival in London in June 1864 was to give an account of his travels to the Royal Geographical Society (RGS) at Burlington House. This was such a success that he was showered with invitations to society dinner parties and to weekends at grand houses in the country. He became 'the lion of the London season'; he met the Prince of Wales (the future King Edward VII); publishers sought him out and he had encounters with Charles Dickens and the poet Swinburne; other explorers like Sir Richard Burton were fascinated by his tales; he was invited to join the Athenaeum Club; his views on Islam were listened to with attention by the foremost Anglican theologian of the time, Bishop 'Soapy' Wilberforce of Oxford (who was to become renowned for wrestling in debate with Charles Darwin about evolution); he exchanged views on foreign policy in Central Asia with Lord Palmerston and even with Disraeli. But he still had many moments of nostalgia for the steppes and deserts he had left behind. He recorded: 'My wanderings have left powerful impressions upon my mind. Is it surprising, if I stand sometimes bewildered, like a child, in Regent Street or in the saloons of British nobles, thinking of the deserts of Central Asia, and the tents of the Kirghis and the Turkomans?'

In a book about British adventurers confronting tsarist Russia, it may at first sight seem strange that Arminius Vambery should find a prominent place. It is true that he was not born British but Hungarian; however, he saw himself as centred on England and was continually on the lookout for British interests – and threats to British interests – in his travels; it was to London he returned to unburden himself of his experiences at the RGS; it was in London that in 1864 he found a publisher, John Murray, for his best-selling account of his trip; it was in London that he was appreciated and lionized; and it was to London he returned twenty years later to continue his campaign to alert the British establishment to the dangers facing India from Russia in Central Asia. It must also be remembered that when he was suspected on his travels of not being a Turkish dervish, it was almost always as an Englishman that he was perceived. He had the outlook and bearing of an Englishman and was proud of it.

That he was an adventurer needs no elaboration: even Sir Richard Burton (who knew something of the perils of disguising oneself as a Moslem) recognized a like spirit in Vambery. And his role in confronting tsarist Russia was to become very explicit from the moment of his publication of his travelogue. His book contains a final chapter entitled 'The Rivalry of the Russians and English in Central Asia', in which he confronts head-on what he sees as British complacency in the face of the advancing tsarist conquest of the khanates and emirates dividing southern Russia from the British Raj in India: 'I disapprove of the indifference of the English to the Russian policy in Central Asia', he writes. He thinks the British argument that, because Russia is a Christian power her influence on Islamic emirates must be benign, is deeply flawed. He draws attention to the inexorable encroaches of Russian power and influence into the region, and foretells – all too accurately – how one state after another (Tashkent, Khiva, Bokhara, Samarkand, Merv and so on) will fall to them in the next few years. He writes of the building of forts and defences, and of the Russian shipping dominating the Aral Sea. He doubts whether Russia will satisfy herself with the Oxus as a boundary, and whether she will not 'seek some richer compensation than is to be found in the oases of Turkestan' – in fact the compensation of India itself.

It was Vambery's misfortune that his arrival in England and the publication of his book in 1864 coincided with a period when 'forward' policies were discouraged in favour of 'masterly inactivity' in Central Asia. The peace-loving Mr Gladstone was a rising force in the government, and the country was still bruised by the heavy losses of the Crimean War and anxious to avoid renewed confrontation with Russia. Vambery went back to Hungary and took up a professorship in oriental studies at Budapest. But he continued to write to *The Times* and to other bodies in England about Russian expansion, and when – by 1885 – many of his gloomy prophesies had been fulfilled, he returned to London and was invited to lecture up and down the country on his favourite theme of the threat to India. This time, his words fell on more fertile ground: the Great Game was launching once more into full swing. His book on the subject, *The Struggle for India*, became an instant best-seller. He was described by Charles Marvin (a notable expert on Russian interests in Asia) as 'England's warmest and most disinterested supporter in her rivalry with Russia [. . .] a model English patriot'.

Towards the end of his life, Vambery's close connection with the sultan of Turkey was exploited by the British government, who even paid him a salary from secret service funds to supply confidential information. He had instant access to the sultan, while accredited ambassadors were often kept waiting for weeks for an audience and – never over modest – he boasted that 'ten ambassadors could not accomplish in years what I have done in days'. His secret paymasters were afraid that he would mention their payments to the Prince of Wales and that, if once the indiscreet prince knew, then 'all London will know'. Eventually he negotiated a pension from the Foreign Office who were afraid he might – in his uncertain old age – release embarrassingly private and confidential letters that had been written to him by successive foreign secretaries over the previous quarter of a century. 'He is not a bad sort but tremendously self-centred and vain' was the verdict of one senior Foreign Office official on the aging self-styled dervish. The pension may have had an element of hush-money in it.

Whatever might be the case, this adopted Englishman and celebrated adventurer had confronted tsarist Russia as directly and effectively as many who had fallen – decked out in their scarlet uniforms or concealed in their shabby disguises – in the passes of Afghanistan or on the steppes of Turkistan.

Chapter 10

Edmund O'Donovan: The Frustrated
War Correspondent

'I had no idea you could become what I became, an
unscathed tourist of wars.'
— Martha Gelhorn (1908–98)

Among the troublemakers on the frontiers of Central Asia there
were many unorthodox characters who were out of step with
their own government's policies. Few however had quite such a
chequered record as Edmund O'Donovan, the special correspondent of the *London Daily News*. Born in Ireland in the
middle of the nineteenth century, his father – who was an
eminent Irish scholar – had his son educated by the Jesuits and
then encouraged him either to join the Royal Irish Constabulary
or to read medicine at Trinity College, Dublin. But it was not to
be. Young Edmund's inclinations were in a very different
direction: by the time he was in his early twenties he was already
involved with the Fenian (Irish revolutionary independence)
movement. In 1866 he was arrested and incarcerated for a year
at Mountjoy Prison, only being released on condition he
immediately emigrated to America. He accepted this condition,
but had no sooner arrived in the United States than he was
making plans to return illegally to his native Ireland. Having

done so, he resumed his subversive activities and was again arrested, this time for possession of unauthorized weapons, and was back in jail at Limerick. After a ten-month sentence, he again went abroad, this time to England where he started plotting with an underground Irish revolutionary movement. When one of his co-plotters was sentenced to fifteen years hard labour, O'Donovan realized that things were becoming too hot and he went abroad – this time to France – with the intention of staying away.

But he did not intend to settle down to a quiet life. In France he joined the Foreign Legion and was soon seeing active service in the Franco-Prussian War. After a period as a German prisoner of war, he moved on to Spain and was involved in the Carlist War, once more being on the losing side and ending up in prison. Perhaps tiring of such regular detention, he now shifted his field of activity from insurgency and soldiering to journalism, resolving to report on military activities rather than participate in them. After covering insurrections in the Balkans and sending dispatches about the Russian-Turkish war of 1877, he moved on to Central Asia just in time to witness the tsarist troops storming and capturing Geok Tepe. He would have liked to have been more closely involved (he only saw the action from a hilltop ten miles away) but determined to be a closer witness to the next Russian assault, as his sympathies were already firmly with the struggling khans and emirs whose territories lay in the path of the tsar's advance. The oasis city of Merv, 'Queen of the World', seemed a sensible place to await further action.

Getting to Merv from Geok Tepe was to prove no easy task. To start with, all the steppe around Geok Tepe was swarming with soldiery on the rampage: some were Turkoman refugees, some were Russian soldiers intent on plunder, others were neighbouring tribesmen who – sensing that there was loot to be had – had swept down from the hills to join the fray. O'Donovan managed to make his way southwards to Ash-khabad and then headed on towards Kelat, passing through 'jungle so thick that it was with much ado that we were able to force our way through'; there were encounters with jackals and leopards and 'snakes, mostly of a venomous kind, glided across our track every moment'. He was not far here from the dreaded swamps which surrounded the banks of the Tejend river, and which made a formidable barrier for those escaping the advancing Cossacks from the north. He made two reconnaissances of the swamp and found that wild boar and leopards abounded and tigers were not uncommon. 'The marsh', he concluded, 'is a treacherous expanse and men and horses are often swallowed in its depths while attempting its passage at night'.

From Kelat he hoped to set out across the desert to Merv before the Russians could get there. But getting out of Kelat was almost as difficult as reaching it. The Khan of Kelat was reluctant to let him travel alone in these parts in case he upset the prospect of some ultimate accommodation with the Russians. Most of the Turkomans and other inhabitants were fairly unconcerned about who claimed sovereignty over their lands, provided that their Moslem faith was not interfered with. O'Donovan records: 'I remember an old man asking if the Russians were likely to build churches and ring bells in their villages [. . .] these were the only points that seemed to interest him'.

To prevent his slipping away and causing trouble, the khan attached an 'escort' to O'Donovan to keep him under surveillance. Indeed any thought of slipping away was made more difficult by the fact that 'Kelat is not a town, properly speaking: but an oval valley, enclosed on all sides by almost vertical cliffs over a thousand feet high. Narrow gorges [. . .] are the only means of access to the valley'. No one could leave through these gorges without a pass from the khan. However, O'Donovan was equal to the challenge. He got permission to go out of the valley on a short excursion, where he managed to shed his escort – who were more frightened than he was of the approaching Cossacks – and then, pretending to be returning to Kelat with his two servants, he managed to give the slip to those who were watching his every move from the ramparts. Having followed the road back to Kelat until out of sight 'among the first ravines and hills spurs [. . .] I turned my horse's head and rode swiftly in the direction of Merv'.

His brief spell at Kelat had had one important effect on his attitude towards the Russians. Here he met refugees from Geok Tepe who reported horrendous tales of General Skobeloff, the army commander, who had told the 15,000 Turkoman women left behind after the rout of the stronghold that, unless their male relatives returned to look after them and accept the rule of the tsar, he would abandon them to the lusts of his soldiery. He had also made them pile up all their gold trinkets and jewellery as 'a war contribution'.

The decision to strike out across the desert to Merv was a bold, indeed reckless one. Not only were there few watering places, but those which there were tended to be frequented by roving bands of Tekke Turkomans. Colourful as these people might be, with their huge black sheepskin hats and their dark red robes, their sabres and carbines, they were in fact more of a serious menace than a picturesque experience. Although they professed to be intent on sowing and harvesting crops (the water came from a stream dependent on the goodwill of the Khan of Kelat) they were clearly in the habit of robbing or capturing anyone rash enough to venture within their range. O'Donovan spent two nights in their encampments.

They were uncomfortable experiences in every sense: the reed huts or broken-down forts that constituted the Turkoman camps were alive with black fleas, cockroaches and scorpions; and the attentions of his Turkoman hosts were alternately embarrassing and threatening. 'A fire of camel's dung smouldered [. . . the hut] speedily became crammed to suffocation by Turkomans, whose curiosity was little short of ferocious [. . .] they literally thrust their noses into my face, and seemed desirous of looking down my throat'.[1] More worrying than this unwanted attention was the fact that the majority of them seemed convinced that he was a Russian spy. They could not think what he could be doing wandering round the desert with a refugee from Geok Tepe and a dubious Kurd (his two servants or guides) unless he were spying out the route for an advancing Russian army – which was known to be all too close. On this occasion he was saved by a Persian visitor who 'having seen a little more of men and things than the nomads' firmly declared that he was not a Russian. Even when this suspicion was lifted, there were other hazards. A well-disposed local chief whispered to him that the greater number of his fellow camp-occupants

---

1. The tendency of Asians to seek closer physical proximity than Westerners are comfortable with is an enduring trait. Asian delegates frequently approach their Western counterparts to within inches of their faces when speaking to them in the delegates' lounge at the United Nations in New York, with the consequence that the Westerners tend to step backwards. When a film-maker recorded this process a few years ago, and showed his film in fast time, it appeared that the entire Western diplomatic corps was in rapid retreat in front of advancing oriental colleagues.

were thieves and that it was 'advisable to look very sharply after my horses [. . .] he had taken the precaution of chaining them together by the fetlocks'.

Having convinced his hosts that he was wanting to warn the inhabitants of Merv of the oncoming Cossacks and make the outside world aware of what was happening (the concept of a foreign correspondent was a totally novel one to them), he was eventually allowed to proceed on his way with four armed Turkomans to guard him. But like his earlier escort at Kelat, these less-than-intrepid companions soon abandoned him to his travels. At his next stopping place he was told tales of the quarrels between the Turkoman and Persian inhabitants of the desert he was crossing; his host explained at length what a generous-hearted man he was, because when the descendant of a Persian who had murdered his great-uncle fell into his hands, he refrained from killing him 'only cutting off his ears and nose, and chopping off his fingers in the middle'. O'Donovan confesses in his book that 'this disclosure of the amenities of border society [. . .] doubled my anxiety to make a final plunge [on to Merv]'.

And press on he did. Again he was allocated an escort, this time 'each of them as truculent-looking a fellow as I ever met with in any part of the world' (and O'Donovan had met a few truculent fellows among his fellow-prisoners and mercenaries). When they eventually came to the Tejend river, which was about fifty yards wide at that point, they found the fording of it quite a problem, the horses zig-zagging across to find the shallowest route and the men kneeling on their saddles with their supplies of tea and sugar on their shoulders to keep them dry. The waters were infested with otters and huge water rats. For the final stages of his journey it was necessary, for reasons of avoiding ambush, to travel whenever possible at night; sleep was difficult by day and interrupted at night; he was periodically soaked through his leopardskin wrap; when he did arouse himself for the next stage of the ride, he frequently found himself to be 'a peripatetic museum of entomology [. . .] there were juvenile tarantulas, stag beetles, lizard-like mantis' and other wildlife to be shaken off or combed out of his hair.

When he finally found himself approaching Merv, it proved to be a grave disappointment at first sight. He had expected a city of minarets and domes, fountains and elegant courtyards. What he found was a series of clusters of kibitkas (round felt tents not unlike Mongolian yurts). But if the city was a disappointment to him, he was not a disappointment to it. Crowds gathered to watch his approach, which must have been a fairly remarkable sight: he rode holding an umbrella (something unseen there before) over himself; he wore 'an enormous tiara of greyish-black sheepskin [on his head . . .] over my shoulders was a drenched leopard skin [. . .] my legs were comparisoned in long black boots armed with great steel spurs, appendages utterly unknown in Turkestan [. . .] a sabre and revolving carbine completed my outfit'. He knew he looked bizarre, but had long ago given up any hope of passing himself off as a native of the region.

But the truly worrying aspect of his arrival was not that he looked bizarre, but that he looked as if he was a prisoner – booty being brought back from a desert raid. And the truculent-looking escort had suddenly transmogrified themselves into not so much a bodyguard as a group of warders. O'Donovan could hear them speculating among themselves about what they should do with him. 'How could anyone know that he was not a Russian? What will our friends say when we bring him among

them? Who knows but he has a brigade of Cossacks at his heels? What is his business here? Who knows but they will kill him at the first village?' For two hours he was kept waiting in the saddle in driving rain while these issues were debated among his escort; periodically some of the party looked daggers at him, and others 'seemed inclined to solve the matter there and then by finishing me off'. Fortunately, the more well-disposed towards him won the day, and he was permitted to proceed further towards the centre of the city.

Unimpressive as the city was, there was plenty of evidence of Merv being the crossroads of desert caravan routes from all over Central Asia: bales of silk, tea, tobacco and other merchandise from Bokhara and bound for Meshed lay stacked around the dusty tracks. He consoled himself with the thought that, whatever problems and dangers lay ahead for him, he had at least reached his long-sought destination: 'Here I was, at last, at the heart of the Turkoman territory. Let the future take care of itself'.

The debate about what was to be done with him continued when he reached another gathering. One local chief asked him directly who and what he was. He tried to explain 'the functions of a peripatetic literary man' and said that if he wrote a letter to the British agent at Meshed, and sent it by the caravan that was about to set out, confirmation would quickly be forthcoming of the innocent nature of his mission. But the mere suggestion of putting pen to paper 'was met by a shout of warning not to attempt to write a single word, or my throat would be immediately cut'. Writing things down and espionage were synonymous in the eyes of his hosts. Nonetheless, under cover of his mantle he did manage to jot down a few notes about his adventures: already he probably had a book in mind. But this was a dangerous occupation because 'fully a dozen eyes were watching me through crannies in the door and walls [of his hut]'.

The following day he was taken on to the very heart of Merv, the seat of the Tekke government, and lodged in a comfortable tent – captured from the Persians on an earlier campaign – where he was received by a mullah who was the brother of one of the khans, as the khan himself was away. The mullah treated him with a reserve which O'Donovan decided reflected the query hanging over his fate: was he about to have his throat cut as a spy, or was he to be considered an honoured guest who was the representative of a potential military ally? This doubt and curiosity about the nature of the Westerner – the first most of them had ever seen – who had so mysteriously appeared among them, extended to some thousands when the inhabitants of the oasis gathered around for a market day. People would crowd into his tent sitting on their heels 'gazing at me with the ludicrous eagerness which may be observed in baboons and apes when some unfamiliar object meets their eyes'. Fresh waves of sightseers arrived to stare at him, abandoning the market for this new diversion. So great was the crowd that the tent pegs got lifted and at one moment the whole tent collapsed on him, prompting the local police to intervene 'striking right and left with sticks' and upbraiding the visitors for their lack of manners towards a stranger.

This state of affairs went on day after day. O'Donovan wrote that he might be said during this time to be living in the interior of a much-patronized peep-show, in which he was the only object of attraction; the way he washed or combed his hair drew forth exclamations of surprise and interest from the spectators. But he had still not met the senior khan in whose brother's charge he was. The first indication that his condition was under review was a visit by the three other khans of Merv.

The first of these was Baba Khan, the chief of the Toktamish division of Turkomans. He was a short man with a cunning aspect, not improved by the fact that he had lost the use of one of his eyes due to the fierce sunlight and dust of the plains; he appeared to be sneering at O'Donovan's protestations that he was not a Russian and, even while ostensibly talking to the him, was in practice seeking the plaudits of the crowd; he pointedly referred to the proximity of the Russian army and the remoteness of the British.

The second khan was called Aman Niaz Khan and was chief of the Otamish people. He was less hostile; O'Donovan decided he 'was evidently more of a natural gentleman'. However, he suffered from all the symptoms of excessive opium consumption. He also was distinguished by wearing a white robe with splashes of bright colours which made him look from a distance as if he were wrapped in a Union Jack; the picture was completed by a carving-knife-like dagger stuck in his sash.

The third of the visiting khans was called Yussuf Khan and was the leader of the eastern division of the Merv Tekke people. He was only some fifteen years old and looked every inch a Tartar with a flat nose and high cheekbones; out of deference to his two older companions, he spoke little and gazed into space.

These were the rulers in whose hands it seemed that O'Donovan's fate rested. They interrogated him all day, repeating the same old weary questions, and then left him, while the crowd enjoyed this variant of the peep-show. His only comfort was a visit from an elderly Jewish merchant – one of the few living at Merv – who brought him a bottle of arrack and some almost-undrinkable wine to cheer him up in this anxious time.

It was only after sunset on the second day of these deliberations that another stranger entered the tent quite unannounced. This turned out to be Kadjar Khan, the missing khan whose mullah brother had been looking after him. O'Donovan decided that this patrician-looking figure was a spitting image of the bust of Julius Caesar in the British Museum. It was some while before he realized that he had met this khan before, in fact the previous year at Tehran where the khan had been a guest of the shah.

The days dragged by. There was not a moment of privacy. He was not able to leave the tent to walk around the oasis because – he was told – 'the dogs might bite you'. In effect he was a prisoner in a glass case. And then on the seventh day after his arrival a grand council of all the khans, chiefs and elders was convened to decide once and for all what O'Donovan's status should be: friend or foe. By then, he was entirely on his own as far as moral or physical support went: his guide from Geok Tepe had found relations at Merv and moved off to be with them, and his terrified Kurdish servant had collapsed in a drugged heap. Before finally succumbing to opium, this Kurd had done O'Donovan a considerable disservice by repeatedly declaring that the latter was an official representative of England 'with the British flag in my pocket [...] and about to summon from Kandahar endless legions of British troops'. O'Donovan's inability to live up to these expectations was to be the cause of much misunderstanding and embarrassment.

After the council of elders had been deliberating for an hour, O'Donovan was summoned to attend and give an account of himself. He was careful to come before the council wearing what were left of his European clothes, and although these were by now fairly bizarre he thought they would deflect any charges that he was in disguise. There was a general whispering buzz of expectation when he appeared. Then a giant of a man with a long white beard who was known as 'The Old Man of the Sword' roared at him the now all-too-familiar question: 'Who and what are you, and what brings you here?' He explained that he was 'a native of that part of Frangistan [western Europe] called England' and having come to report on the Russian campaign had fled before General Skobeloff's advancing army from Geok Tepe to Merv. He was asked for proof of this identity and produced some convincing papers, but it was then suggested that perhaps he had just murdered an Englishman and stolen these; he was asked to explain – no easy matter – the exact status of the East India Company; and there was general incredulity about the claim that England was ruled over by a woman. After an hour of such interrogation, he was led back to his tent and could hear his case being debated for a further half hour. When he was re-summoned, it was to be told he would not be killed, at least for the present, but would remain a prisoner until a message could be sent and a reply received from the British agent at Meshed.

Meanwhile he was moved into more comfortable accommodation, and felt sufficiently self-confident to be able to adopt native dress – a long crimson tunic of coarse Bokharan silk – which enabled him to move around with at least a little less obsessive attention from the locals; he now only had 'a following of not more than two hundred persons'. The risk of being attacked by dogs also seemed to have been forgotten.

But the real moment of relief came with the arrival of the reply from the British agent at Meshed. This confirmed that he was British and had no connection of any sort with the Russian military campaign. Although he was still under surveillance, he was now in comparative liberty. Indeed, the Kadjar Khan took him on a tour of the fortifications under construction and showed him the guns they had captured from the Persians and others. Some 8,000 local men were working on improving the fortifications, focused on their task by the perceived Russian advance. But O'Donovan was rather sceptical about the effectiveness of the defences – 'the smallest mountain gun would pierce as through cardboard' – and thought that any army with howitzers would annihilate the breastworks that were being so laboriously constructed and leave 'a gently sloping path to an assaulting column'. The captured guns were also in an awful state, having been used to fire such 'heterogeneous projectiles' that their barrels were eroded beyond repair; they were counting on traders' scale-weights from the bazaar to use as ammunition.

Almost the only feature in favour of the defence was the fact that internal wells could provide the water required during a siege. He ended up very disillusioned; having thought that the experience of Geok Tepe would have given the citizens of Merv a more realistic sense of what was required to resist the Russians, he now found quite to the contrary that 'each man thought that, armed with his curved brittle sabre, his antiquated, cumbrous muzzle-loader with its forked rest, a half pound of bad gunpowder, and the bullets he founded from the material dug up on the battle-fields of his ancestors, he was amply provided with all the necessities of war'.

It is clear O'Donovan now identified himself with the inhabitants of Merv in opposition to the Russian invaders. Any traces there might once have been of an impartial reporter were long since abandoned. The local khans too, however ambivalent in their former attitude towards him, were also becoming convinced he was now wholly on their side. One of the three khans in fact suggested that O'Donovan should take command of their rickety artillery in the event of an attack. He responded politely by standing up and bowing profoundly, but he added for the record that he felt he 'might accept the position of artillerist-in-chief without in the least compromising my national neutrality'. Few in London would have agreed with this last statement: O'Donovan was again getting out of step with the British establishment.

Ironically, it was only now that he was 'firmly established in the good graces' of the locals that he decided he wanted to get out of the place as quickly as possible. Perhaps he felt that there would be few survivors of a Russian assault and there were limits to the sacrifices he should make even for a good news story. He therefore wrote to the British agent at Meshed asking him to send a letter explaining that he was 'instantly required at

Meshed'; and he wrote a parallel letter to the British Minister at Tehran asking for his support also. A natural messenger for these letters presented himself in the form of his drug-addicted and recalcitrant Kurdish guide, who was only too glad of any excuse to get out of Merv. The local khans were happy to let him go, as they had long ago concluded that the Kurd would have no ransom value. The same was not the case with O'Donovan himself; he was only too aware that, however friendly they might now be, the local khans were not prepared to let him leave; he was part talisman, part hostage, part military adviser; he was going to need a very convincing reason for his eventual release from this Queen of the World city.

However much he might be in the good graces of his hosts, there were always occasional incidents which triggered the oft-repeated – but now rejected – charges about his being a Russian agent. One such incident arose when an elderly Russian officer from Circassia was captured and brought to Merv. He was wearing an Astrakhan hat and gold epaulettes which, taken together with his age, led his captors to assume that he was a general. As such he would be worth a handsome ransom and all those involved with his capture would be greatly enriched by the event. But O'Donovan knew from his experience of military matters that the gold epaulettes, with a single black stripe and a solitary silver star, were not those of a general (commanding an army) but of a second-lieutenant (commanding a platoon of twenty men). He explained this to the consternation of his hosts, who realized that the ransom value of their prisoner was drastically reduced by this knowledge. Their annoyance momentarily resuscitated the old accusations of his knowing suspiciously much about the Russian army; but these charges no longer stuck.

Events were now about to take an unexpected turn, and O'Donovan found himself in the thick of internal intrigues between the various khans. It transpired that Kadjar Khan, in whose tent he had been originally lodged and by whose brother he had been befriended, was not in reality a hereditary khan at all; he had been given the title to enable him to go to Persia and negotiate on behalf of the people of Merv in circumstances in which none of the other khans wished to go, because they feared they might end up as prisoners or hostages. Now the three other khans, who had all called on and interrogated O'Donovan before, turned to him for support in their plotting to re-establish their pre-eminent power. They were encouraged to do this by the fact that, having once decided O'Donovan was not a snake in the grass, they swung the other way and decided, with no justification beyond the exaggerated boasts of his Kurdish servant, that he was an influential emissary of the British government who could ensure not only financial support but also that British troops from Kandahar came to the rescue of Merv.

Kadjar Khan poured poisonous gossip into O'Donovan's ears: the other khans were really in league with the Russians, and if they resumed power 'his life would not be worth a moment's purchase'. However, Kadjar Khan did not endear himself to O'Donovan by taking advantage of the generally disturbed situation firstly to drop broad hints that he expected an expensive present, and then – when presented with a handsome silver casket containing jewels – rudely rejecting this and asking for its cash value in gold sovereigns instead. O'Donovan wryly comments: 'I had, at a bound, gained an enormous insight into the mental temperament of Turkoman chiefs'. One of the other rival khans who had seen what was going on observed: 'Sahib, you can see that Kadjar is no true Khan!'. The effect of his remark was however slightly spoiled when a moment later he dropped a heavy hint that he would like the silver casket for himself. These were just some of the incidents which were a prelude to the bloodless revolution that was to alter dramatically O'Donovan's standing. Suddenly everyone seemed to be seeking his support or goodwill. An outsize bottle of arrack arrived from the Toktamish chief. And a request for money from the keeper of a Russian prisoner was coupled with a message to the effect that 'I had only to say the word, and the throat of the captive would immediately be cut in my honour'. (O'Donovan was so disturbed by this last message that, even at the risk of appearing pro-Russian, he remonstrated that he would consider such an act the very reverse of an honour.) Kadjar Khan came and sat up all night with him talking politics and spreading slanders about his rivals for power.

The following day there was a council of the hereditary khans – excluding Kadjar – and O'Donovan was required to attend to answer questions, this time not about himself but about the likely course of international affairs. Were the Russians about to advance on Merv? He said, as nothing had happened so far, he thought not for the next few years. Were the British about to advance from Kandahar? He said he thought only if they went to war with Russia. What should the people of Merv do to preserve their independence? He said they should stop launching raids on their neighbours. Would the Queen of England be prepared to receive the people of Merv as her subjects? He said they should write via the British agent at Meshed to inquire. Would the queen send them breech-loading rifles and a cannon? He said she would, if they were her subjects, and that she would then send troops too. If the people of Merv were to stop launching raids, would the queen pay them a subsidy to make up for their loss of income? He said they had better ask that too. Having given all these answers, he again repeated that he had no authority to speak for the British government – a statement which they clearly thought was over-modest and inaccurate.

When he was accompanied away from the council, he was not taken back to his former tent, but was instead led to a new redoubt, some seventy yards square complete with a moat, which was being rapidly constructed by over a hundred men while half a dozen women were busy with the felt walls and roof. His saddles, arms and bedding had already been installed. His first thought was that he was being relocated to a more secure building to prevent him making a getaway. But he then noticed that instead of being addressed as formerly as 'sahib', he was now being called 'khan'. He inquired what was going on, and was told that the council of Merv had decided that, among the other changes they were making, he should henceforth be considered as the personal representative of the Queen of England and as such should be granted the dignity and rank of being one of the khans of Merv. The new redoubt was to be his palace. O'Donovan decided that, since all his protestations to the contrary had been of no avail, he could only go along with this: 'I simply bowed, as if it were only a matter of course'. He sat down on the special rug prepared for him and promptly fell asleep.

The reason behind the sudden elevation of O'Donovan to the rank of khan was of course that the other khans wished to establish some formal link with England which would ensure her support if and when the long-expected Russian advance materialized. Short of military support, financial support was the next best thing. And the people of Merv soon saw what they took to be evidence of this – evidence based on a very curious misapprehension.

At about this time O'Donovan received a package of newspapers from Tehran via Meshed. No one in Merv had seen newspapers before; in fact, almost the only printed paper they had seen had been some Russian bank notes captured near Geok Tepe. Being unfamiliar with paper money (silver was the coinage of use) they had at first been inclined to think the Russian paper money of no value, and had then been mystified and impressed by a streetwise Jewish dealer buying up the notes for almost nothing and later exchanging them with a visiting caravan for goods of substantial worth. If such small pieces of printed paper were really of such high value, surely, they argued, these large (broadsheet) pages of newsprint must be worth a fortune? Was not this the first evidence of the British exchequer sending substantial material backing to the beleaguered people of Merv? O'Donovan did his best to disillusion them by explaining that the vast printed pages were conveying information – news – rather than incorporating intrinsic value. But the inhabitants of the oasis were almost as unfamiliar with the concept of news as they were with the concept of paper money. He was thought to be playing down the significance of the package he had received, possibly to safeguard it. It was only when later they saw 'the heterogeneous purposes to which this paper was applied, and the total disregard which I showed for it' that they began to accept that he was not in receipt of a sudden fortune. But still they had high hopes of material British support.

In a different sense altogether, the newspapers did give substance to the concept of Britain being a valuable ally, because these papers brought news of British successes in the Second Afghan War. With General Roberts and a British army at

Kandahar, the Russians at Geok Tepe seemed a less imminent menace. In these more relaxed circumstances, O'Donovan was able to persuade his hosts to take him on a visit to the ancient ruins of the former cities of Merv, which lay less than a day's ride from the existing capital. On such rides through the desert, he was disconcerted to witness how the warriors from Merv would dash at full gallop through settlements of their own tribesmen, terrifying all in their wake, purely for the purpose of exercising their military and equestrian skills. He was obliged to participate in these mad charges because, if he had loitered behind, he would have fallen into the hands of the frightened and enraged villagers, who would have taken their revenge on him. But when asked by his hard-riding hosts whether such amusing exercises were carried out in Western countries, he told them in no uncertain terms that they were not, and then fell silent. They appeared to get the message and in future saved their energies for attacking real enemies. O'Donovan was beginning to have some influence.

He was soon to have an opportunity to use this influence because, shortly after his visit to the ancient ruins, a formal ceremony was set up by which he was not only installed as a khan of Merv but invited to advise about their foreign and domestic policy. All his protestations about not being a formal representative of Britain having been brushed aside, a flag pole was erected outside his new residence with a bright crimson silk banner floating from it; this – he was told – was both an emblem of his office and 'supposed to represent the English flag'. The hoisting of the flag was intended to indicate the formal adhesion of the Merv nation to the British government. Rich carpets were spread around and when the other two khans joined him in council, one of them 'took from his finger a singular looking ring and placed it upon mine'. They then invited him to speak publicly, both to them and to the listening crowd which had assembled. It was a strange privilege.

O'Donovan was well aware that part of his influence stemmed from the fact that, quite coincidentally, the Russian advance towards Merv had been halted just at the moment when he arrived at the oasis. With the authority that this gave him, and with the audience set up for him, he decided to make the most of the opportunity. He reminded them that there was very little use in putting themselves under the protection of England unless they ensured that news of their gesture had been communicated to the Queen of England. He suggested a further channel for such communication – a formal document adorned with seals and transmitted by their own ambassador at Tehran to the British minister.

The next point that he emphasized was that they must ward off anything provoking hostilities with Russia, and he reminded them that most of the other khanates and emirates of Central Asia had, at least in part, brought their ill fate upon themselves by continuing to launch raids across the Russian frontier and against passing caravans. If they wished to deflect a Russian invasion they must not fight or harass her either as a state or privately by individual raids. He reminded them that Bokhara was already under Russian protection, so attacks on such a neighbour were equally taboo. Holding prisoners was a further provocation.

At this stage he was interrupted by a member of the assembly who angrily interjected, 'How in the name of Allah were they going to live if raids could not be made?' O'Donovan replied that if they were overrun by Russia they would have all their raiding stopped, so they might as well learn to stop it first and so avoid being overrun. He went on to say that trade was the answer: the ancient cities whose ruins he had just visited were built on the proceeds of legitimate trade with passing caravans, and Merv could thus regain the lost glories of earlier times and be once more Queen of all the World! They should take advantage of the fact that Russia had halted her advance at Ashkhabad and Britain had halted hers at Kandahar. (Little did he know that within a year Russia was to send a trading caravan to spy out the land, and follow it with an invasion force.[2])

After this very public meeting, some heed seems to have been taken of O'Donovan's advice: attempts were made to impose charges on passing caravans instead of turning a blind eye to the plunder, and a long-standing Russian prisoner-of-war was released from his shackles. The same prisoner was eventually brought under escort to see him, and he discovered that, as he had thought, the prisoner was a humble artillery man and neither a senior officer nor the son of a Russian general as they had been led to believe. The misunderstanding of his rank and significance as a hostage, which had led to exorbitant and unrealistic ransom demands, was at least in part the fault of the prisoner himself who (although only aged seventeen at the time of his capture) had claimed to his captors that he was more important than was the case, in the hope of better treatment. After O'Donovan had explained that there was no hope of the Russians paying up the sort of sum demanded, and that his continued detention and bad treatment (he had been tortured) could only prove a provocation and excuse for further aggression, he was eventually set free near the Russian frontier. Though still implacably opposed to tsarist policies, O'Donovan

---

2. For details of that expedition, see the author's book *Shooting Leave* (2009).

was sufficiently humane to come to the aid of individual distressed Russians; perhaps his own various times in prison had given him a certain sympathy with all prisoners – whether criminals or prisoners-of-war.

Popular celebrations also took place following the public meeting, with horse racing and wrestling matches. For the latter the khans (now of course including O'Donovan) had to present prizes. They also had to present each other with gifts, and this was becoming a problem for O'Donovan since 'I was at the end of my selection of presents brought out from Meshed, and all my European goods had long since been given away'. However, he scratched around and managed to find a prismatic compass for one of the other khans, and he dipped into his remaining supply of silver coinage. It was not only his fellow khans who looked for gifts on such a festive occasion: everyone from the town-crier, itinerant poets and 'hook-nosed ruffians [. . .] like stage brigands', all lined up for presents, tips or merely to gorge themselves at his expense on glasses of arrack and portions of freshly slaughtered mutton. Their appetites seemed insatiable, as most of the inhabitants of the oasis were permanently hungry.

Despite all the caveats that O'Donovan had expressed about not being an official representative of the Queen of England, the people of Merv were determined to make use of him in every possible way as an emblem and guarantor of British support. Realizing that the scarlet banner they had erected outside his redoubt was not in fact the national flag of Great Britain, they invited him to design a Union Jack which they would then arrange for their ladies to embroider to replace the existing banner. He was wary of doing this as he thought it might amount to 'an unauthorized hoisting of the British flag' which could lead to accusations of attempted colonization, so he asked that this too should be referred to the British minister at Tehran for authority. But he was less successful in preventing the usage of a branding iron – inscribed with VR and surmounted by an imperial crown – being used on the local horses in the hope that if they were stolen or captured it would indicate a measure of protection by the Queen of England (Victoria Regina). In the event, they forgot to reverse the design and applied it upside down, so it would have been unlikely to convey any meaning to anyone.

On all counts, O'Donovan was now being treated as part of the establishment in Merv, 'as naturalized among them'. He had become so proficient at talking about Islamic doctrine that one of the mullahs called on him and asked why he should not now openly embrace the true faith. The mullah promised that once he had acknowledged that he was a Moslem 'we will find you another wife here, or two if you wish'. It was clear that they assumed O'Donovan had a wife at home – 'they could not believe it was possible I was unmarried' – so he used this imagined wife as an excuse for not following up the kind suggestion of conversion and the acquiring of more wives. The Christian religion forbade it, he explained, and he could not betray his existing wife.

This approach, like others, was all part of his hosts' plan to stop him leaving Merv. Having decided in their own minds that he was a representative of the British government, they saw his presence among them 'as a kind of security for the co-operation of England', and were determined he should not leave unless or until another such representative came to live among them. In any case, they could not see why – when O'Donovan had faced such risks and dangers to reach them – he should now consider going away. He himself knew, from news reports reaching him from Meshed, that the British were already considering with-drawing from Kandahar; he thought that if this were to happen the rulers of Merv might react very badly; they would feel more vulnerable to Russian attack and they would blame O'Donovan – a situation that 'might possibly terminate fatally for myself'.

From now on, he was therefore determined to get away. He requested the British agent at Meshed to write again, this time explaining that his temporary presence was required there for a short meeting. When such a letter arrived, the other khans argued that surely any business could be conducted by correspondence and it was not necessary to go to Meshed in person. O'Donovan pointed out that other envoys (those of Persia and Bokhara) were allowed to come and go freely, and any detention of him would be taken as evidence of bad faith by the British authorities. The determination of the khans to keep him in Merv was graphically illustrated when he tried to join a mounted expedition to reinforce the frontier with Persia when a 'genuine border fray bade fair to take place'. Ever the frustrated war correspondent, O'Donovan was anxious to witness and report on the event. But the other khans would not let him go, saying that his life was too precious to be put at risk, but in reality fearing that he might do a runner if he got too close to the Persian border.

Matters got worse when the British agent at Meshed sent three letters to Merv, addressed to different people and all saying very different things about the possible alliance of Merv to Britain or Persia. Predictably, all three letters fell into the hands of Baba Khan, who was furious at the apparent double-crossing and who stormed in to O'Donovan saying 'The British Agent at Meshed is a traitor [. . .] you must have no dealings whatever with him [. . .] he is evidently in the pay of the Persians'. From now on it was going to be necessary for him to get any letter – extricating him from Merv – direct from the British minister in Tehran, and an exchange of messages would take at least a month. He wasted no time in getting off such a letter requesting the minister should 'attach to his reply seals and signatures which they [the other khans at Merv] could understand, and whose importance they could realize'. In the meantime and while still waiting for an answer from Tehran, some of the old caravan-raiding practices were resumed, and O'Donovan threatened to pull down his scarlet banner and break off all relations between Britain and Merv. He was looking for any pretext to leave before the British withdrawal from Afghanistan became public knowledge.

One of the reasons why the other khans would not give their consent to his leaving was that they all thought they stood to benefit from the presents that he was still expected to distribute. He therefore decided he would declare himself broke: no longer able to hand out largesse to the more distinguished citizens, no longer able to feed the hungry mob who frequented his redoubt on a daily basis, unable even to support himself and his horse. He put it about that his horse was for sale, and he and his horse went without food for a whole day. As he anticipated, this thoroughly embarrassed the other khans. They levied a compulsory contribution on the leading local citizens, obliging them to provide for their 'guest khan'. O'Donovan felt that a mixture of embarrassment and meanness would soon persuade one and all that he should be allowed to go on his way.

Until that came about, or until a message summoning him to Meshed was received from the British minister in Tehran, he tried to pass the time by writing up his notes – the notes that were to be the foundation of his two-volume, thousand-page account of his adventures. But not even this was easy. Although he was no longer suspected of espionage whenever he wrote anything down, the constant stream of curious visitors never left him alone for a moment, and his supplies of ink and paper soon ran out. The final straw was when he found one of his servants using his last steel pen nib to remove a thorn from his foot. What entries he did manage to make in his notebook were ever more vitriolic about the manners and practices of the Mervli (the people of Merv).

Some time in June 1881 (exact dates were beyond the calculation of the Mervli) when O'Donovan had already been some six months at Merv, the long-awaited reply from the British minister at Tehran was received and delivered with much ceremony by the other two khans to his redoubt. It was along the lines O'Donovan had requested. While stating that he was not 'an emissary of the British government, but an agent of the British public' it went on to say firmly that 'it is now both desirable and expedient that you should send Mr O'Donovan at once to this country in order that he may personally communicate to me such information as may have been furnished to him during his stay at Merv'. Baba Khan declared he was at liberty to go when he pleased, but then added in the same breath that there would have to be a council of elders called first. This would cause another week or two's delay at least, during all of which time he felt more like a hostage than an envoy. Finally, in exasperation, O'Donovan declared he was going to leave in three days' time, and if stopped would 'haul down my flag as a declaration of war'. He was helped by the fact that rumours had reached the oasis of Cossack patrols surveying the road eastwards across the desert; this looked like the precursor of more trouble. O'Donovan seized on the reports and announced that the reason why he had to reach Meshed so quickly was because a meeting of European ambassadors had been convened to decide the new frontier and frustrate the Russian plans. It was essential he was there. No one else could both speak English and convey the concerns of Merv. Even then, it was a close run thing: he had to distribute a final delivery of silver coins to his fellow khans as a sweetener, and he had to disregard an impassioned plea to the effect that the ladies of Merv would lament his departure.

The council of elders, to which O'Donovan was summoned to make his case for the last time, lasted six hours. He thought that among the elements urging his release were a few covert Russian sympathizers; they did not want a British agent continuing to haunt the oasis. Be that as it may, the verdict was in his favour. Even after this decision, there were endless prevarications and delays. If he left now would he be intercepted by Cossack patrols? Should he not postpone his departure till more farewell presents were ready? (In the end he was given eight magnificent Tekke Turkoman carpets, on which he had to pay duty when he arrived in Persia.) A last-minute gift was a suit of chain armour and 'a huge steel helmet like a dish cover'. Considerations of practicality before a long desert ride do not seem to have occurred to his hosts. He for his part gave away the small menagerie he had assembled during his six-month stay: a tame antelope, a ger-falcon, a jackal and some wolf cubs.

When eventually they mounted and rode away from the oasis he had an armed escort of some fifty warriors, who reduced themselves to thirty before the end of the journey. The escort slowed down the pace of the journey so much that at times he feared they were deliberately marking time in the expectation of being overtaken by a messenger demanding his return to Merv for some spurious reason. There were however a couple of days when he was quite glad of the gentler pace, because he had been stung by a scorpion and developed a mild fever. There were also the periodical alarms which were a part of any journey across Central Asian deserts and tamarisk jungles: 'in the midst of the thicket we heard the tramp of many hoofs, and all prepared their arms'. This particular scare turned out to be caused by an innocent group of donkey men who had been equally scared by O'Donovan's party. In another encounter with some caravan camel-drivers it was revealed that they were much alarmed by the current Cossack movements in the region, and thought it was wholly irresponsible of O'Donovan to be leaving Merv at such a moment: 'had it not been for my formidable array of Tekke horsemen, these caravan people would have seized upon me bodily and brought me back [to Merv]'. Another caravan they encountered had a package of letters for O'Donovan, bringing the dreaded news that the British were indeed withdrawing from Kandahar; this made him doubly glad he was well quit of Merv before the unwelcome news reached the khans there. But there were happier aspects of the journey too: the banks of the Tejend river were alive with pheasants which provided much-welcome game for the pot; the reeds along the riverside provided comfortable bedding; and there was enough wood to light big fires at night designed to keep away the mosquitoes by the smoke, and by the flames to deter the attentions of the leopards and tigers that were known to frequent the more jungly regions. Their final problem was being mistaken for a bunch of desert marauders by the sentries at the outskirts of the Persian city of Meshed. This overcome, they had arrived. O'Donovan was once more a free man.

After a short period of recuperation, he went on from Meshed to Tehran and then returned via Odessa and Constantinople to

England. Although he received various communications from the khans of Merv before he left Meshed, informing him of approaches by Russian agents and reminding him that 'the tribes of Merv firmly grasped the skirt of submission to the Queen of England', he neither wrote back with advice nor contemplated returning to Merv. For him, this chapter was closed.

But as if his adventures had not been enough, the intrepid war correspondent then signed up to go for the *Daily News* to the Sudan, where the Mahdi had recently emerged as both an extremist Islamic leader and a threat to British and Egyptian interests. So it came about that he was with the Egyptian expeditionary force sent up the Nile under command of Hicks Pasha when they were massacred in November 1883. At his death O'Donovan was just thirty-nine years old.

O'Donovan had broken all the rules in his Central Asian escapade. He had put himself in a position where his capture by the Russian army of General Skobeloff would have been an embarrassment to his own government. He had allowed himself, despite protestations to the contrary, to be unjustifiably hailed as a representative of the British government and of the Queen of England and Empress of India. He had been seen as an earnest of his government's intention to intervene in Central Asia to protect the independence of a Turkoman khanate (Merv), whereas in reality Lord Granville, the British foreign secretary of the day, had no wish to risk a confrontation with a major European power such as tsarist Russia. He had been the sort of war correspondent that, in the eyes of generals and politicians, cause more trouble than they are worth. But even if his sudden and unexpected appearance in Merv had not – as the other khans of Merv liked to believe – stopped the Russian advance dead in its tracks, his presence there for more than six months had at least temporarily stiffened resistance to further Russian incursions. He had been a brake on the Cossack troika careering across the steppes. In short, he had earned a place in the pantheon of players in the Great Game.

Chapter 11

Ney Elias: The Odd Man Out

'We shall not cease from exploration
And the end of all our exploring
Will be to arrive where we started
And know the place for the first time.'

— T. S. Eliot (1888–1965)

When two travellers, carrying a considerable sum of money, were murdered outside the eastern Persian city of Meshed in 1892, the local authorities accused three Turkomans working for the British consul-general of committing the crime and set about trying to arrest and charge them. It transpired that all three Turkomans had watertight alibis, but that the Russian consul-general had instigated the charges, claiming that the accused were Russian citizens working as spies for his rival for power and influence – the British consul-general. It was a deep laid plot which was only unravelled by the assiduous work and ingenuity of the British consul-general himself, who was convinced by evidence he had that the money the murdered travellers had been carrying was intended to finance the sending of a tsarist secret agent into Herat in Afghanistan. The British official also discovered that his correspondence with the Persian government was being intercepted and read by his Russian rival. The whole affair was deeply sinister and called for action on a much more sensitive and sophisticated level than was usual with the conduct of consular affairs. This was espionage and intrigue on an international scale.

The British consul-general concerned had the strange name of Ney Elias. He was an unusual figure to be a British consul, and he was also very different on a number of grounds from his fellow protagonists in this book. He was modest and self-effacing to the degree that – unlike most of the other explorers and adventurers of his day – he did not write any popular accounts of his travels and exploits. There were no two-volume best-sellers to tell the world of his achievements, only a series of official (and usually confidential) reports to the Foreign Office in London or the viceroy's office in India, or else scholarly articles (frequently anonymous) in the journals of the Royal Geographical Society and other learned bodies.

At first sight he might appear scarcely eligible to join the ranks of British adventurers who confronted tsarist Russia and who acted in defiance or disregard of their official instructions. But on closer inspection he was eligible on all grounds. Despite his name, British he was; his parents were both from well-established Jewish families and he was born in Bristol in 1844; when he was still a young child, both his parents renounced their Jewish faith and became Christians and Ney himself, in later life, was to resent being labelled as Jewish (which he inevitably was in Victorian England on account of his origins and name). That he was an adventurer is also beyond dispute, as even the briefest study of his exploits throughout Central Asia will confirm. That he confronted tsarist Russia will emerge clearly, particularly when one considers the later part of his career as an agent of the Indian government and a British consul in such posts as Leh and Meshed, where his entire raison d'être was to attempt to contain and undo the aggressive and often nefarious activities of his Russian opposite numbers. Less easy to establish is, perhaps, his character as a maverick operator who acted independently of official guidance and authority; but there are clear instances when he was to do this, trusting his own judgement rather than that of his superiors.

Elias had the advantage of a very cosmopolitan education: he went to school in London, Paris and Dresden, and was soon adding oriental languages to his grasp of European ones. After starting his professional life working in the family business in Shanghai, he concluded early on that, despite his ancestry, commerce was not for him. Taking advantage of his foothold in the Far East, he turned his mind to exploration. It was known that the Yellow River had changed its course, but it was not until Elias made a number of exploratory trips into the region that the new course was mapped and identified. He was already a Fellow of the Royal Geographical Society (RGS), and he received the congratulations of the Society on this achievement.

An even more remarkable journey was to follow, which confirmed his standing as an explorer. He set off for 2,500 miles through Mongolia and across the Gobi desert into Russia, and then a further 2,000 miles across Russia to Nijni Novgorod (later named Gorky) which was the terminus of the railway from Moscow and St Petersburg. In fact, he was traversing the famous Silk Route from east to west, most previous European travellers having gone in the opposite direction. His objectives were to try to find the ruins of Karakoram (the capital of Genghis Khan's son) and, more importantly, to visit Ili, a Chinese settlement on the Silk Route which had been overrun by Russian forces, and to find out what was going on there. Was it a sinister new probe by the Cossacks?

From the outset, the Chinese were very suspicious of his intentions. Was he charting a route for an invasion force? The only available maps were very inaccurate Russian ones, and Elias found that he could not be seen correcting these or drawing his own maps without risking being stopped in his tracks. He had to do all his cartography at night by candlelight. He was a conspicuous stranger: declining to wear local dress, refusing to pose as a holy man or missionary, not speaking any Mongolian, and not even having the rudimentary medical skills that often helped ensure a safe passage for Westerners. In all this he was unlike most of his fellow-countrymen players of the Great Game; he was indeed an odd man out.

His main problem however was that he was entering a war zone. The Moslem population was in open revolt against the Chinese and were moving round the Gobi in large rebel gangs intent on plunder and disruption. And his was a vulnerably small party, consisting of just four men, six camels and two ponies. To make matters worse, he was only able to start later than was sensible, in September, when harsh winter conditions were sure to set in while they were still in the Gobi desert. Although they encountered large flocks of wild sheep and herds of wild horses and gazelle, by the time they reached the all-important wells, which were often not much more than muddy pools, these were often dried out or drunk dry by the passing flocks and herds. The camels managed to survive on minimal sustenance, but the men and horses were in dire straits. The temperature fell below the lowest point that their thermometer could register.

Despite all these hazards and difficulties, Elias kept meticulous records of the heights of the hills, the bearings of the tracks, and the boiling point of his kettles. He was collecting just the sort of geographical information that his Chinese hosts had

SABRES ON THE STEPPES

feared he would. The guide he had recruited proved useless, 'more or less an imposter', and relied for any sense of direction on the camel driver, who could not be expected to know the route. But worse was to come: the useless guide (who was also supposed to be an interpreter) slipped away in the night, taking with him a large share of the remaining provisions. Now there was no one who could explain to whoever they encountered – be it Mongol settlers, rebel bands or Chinese garrisons – who they were, what they were doing, or why they should not be arrested or taken hostage. As three hungry and scruffy travellers, they must have looked like vagabonds or people on the run. Elias recorded that 'it was only by a constant parade of arms and the most careful vigilance by day and night that a collision [disastrous encounter] was avoided'. Indeed, the fact that he survived at all was attributed by the Chinese garrisons to his having some sort of 'improper understanding' with the Moslem rebels to protect him: if he was safe, he was suspect.

But he had one stroke of extraordinary good luck. When he reached the Mongol settlement of Kobdo on the edge of the Altai mountains which formed the western fringe of the Gobi desert, he found it had been attacked by two hundred Moslem rebels just three days before. They had scared the garrison into thinking they were a much larger force, by driving a thousand camels ahead of them. Although the garrison consisted of nearly two thousand Chinese infantry and cavalry, this body of not very gallant men had retreated into their fortress and watched while the rebels pillaged the settlement and slaughtered the merchants and other Mongol inhabitants. If Elias and his tiny party had been there any earlier they would undoubtedly have been among the unrecorded victims.

As it was, the frightened survivors and garrison of Kobdo

refused to allow Elias entry to their settlement, and he camped outside without food or firewood until an old Mongol woman appeared and offered to act as a go-between. Once admitted within the walls, Elias and his party were fortunate not to have been dubbed as agents of the rebels and summarily executed – as had happened to most visitors who could not give a proper account of themselves. They were provided with a minimum of food, water and firewood and dispatched on their way with all haste: even if they were not enemy agents, such a dubious little party heading for Russia was an embarrassment as well as a drain on resources.

When eventually they reached the Russian frontier, after eighty days of marching in all, they were still not out of danger. The border region was infested with Kazak sheep stealers and horse and cattle rustlers. The prudent Elias had already taken the precaution of obtaining a Russian visa, so once inside that country he was able to join up with other caravans and even make use of the troika-driven sleighs which acted as the official mail carriers. He had another two thousand miles to go, mostly round the southern edge of Siberia, and still in winter, before he reached Nijni Novgorod, the longed-for railhead. He had not managed to discover the extent of the Russian military activity at Ili, but he had acquired a vast compendium of knowledge of potential strategic value. It was little wonder that for the completion of such a journey, even if his designated objectives had not been formally achieved, he was awarded the Founder's Medal of the RGS.

Having by now renounced his business career, and having established his reputation as an intrepid traveller, Elias now needed some regular and gainful employment. He was therefore fortunate that Sir Henry Rawlinson, the president of the RGS, arranged for him to be taken on by the government of British India. His early appointments included assignments in Calcutta and Mandalay, from where he joined a mission to open up trade between Burma and China. Plans for an expedition to Tibet failed to materialize in 1876, and the following year he was attached to another abortive mission, this time to Kashgar. By now, Elias was beginning to become preoccupied with Russian expansionism and intentions in Central Asia, and particularly with their bearing on the security of India.

He was therefore gratified to be appointed to a post where he could spend more of his time and energies on countering this growing Russian influence. The post in question was a curious one: he was to be an agent of the Indian government and a 'joint commissioner' at Leh in Ladakh, from which listening post he would be expected to report on developments in Kashgar (where the Chinese had recently re-established their control after the death of the Islamic ruler Yakub Beg). The task was not made easier by the fact that Kashgar was some four hundred miles north of Leh and the other side of the formidable Karakoram mountain range with its precipitous pass.

It was now that he began to set out on unauthorized missions of his own initiative. He made contact independently with the Chinese official resident in Yarkand (north of the Karakorams) but even so it was some time before he heard the news of Yakub Beg's death – he was said to have been poisoned by his enemies – and of the Chinese takeover, as all caravans took nearly two months to cross over the passes between Leh and Yarkand. But distant and inaccessible as Kashgar, Yarkand and Leh were from each other, it was still the case that all the caravans going to India from western China came by this route, so Elias was well placed to pick up the news, gossip and intelligence that flowed with the merchandise and caravan traffic. He also had the full support of the viceroy, Lord Lytton, who wrote to the secretary of state for India expounding the merits of Elias and thus managed to procure for him a permanent place in the Indian civil service without going through 'the usual channels'. This was

an exceptional, if not unique, preferment.

But despite his good relations with the viceroy, Elias did not wait for official instructions or authority to take off on his trans-Karakorum mission to Yarkand and Kashgar. Ostensibly, the reason for his expedition was a commercial one: to see for himself the problems of establishing a profitable trade route and to find out why the traffic was so slow. In reality his reasons were far more political and military: to determine whether or not the route was a viable one for an invading army – and the army he had in mind being not a Chinese one but a Russian one. He did not have much difficulty in finding out why the commercial caravan traffic was so sporadic: there were no less than five narrow passes of over 15,000 feet altitude to be crossed, the highest being the Karakorum at nearly 19,000 feet; some of the passes were no more than narrow clefts in the rock where both mules and camels had to be unloaded before they could squeeze through. If trade caravans were a problem, Elias was comforted by the thought that there could be no question of an army with artillery and heavy equipment passing that way.

When he reached Yarkand, Elias had extensive talks with the Amban (the local Chinese government representative) and emphasized the British wish not only for good commercial relations but also for close political links. He took the opportunity to listen sympathetically to Chinese complaints about the Russians stirring up rebellion among the Tungan tribesmen and about their permitting Kirghiz tribesmen to make raids across the border into what was now again a western province of China. The Chinese clearly felt that the Russians were pressing in on their frontiers, and Elias lost no time in capitalizing on this feeling, which reflected his own concern over the long-term threat this posed to British India. He also managed to recruit a local agent who could send him ongoing reports about these border matters. He took the opportunity of his visit to be the first to congratulate the Chinese on the recovery of their lost province, thereby scoring a diplomatic point over the Russians. Elias had hoped to move on from Yarkand to Kashgar and have further talks there. But no firm invitation arrived and so – thinking it would be a mistake to arrive with no credentials and no invitation – he returned the way he had come. All in all, it had been a useful visit and one that had been entirely on his own initiative.

Elias was to make two further trips to Yarkand and reached Kashgar in 1880. He found that anti-Russian feelings had increased, and he was approached about the possibility of buying arms from India for use against any possible Russian incursions. Indeed, there were more ambitious hopes in London and Calcutta that the British and Chinese might cooperate in other military matters; there was talk of attaching British Indian-army officers to the Chinese to help train their troops in Kashgar; there was even a proposal that some Chinese units might be commanded by British officers. Elias was highly sceptical about these ideas. He had seen something of Chinese troops – they had provided a sloppy, chattering and abusive guard of honour for him at Yarkand – and he commented in his private journal, 'These are the people we are asked to ally ourselves with against the Russians – Ye Gods!'. He could think of better ways to pursue the Great Game.

While still based at Leh, Elias had continued to collect and collate intelligence received from his numerous visitors from all over Central Asia; perched at this junction of caravan routes he had, like Sir Walter Bullivant in John Buchan's *Greenmantle*, 'heard reports from agents everywhere – pedlars in South Russia, Afghan horse-dealers, Turkoman merchants, pilgrims on the road to Mecca, sheep-skinned Mongols, Hindu fakirs, as well as respectable consuls whom use cyphers'; all these reports confirmed that, whatever the likely problems of launching an invasion through the Karakoram or Pamir mountain ranges, the Russians were far from giving up their ambitions in the region. He learnt from such sources as these and from his own agents how the Russians had sent spies into Hunza and Chitral (near the Indian, now Pakistani, border with Afghanistan and China). Elias was strongly in favour of a British agent being appointed at Kashgar, and doubtless saw himself in that role. But Lord Lytton's successor as viceroy of India was of a cautious disposition: Lord Ripon opposed the idea of such an appointment and even was reluctant to authorize any further exploration. It was therefore only in 1885 (after his return from sick leave in England and Lord Ripon's recall) that Elias was able to embark on his next great adventure.

This was a journey over the Pamirs and along the upper Oxus river. It was an undertaking he had been quietly planning for years from Leh. He made a survey of over 500 miles from the Chinese frontier to that part of Afghanistan where there had always been controversy about the main stream of the Oxus. In helping to define this, he also helped to define the contentious frontiers between Russia, China and Afghanistan on which the peace of the region largely depended. The main recommendation in his report was that China and Afghanistan should establish a common frontier which cut off Russia from the Hindu Kush; the so-called Wakham Corridor (a narrow strip of land belonging to Afghanistan between Russia in the north and India in the south) was an essential ingredient in any solution, and Elias was anxious to reconnoitre it, but the various boundary commissions that had been set up greatly complicated his task.

By any standards, Elias had by now done great service to the British Raj. Other boundary arbitrators had been knighted; other explorers had been knighted, and other diplomatic officials left in remote and lonely stations were to be knighted in the next few years. Knighthoods were distributed generously by the queen and her viceroy at the high-water-mark of the British Empire – far more so than in modern times. There were two distinct orders of chivalry devoted exclusively to India: the Order of the Star of India (which was awarded to Indian princes and an elite of British officials) and the Order of the Indian Empire (which was awarded to lesser officials). The lowest rung of the latter order was that of Commander: C.I.E. This was the award that it was deemed right to give to Elias at this juncture. He thought otherwise. He wrote to a colleague who had learnt of his award before he had and addressed him with his new initials after his name: 'I hope I have not been made the victim of any such damning mark of faint praise'. He declined to accept the order.

It is difficult to judge at this distance of time whether he was justified in responding so negatively and ungraciously. Part of the reason for his not being offered a higher award was undoubtedly that he had always been a very private person; he had not indulged in self-glorification in his reports of his achievements; he had not written popular books which might have drawn him to the attention of a wider readership and converted him into a public figure. But it seems all too likely there was also another underlying reason for his failure to achieve more elevated recognition: although Elias had converted with his family to Christianity, he was still thought of by many as a Jew; his Jewish surname and strange first name would not have resonated readily with a title. Although England had accustomed herself over the past decades to a Jewish prime minister in Benjamin Disraeli, there was still a strong latent anti-Semitism, particularly among the ranks of imperial administrators. Be that as it may, his unusual behaviour in rejecting an honour did not seem to impede his subsequent career.

His next appointments were somewhat out of line with his previous role in containing Russia in Central Asia. He was sent on special duty to Sikkim, and later to the Burma-Siam frontier. But by 1891 he was installed in a post that completely fulfilled his ambitions to counter the spread of Russian influence on the fringes of the British Raj, and which also enabled him to use all his previous experience and skills to good advantage. He was appointed as agent of the viceroy of India in Meshed and simultaneously consul-general of Britain in the surrounding Persian provinces of Khorasan and Seitan. This region of Persia had previously been dominated by tsarist influences, and it was Elias's role to redress the balance. But as well as this general objective, there were many more specific tasks to be accomplished in the field of intelligence gathering and espionage which were to exercise all his ingenuity.

One of the first of Elias's objectives was to impress the Persian government and community by building a consular residence that would not only match but would outshine the Russian consul-general's spacious accommodation. He was helped in this aim by the remarks – both in his book and in letters to *The Times* – of George Curzon (the future Lord Curzon and viceroy of India) who had noted on passing through the previous year that the British residence was a discredit to a great imperial power. With this support, Elias got a handsome and colonnaded British residence constructed, into which he promptly moved. His prestige was also helped by the secondment of a personal escort of mounted cavalry in the colourful uniforms of the Queen's Own Corps of Guides. These measures helped him establish himself as a person of respect, but were to prove the least challenging of his tasks.

The Russians had perfected the art of intriguing behind the backs of the British. His Russian counterpart, Consul-General de Vlassow (whose rank equated with that of a major-general), had already set up a network of spies and agents who reported to him not only on developments inside Persia but along the frontier with Afghanistan in the east. He was also engaged in infiltrating Russian troops and railway engineers in Trans-Caspian Russia, which lay directly to the north of Meshed. To assist in this process, and to avoid detection, de Vlassow arranged for all the Indian traders and clerks ('babus') to be expelled from Trans-Caspian territory; this action caused so much upset and offence that he had to rescind the order eventually. His objective in all this was to pave the way for such an expansion of tsarist influence that, when the time was deemed ripe, a Russian army could quietly advance across this hinterland to the very frontiers of the British Raj. Insider knowledge and influence was seen as the key to later aggression.

Elias was a match for his Russian opponent. He too set up a network of native agents and of 'newswriters' (reporters) who not only sent him their own version of developments, but who also managed to detect the machinations of Persian officials who had been seduced or suborned by the Russians. One of their nefarious schemes which he uncovered with the help of his agents was an arrangement by which Persian officials in the telegraph office – who it transpired were also in the pay of the Russian consulate – were making a practice of passing copies of all telegrams between Meshed and India to de Vlassow. The latter had been reading Elias's reports for some time before he became aware of this.

Despite all these surreptitious moves and counter-moves, very few complaints were passed back to London or St Petersburg. This was largely because, at a personal level, Elias and de Vlassow got on well together and saw a lot of each other on the limited social circuit of Meshed. Their contact was increased and enhanced by the fact that both de Vlassow and his assistant had English wives – a fact that occasionally resulted in indiscretions, as when one of the English wives gave away that it was a Russian-inspired rumour of an impending bread shortage that had given rise to riots in the town. Mischief making was part of the Russian brief, because they felt it was in their interest that the tense relations between Persia and Afghanistan should be further sharpened. The excessively cruel behaviour of the ruler of Afghanistan – who regularly threw offenders down deep wells, gouged out their eyes and had them fired from cannons – meant that there were many unwelcome exiles from Afghanistan in Persia, who were afraid to return to their own country across the ill-defined frontiers. They helped to unsettle the authority of the shah, and so – in de Vlassow's view – made it easier for the tsar rather than the viceroy of India to exercise influence over the troubled kingdom.

It was against this background that Elias had uncovered the Russian plot to implicate two of his staff in the murder of the travellers who were carrying suspiciously large sums of money between Meshed and Herat (referred to in the opening of this

chapter). On the one hand, the gloves were off in the fierce contest for power and influence in Persia; on the other hand, the two consuls-general continued to take tea together and exchange cutlets in the best diplomatic tradition. When eventually Elias had to go home for reasons of health, de Vlassow invited him to travel on the newly built Russian Trans-Caspian railway and – having crossed the Caspian – to return home through Russian territory to save him from the rigours of a more round-about journey. The courtesies between Europeans took precedence over their political rivalries.

There must have been some recognition in London and Calcutta that Elias was doing a difficult job uniquely well, because when his sick leave in England was extended again and again on medical grounds, the Foreign Office and the viceroy kept his post open for more than two years until he was fit enough to return. Meanwhile, de Vlassow and his Russian staff at Meshed had not failed to take advantage of his prolonged absence: more of the tsar's troops had been moved into Trans-Caspia; the Russians were looking for any excuse to intervene across the Afghan frontier if given the slightest provocation; more plots – involving Russians entering Afghanistan disguised as Turkomans – came to light; threats were made of sending for 300 Cossacks to support de Vlassow's staff in their machinations; the Persian province of Khorasan had been in danger of defecting to Russia; Elias's stand-in and deputy took to drink under the strain. Elias had been away too long. Return he did, but not for long. Ill health finally led to his retirement in 1896, and he died in London a few months later.

The shy, Jewish-born explorer and confidential agent of the Indian government had worn himself out, playing the Great Game beyond his strength, by the age of fifty-three. But he had worn himself out on his own initiative and without recording his feats for posterity. As Sir Francis Younghusband said in his obituary in *The Times*, 'he was restless and sensitive of constraint from his superiors'; his career had shown that the driving force behind his achievements had been himself and not his political masters. But he had paid a price for this independence: as the author of another of his obituaries said: 'His true distinction was to die undistinguished.'

Epilogue: Why and Wherefore?

'You shall judge a man by his foes as well as by his friends.'
                                          – Joseph Conrad (1857–1924)

So why did the disparate collection of protagonists in this book – often middle-aged men from a variety of professions – risk their lives, and often their fortunes and reputations, in challenging the might of tsarist Russia? It is a much harder question than it would have been about the characters in my book *Shooting Leave*, which concerned young officers who volunteered to spy out Central Asia at the behest of their government, while pretending to be on safaris in the Himalayas. Those characters in the earlier book had obvious motivation – usually ambition to do well in the service of their country, and to enjoy the kudos that followed on their achievements.

But the protagonists in this book were distinguished by *not* following the approved path to professional and public recognition: in their own way, they each and every one got out of line with the authorities on whose patronage their advancement depended. Career ambition was certainly not their driving motive. What then was it?

Perhaps three different motives could be defined. First, most of the adventurers whose exploits have been recounted in the previous chapters had become aware through their extensive travels in Central Asia or the Caucasus of the encroaching ambitions of tsarist Russia in these regions. As Englishmen – or Scotsmen, or Irishmen or adopted Englishmen – they resented this process, which they saw as constituting a long-term threat to the frontiers of British India, where many of them had spent the formative years of their lives and which all of them regarded as the jewel in the crown of an empire of which they were proud. Although they were not docile or even disciplined agents of the British or Indian governments, it nonetheless seemed natural and right to them that they should confront this aggressive movement.

But for many of them there was another, second sentiment which was, if not equal, at least an important strand in their motivation, and which was briefly referred to in the introductory chapter. This was their concept of their own country and their very different concept of Russia. Nineteenth-century English gentlemen – whether soldiers, writers, merchant-adventurers or explorers – saw themselves as part of a great liberal tradition, fuelled by the writings of Macaulay and the politics of Gladstone, with a mission to bring these enlightened principles to the service of less fortunate peoples. The khanates and emirates of Central Asia and the independent-minded highlanders of the Caucasian mountains came into the category of such peoples in their minds.

When they turned to their concept of Russia, the picture was very different. There was no liberal tradition: quite the opposite. Count Munster quoted in 1868 an anonymous Russian who had remarked to him: 'Every country has its own constitution; ours is absolutism moderated by assassination'. And it was not only in metropolitan Russia that this applied: as the tsar's land-bound empire expanded, so this domestic claustrophobia was extended. Baron Brunnow (a diplomatic adviser to the Russian foreign minister Nesselrode) had written in the 1830s: 'The English always remember that countries taken under the protection of Russia have all ended by losing their independence [. . .] she freed the Georgian tribes from Ottoman dominion only to subjugate them to herself [. . .] she recognized the independence of the Crimea in order to annex it to her empire'. And it was clear to all – particularly to liberal Englishmen – that the Russian Empire was run on very different lines from the British.

In fact, the Russian autocracy was the very antithesis of those English standards of liberty and independence which meant so much to the British. For the first half of the century, the tsar was Nicholas I, who tended to view his people as a regiment and his country as a parade ground. He had been badly shaken by the mutiny against him by the so-called Decembrists at the moment of his assuming power, particularly as many of the leaders of that movement were members of the aristocracy or officers in the elite corps of Guards – the very people on whom he had thought he could rely for support. He had been savage in his retribution: many of the leaders had been hanged, most of the rest sent for indefinite exile in Siberia, and the rank and file who had meekly followed their orders were mercilessly flogged. These facts were known to the British adventurers who feature in this book; many of them, as recounted earlier, had encountered former exiles who were working or fighting their way back to favour.

Already in England there was a tradition of free expression in speech or writing, which dated back at least to Milton's diatribe in defence of unlicensed printing – his 'Areopagitica' published in 1644. But in Nicholas I's Russia, two hundred years later, censorship was almost total: not only was criticism of the government or the administration prohibited, but even favourable remarks were not allowed on the grounds that it was disrespectful to the tsar to comment on his decisions. Social commentary from abroad equally fell under censorship; among the authors whose works were not allowed to be imported or read were Nathaniel Hawthorne and Harriet Beecher Stowe of *Uncle Tom's Cabin* fame.

Nor, as the century progressed, did things get much better in Russia. When Nicholas I died in 1855, a man disappointed and broken by the failure of the Crimean War, he was succeeded by his son Alexander II. Although it was Alexander who presided over the legislation for the abolition of serfdom in 1861 (one year before Abraham Lincoln's proclamation of emancipation of slaves in the United States) it was some time before the beneficial effects of this were widely felt. And instead of an independent and politically aspiring middle class as in England, in Russia the social gulf between the landowning aristocracy and the peasantry was largely filled by a class of bureaucrats and military officers who were the instrument of the tsar and his hierarchy. Whatever his credentials as a reformer, this did not save Alexander II from being the victim of an anarchist assassination in 1881. With the ascent to the throne of his son, Alexander III, a period of resistance to progress was the reaction against the revolutionaries who had killed his father. As the historian Hugh Seton-Watson was to comment, his reign was characterized by 'russification of the non-Russian half of the empire's population, and an overall attitude of nostalgic, obscurantist, and narrowly bureaucratic paternalism'. There are echoes of this world in the plays of Chekhov. So this was the Russia of Alexander II and III which the later protagonists in my book – Vambery,

O'Donovan and Elias among others – were confronting. It was little wonder that they saw it as an alien world deeply different from their own and meriting their opposition.

The third motive was perhaps more introspective. They were not only resisting Russian aggrandizement and Russian obscurantism, but they were also trying to live up to an ideal of Victorian manhood which was reflected in the literature, particularly the boys' literature, of the period. Although G. A. Henty only started his prolific career of writing military adventure stories for boys in 1868 (he was to write eighty such novels in all), the ethos of adventure and empire-building that was to characterize these novels was already well established. Sir Henry Newbolt in his famous poem telling of a young ex-public-schoolboy rallying his troops with the cry of 'Play up! Play up! And play the game!' was speaking for a generation of young Victorians who were intent on seeking honour, preferably coupled with excitement and glory. Many had been weaned on Tennyson's poem 'Morte d'Arthur' and the retelling of the tales of King Arthur and his knights of the Round Table. This was their ideal. They may seem strangely one-dimensional figures to the twenty-first-century eye, but they were instantly recognizable to their nineteenth-century contemporaries. It was from the ranks of such characters that the protagonists of this book are selected. Their spirit was to be invoked by later writers such as John Buchan, whose novel *The Half-Hearted*, about just such a hero, was first published in 1900, only three years after the death of Nye Elias and while Buchan himself was still an undergraduate at Oxford.

To those who may ask themselves what therefore is the mainspring motive and common denominator between the British adventurers confronting tsarist Russia in this book, I would say not only their objection to Russian expansion, not only their missionary zeal to bring British standards of freedom and decency to a superpower which sadly lacked these qualities, but also a desire to emulate and replicate the heroic qualities that Victorian England most admired and celebrated.

These were the reasons for the risks they took: these were the Why and Wherefore.

Select Bibliography

ALDER, Dr Garry, *Beyond Bokhara: The Life of William Moorcroft* (London, 1985).

ALDER, L. and Dalby, R., *The Dervish of Windsor Castle* (London, 1979).

BADDELEY, J. F., *The Russian Conquest of the Caucasus* (London, 1908).

BELL, James Stanislaus, *Journal of a Residence in Circassia during the years 1837, 1838 and 1839*, 2 vols (London, 1840).

Blackwood's Magazine (Edinburgh).

BULLOUGH, Oliver, *Let Our Fame Be Great: Journeys among the defiant people of the Caucasus* (London, 2010).

CAMERON, G. Poulett, *Personal Adventures and Excursions in Georgia, Circassia and Russia* (London, 1845).

CONOLLY, Lieutenant Arthur, *Journey into the North of India, overland from England through Russian, Persia and Affghaunistaun* [sic], 2 vols (London, 1838).

CRANKSHAW, Edward, *The Shadow of the Winter Palace* (London, 1976).

CURZON, George N., *Russia in Central Asia* (London, 1889).

Dictionary of National Biography (Oxford).

ELIAS, Ney, *A Journey through Western Mongolia* (London, 1873).

Foreign Office Records.

GLEASON, John Howes, *The Genesis of Russophobia in Great Britain* (Cambridge, Mass., 1950).

HOPKIRK, Peter, *The Great Game: On Secret Service in High Asia* (London, 1990).

India Office Records.

KEAY, John, *When Men and Mountains Meet* (London, 1977).

KELLY, Laurence, *Lermontov: Tragedy in the Caucasus* (London, 1977).

LONGWORTH, J. A., *A Year Among the Circassians*, 2 vols (London, 1840).

MACLEAN, Fitzroy, *A Person From England* (London, 1958).

—, *To Caucasus: The End of all the Earth* (London, 1976).

MOORCROFT, William, and Trebeck, G., *Travels in the Himalayan Provinces of Hindoostan and the Panjab; in Ladakh and Kashmir; in Peshawar, Kabul, Kunduz, and Bokhara from 1819 to 1825*, 2 vols (London, 1841).

MORGAN, G., *Ney Elias: Explorer and Envoy Extraordinary* (London, 1971).

—, *Anglo-Russian Rivalry in Central Asia* (London, 1981).

O'DONOVAN, Edmund, *The Merv Oasis: Travels and Adventures East of the Caspian, 1879–80–81* (London, 1882).

PEARSE, H. (ed.), *Memoirs of Alexander Gardner* (Edinburgh, 1898).

ROBINSON, G., *David Urquhart* (London, 1920).

Royal Geographical Society proceedings.

SPENCER, Edmund, *Travels in Circassia, Krim-Tartary, etc.*, 2 vols (London, 1839).

URE, John, *The Cossacks* (London, 1999).

—, *Shooting Leave: Spying Out Central Asia in the Great Game* (London, 2009).

URQUHART, David, *The Spirit of the East*, 2 vols (London, 1838).

VAMBERY, Arminius, *Travels in Central Asia* (London, 1864).

WINT, Guy (ed.), *Joseph Wolff's Mission to Bokhara* (London, 1969)

WOLFF, Joseph, *Journal of Missionary Labours* (London, 1835).

—, *Narrative of a Mission to Bokhara* (Edinburgh, 1852).

—, *Travels and Adventures*, 2 vols (London, 1860).

WRIGHT, Denis, *The English Amongst the Persians* (London, 1977).